LAW, LIFE, AND THE LIVING GOD

To Betsey -
Friend in Christ !

Geoff Murray

Soli Deo Gloria !

LAW, LIFE, AND THE LIVING GOD

THE THIRD USE OF THE LAW IN MODERN AMERICAN LUTHERANISM

SCOTT R. MURRAY

SAINT LOUIS

In memory of my father, Ray Jack Murray
μακάριοι οἱ νεκροὶ οἱ ἐν κυρίῳ ἀποθνήσκοντες ἀπ᾽ ἄρτι
(Apocalypse 14:13)

With thanks to God for the love and patience of Maryann,
Anastasia, and Hilary

Scripture quotations taken from the HOLY BIBLE, NEW INTERNATIONAL VERSION®. NIV®. Copyright ©1973, 1978, 1984 by International Bible Society. Used by permission of Zondervan Publishing House. All rights reserved.

Copyright © 2002 Scott R. Murray
Published by Concordia Publishing House
3558 S. Jefferson Avenue, St. Louis, MO 63118-3968

Manufactured in the United States of America

Library of Congress Cataloging-in-Publication Data

Murray, Scott R.
   Law, life, and the living God : the third use of the law in modern American Lutheranism / Scott R. Murray.
      p. cm.
   Includes bibliographical references and indexes.
   ISBN 0-570-04289-5
   1. Law and gospel. 2. Lutheran Church—Doctrines. 3. Lutheran Church—United States—History. I. Title
   BX8065.3 .M87 2001
   241′.2—dc21   2001006195

1 2 3 4 5 6 7 8 9 10   11 10 09 08 07 06 05 04 03 02

CONTENTS

ABBREVIATIONS

AC	Augsburg Confession
AELC	Association of Evangelical Lutheran Churches
ALC	American Lutheran Church
Ap	Apology of the Augsburg Confession
BFCT	Beiträge zur Förderung christlicher Theologie
BS	*Die Bekenntnisschriften der evangelischen-lutherischen Kirche.* Göttingen: Vandenhoeck & Ruprecht, 1979.
CJ	*Concordia Journal*
CR	*Corpus Reformatorum.* Vols. 1–28: *Philippi Melanthonis Opera Quae Supersunt Omnia.* Halle and Brunswick: C. S. Schwetschke, 1834–60.
CTM	*Concordia Theological Monthly*
CTQ	*Concordia Theological Quarterly*
CurTM	*Currents in Theology and Mission*
Di	*Dialog*
ELCA	Evangelical Lutheran Church of America
Ep	Epitome of the Formula of Concord
FC	Formula of Concord
JRH	*Journal of Religious History*
LC	Large Catechism
LCA	Lutheran Church in America
LCC	Library of Christian Classics. Philadelphia, 1953–.
LCMS	The Lutheran Church—Missouri Synod
LQ	*Lutheran Quarterly*
LW	Luther, Martin. *Luther's Works.* American Edition. Gen. eds. Jaroslav Pelikan and Helmut T. Lehmann. 56 vols. St. Louis: Concordia, and Philadelphia: Muhlenberg and Fortress, 1955–86.
ProEccl	*Pro Ecclesia*
RelEd	*Religious Education*
SA	Smalcald Articles
SC	Small Catechism
SD	Solid Declaration
Tr	Treatise on the Power and Primacy of the Pope

Trig	Friedrich Bente and W. H. T. Dau, trans. and eds. *Concordia Triglotta.* St. Louis: Concordia, 1921.
TS	*Theological Studies*
WA	Luther, Martin. *D. Martin Luthers Werke: Kritische Gesamtausgabe. Schriften.* 68 vols. Weimar: Hermann Böhlaus Nachfolger, 1883–1999.
WABr	Luther, Martin. *D. Martin Luthers Werke: Kritische Gesamtausgabe. Briefwechsel.* 18 vols. Weimar: Hermann Böhlaus Nachfolger, 1930–85.
WADB	Luther, Martin. *D. Martin Luthers Werke: Kritische Gesamtausgabe. Die Deutsche Bibel.* 12 vols. in 15. Weimar: Hermann Böhlaus Nachfolger, 1906–61.
WW	*Word and World*

FOREWORD

The Formula of Concord is the one confessional writing of the Lutheran church over which there has been little debate regarding its meaning and content. It carefully lays out the point of contention in each of its articles. In a fair-minded and accurate manner, it describes the position of the various parties in the debate. It then sets forth the position of the formulators along with their thorough argumentation. It draws extensively upon the Scriptures as its fountain and cites the other confessional writings as corroborating witnesses. Its authors offer counsel on the dangerous ambiguities of various slogans, catchphrases, and theological terminology, all the while urging that readers follow the pattern of sound words. As a result, there has rarely been debate over the content and meaning of the Formula of Concord on its various issues. As a rule, the question facing the readers is not, "What does this mean?" but "Do you agree or disagree with its teaching?" In other words, most people either embrace the Formula of Concord wholeheartedly or they dismiss it out of hand.

Article VI of the Formula of Concord on the "Third Use of the Law" is the exception to the rule. Particularly in the 20th century, there arose a significant debate over the meaning of the so-called third use of the Law among Luther and confessional scholars. Arising out of the Luther renaissance, and perhaps motivated by thinkers such as Werner Elert, many rejected the third use of the Law and denied that Luther ever taught it. Often they would cite the Smalcald Articles as evidence that Luther only taught two uses of the Law. Interestingly, people on both sides of the issue—those who affirmed a third use of the Law and those who denied a third use of the Law—claimed that the Formula of Concord supported their respective positions! On the one hand, Article VI comes with the title "Concerning the Third Use of the Law." On the other hand, it seems to focus much of its discussion on the application to the Christian of the first and second uses of the Law.

The debate over a third use of the Law was not merely of academic interest. In some ways, the debate over a third use of the Law was an equally important debate that contributed to the troubles within The Lutheran

Church—Missouri Synod during the late 1960s and early 1970s. To this day, the debate continues. Biblical scholars will point to the exhortations of the Pauline Epistles as evidence as to why we should instruct and inform people about God's will for how they should live their lives. They will challenge the good tree metaphor and ask, "Why exhort a good tree to bear good fruit?" Others will cite the axiom, "The Law always accuses!" In other words, to speak of a third use of the Law is to defang the Law and relegate the Gospel to the past tense.

In this book, Scott Murray provides a most helpful service in helping American Lutheranism to see how we arrived at the point we now find ourselves. To that end, he sorts out the various tangles and weaves himself through the complex labyrinth of theological discussions on the third use of the Law that we might better understand the issues, the terminology, and, most important, what is at stake in the entire debate. As a result, it can serve as the starting point for a new consideration—and, it is hoped, a resolution—of the matter!

—Charles P. Arand
Concordia Seminary
St. Louis, Missouri

PREFACE

This book is the rebirth of my dissertation written at New Orleans Baptist Theological Seminary for the degree of Ph.D. (1998). The topic of the book and the institution at which it was written appear not to be appropriate to each other. In large part the dissertation topic arose out of my attempt to rationalize for a primarily Southern Baptist audience the uniquely Lutheran ethic of Law and Gospel. That original attempt was printed in the pages of *Logia* ("Law and Gospel: The Lutheran Ethic," *Logia* 4 [July 1995]: 15–24). A second reason for this dissertation topic was the loud media coverage given to the 1994 draft statement "The Church and Human Sexuality" written by the ELCA's "Human Sexuality II" task force. The task force was to give the ELCA guidance in matters of human sexuality and Christian morals, but the draft was remarkably permissive to say the least. Upon arriving on campus for classes the day after news coverage of the statement appeared in the local paper, my Baptist colleagues wanted to know why Lutherans would write and release such an apparently antinomian statement. I wondered the same thing. So this topic arose quite naturally in that context from genuine pastoral, theological, and apologetic concerns.

Of course, the people who helped form the ideas here presented and the minds that produced them are too numerous to mention. However, I would like to express my appreciation for the kindly encouragement and dogged criticism provided to my thinking and mode of expression by Professor Paul Robertson, my dissertation advisor at New Orleans Baptist Theological Seminary. The cadre of graduate scholars at NOBTS provided an open community of thought in which lively theological discourse was possible. Earl Waggoner, a fellow graduate student, offered helpful insight into the Baptist context and encouragement at every turn.

My friend and colleague Ken Schurb served as a sounding board as the project progressed. His enthusiastic engagement with the topic and encyclopedic knowledge of the literature was a constant source of aid.

I would like to thank for their patience and support the congregations I served while I worked on this project: Salem Lutheran Church of Gretna,

Louisiana, and Memorial Lutheran Church of Houston, Texas, which I am presently serving. Pat Hatteberg, my executive assistant at Memorial, took care of logistical and organizational tasks with her characteristic efficiency. The Reverend J. Bart Day, associate pastor at Memorial, covered my pastoral deficiencies, a task he continues to take up daily.

Ken Wagener, the acquisitions editor of professional books at Concordia Publishing House, guided the project through CPH and was a constant advocate for the book's publication.

My wife, Maryann, had the tedious task of proofreading the text. Despite this, she appears none the worse for the experience. Perhaps she now knows more about the third use of the Law than many professionals in the theological world. As the writing project progressed, her unstinting emotional support was a work of love, patience, and sacrifice, even as she fulfilled the more basic challenge of just being married to me.

As should be expected, while acknowledging these gifts of help, the errors of fact and interpretation remain my responsibility.

—Scott R. Murray
The Presentation of the Augsburg Confession, 2001

1

INTRODUCTION

LAW AND GOSPEL: CENTRALITY AND TENSIONS

The proper distinction between Law and Gospel is central to Lutheran theology. The Law is God's verdict of guilt spoken against the sinner. The Gospel is God's gracious message of forgiveness for the sake of Christ to the sinner or the imputation of Christ's righteousness. This is justification *coram Deo*. While in Lutheran theology these two, the Law and the Gospel, are conceived of as absolute opposites, they still relate to each other.[1] For example, the Law, by crushing human self-righteousness, prepares the heart for the gracious message of forgiveness in Christ alone.

These two opposites are difficult to hold in tension on at least two planes. First, in pastoral practice, Christian people are often plagued by the struggle to find peace with God in forgiveness without succumbing to moral laxity on the one hand or utter despair on the other. The Gospel without the Law leads to moral laxity and the Law without the Gospel leads to despair. Knowing when the Law or the Gospel applies to our own hearts, not to mention the hearts of others, is difficult in actual practice.[2] Second, how do Law and Gospel relate to each other as they are applied to Lutheran doctrine? The apostle Paul taught that "Christ is the end [*telos*] of the Law so that there may be righteousness for everyone who believes."[3] If Christ has made an end of the Law, it is especially difficult to decide how, if at all, the Law applies to the Christian after conversion. This problem broaches the issue of a third use of the Law, which is the use of the Law that applies to Christians after conversion.

According to the Formula of Concord, there is a separate and distinctive *tertius usus legis*. In Lutheran theology the three uses of the Law have been defined in the following way: The *first use* of the Law is the threat to punish sin with temporal and eternal penalties. The first use is for unbelievers for whom threats of punishment can coerce only into outward obedience.[4] The *second use* of the Law is the distinctively theological use of the Law that lays bare human wickedness and makes clear the need for a

13

Savior.[5] The *third use* gives direction for the impulses of the Christian to do good works.[6] However, not all Lutherans have taught a third use, and those who have taught a third use have often disagreed about either its meaning or its purpose.

THE PROBLEM

This lack of uniformity on the third use of the Law has been pronounced among American Lutheran theologians of the 20th century. In this book I investigate approaches of American Lutheran theologians[7] to the doctrine of the third use of the Law from 1940 to 1998. I will evaluate how and why the approaches differ. Because the third use applies to the issue of church authority in imposing doctrinal norms and standards, how the third use affects prolegomena among American Lutherans is important. The third use also impinges on the doctrines of justification and sanctification because Law and Gospel plays a canonical role in shaping Lutheran theology. American Lutheran approaches to the third use of the Law will be studied to determine how they relate to the doctrines of justification and sanctification.

Dividing the study according to historical periods will be fruitful because different approaches were taken to the third use of the Law in each of the periods of 1940 to 1960, 1961 to 1976, and 1977 to 1998.[8] Furthermore, within each period there were three basic approaches to the third use of the Law: ELCA[9] theologians took one approach, the Valparaiso[10] theologians another, and LCMS theologians still a third. How and why these approaches differed from one another and how the different doctrines of the third use of the Law affected and were affected by prolegomena and the doctrines of justification and sanctification will be evaluated. I also will consider how and why these approaches differed from period to period.

WHY STUDY THE THIRD USE OF THE LAW?

The dialectical relationship between the Law and the Gospel has affected Lutheran theology since the Protestant Reformation.[11] The question of the relationship between Law and Gospel in the life of the Christian led to the eruption of two major antinomian controversies among Lutherans in the 16th century.[12] The authors of the Formula of Concord resolved these antinomian controversies by including Article VI, "Concerning the Third Use of the Law."[13]

The framers of the Formula of Concord sought to navigate between the Scylla of legalism[14] and the Charybdis of antinomianism.[15] The problem for the Lutherans was whether the Law still applied to Christians after conversion and, if so, how. Although this article resolved the problem in the 16th century, this has not been true of later centuries, especially the 19th and 20th centuries. The Formula of Concord might only begin to answer the abiding problem of the use of the Law in the Christian's life.[16]

The problem of the meaning of the third use of the Law in American Lutheranism is important for several reasons. First, 20th-century American Lutheran ecclesiastical conflict included battles over the applicability and meaning of the third use of the Law.[17] Second, divine direction to the Christian through the Law remains a blessing from God, though the Christian's standing before God is established by the Gospel. Third, the rejection of the third use of the Law leads to antinomianism, which is detrimental to the church and her Gospel message. Fourth, overemphasis on the third use of the Law leads to legalism and, thus, obscures the Gospel. Fifth, the classical teaching of Lutheran theology on the third use of the Law needs to be researched to see how it might apply to and be valuable for 21st-century Lutheran theology. Sixth, this book will respond to a new generation of Lutheran theologians who, in the name of the pure Gospel, are jettisoning the third use of the Law.

SITUATING LAW AND GOSPEL IN LUTHERAN THEOLOGY

The Formula of Concord claims to provide the correct interpretation of Luther's doctrines on all the points at issue. Therefore, Luther sets the groundwork for the use of Law and Gospel in Lutheran theology upon which the Formula builds, primarily by definition and clarification. Reviewing the historical context in which Law and Gospel is set is necessary so its ultimate meaning and the Lutheran approach to the third use of the Law in its embryonic state might be made clear.

LUTHER AND THE LAW-GOSPEL DIALECTIC

Martin Luther's doctrine of justification by faith is inseparable from his discovery of the distinction between Law and Gospel.[18] Justification implies and entails Law and Gospel.[19] The Gospel brings justification. The Law threatens the sinner with divine wrath and damnation. In his 1535 commentary on Galatians, Luther made the stark distinction: "The truth of the Gospel is this, that our righteousness comes by faith alone, without the works of the Law. The falsification or corruption of the Gospel is this, that we are justified by faith, but not without the works of the Law."[20] Any mingling of justification and works was for Luther a falsification of the Gospel itself. This distinction is essential to Lutheran theology. Luther had high praise for the person who divided Law and Gospel properly: "Place any person who is well versed in this art of dividing the Law from the Gospel at the head and call him a doctor of Holy Writ."[21]

Like justification,[22] the Law and Gospel dialectic has a canonical or normative use in Luther's pattern of thought. "The knowledge of this topic, the distinction between the Law and the Gospel, is necessary to the highest degree; for it contains a summary of all Christian doctrine."[23] Law and Gospel summarizes the whole body of Christian doctrine, giving shape to the entire theological task. Law and Gospel is the necessary corollary to the Reformation doctrine of justification.[24] The distinction between Law and Gospel is not a single locus of Lutheran theology. Instead, Law and Gospel form and affect the whole of Lutheran theology from prolegomena through eschatology.[25] For Luther, Law and Gospel interpenetrates the doctrinal corpus. Law and Gospel is not a doctrine, but a way of looking at doctrine.[26]

Because of Law and Gospel's thematic significance to Lutheran theology, Lutheran theologians cannot afford to take for granted either its meaning or its functions. Thus, the problems of definition and applicability arise for both the Law and the Gospel in Lutheran theology. What is the Gospel? What is the Law? How are they to be used?

Luther and Antinomianism

Luther faced the problem of properly defining and using the Law in his career as a reformer of the church. What beset him is now called the first antinomian controversy.[27] The teaching of the erstwhile and sometime friend of Luther, John Agricola (b. 1492), precipitated this controversy. Agricola studied at Wittenberg in 1515–16 where he became an adherent of Luther's theology. A man of exceptional talents, Agricola moved to Eisleben to teach in a Latin school there. He became a preacher of renown during his time in Eisleben and was engaged to preach on momentous occasions by the Elector of Saxony. In 1525 a new theological professorship was created at the University of Wittenberg, for which appointment Agricola thought he had the inside track. When Philip Melanchthon was appointed instead, Agricola was deeply disappointed. He felt slighted because he was passed over in favor of Melanchthon.[28] At this time Agricola commenced his attacks on Melanchthon, who insisted that the Law still applied to Christians after conversion.[29] Melanchthon, following the wishes of Elector John Frederick of Saxony, drew up the Saxon Visitation Articles,[30] which were to serve as the basis for a pastoral visitation to the parishes of Electoral Saxony. Melanchthon urged pastors to preach the Law in all its severity to bring the people to repentance. Repentance prepared for faith. The people would not trust Christ unless they despaired of their own righteousness. The visitation articles included this instruction:

> Pastors must follow the example of Christ. Since He taught repentance and remission of sins, pastors also must teach these to their churches. At present it is common to vociferate concerning faith, and yet one cannot understand what faith is, unless repentance is preached. Plainly they pour new wine into old bottles who preach faith without repentance, without the doctrine of the fear of God, without the doctrine of the Law, and accustom the people to a certain carnal security, which is worse than all former errors under the Pope have been.[31]

Melanchthon perceived that conditions in the Saxon churches had changed from the days under the papacy when an unrelenting preaching of the Law had terrorized the people so they despaired of their salvation. The evangelical insight of justification apart from the works of the Law dictated that the Gospel be applied in liberal measure to rescue the people from bondage and damnation. Now, however, without the Law, people would slide into a carnal security that discounted the importance of the Law and repentance. Under such changed circumstances the Law was to be urged for the sake of the Gospel.

Agricola thought that Melanchthon's approach was an absolute abandonment of the evangelical doctrine of the Gospel, which brought salvation apart from the Law. Agricola concluded that the Law could no longer be preached among Christians.[32] Agricola or his followers stated—allegedly—that the Law belonged only to the *Ratthaus*.[33] The only place for the Law was civil government. In this way the "antinomians," as Luther called Agricola and his followers, denied not only a third use of the Law, but also the first use as well as the theological, or second, use.

Agricola still admitted the importance of repentance to the Christian life. He asserted, however, that the Law, which has no place in the church, does not work repentance. Only the Gospel produces repentance in the church. This stunning denial of the validity of the Law and the proposal that the Gospel works repentance goaded Luther into action to defend his friend Melanchthon. Luther attempted a reconciliation between Agricola and Melanchthon, an effort that had the appearance of being achieved. The visitation articles they agreed to, together with some necessary clarifications, were published and employed. Luther thought the reconciliation was genuine.[34] In time Luther was proved to be gravely mistaken.

In 1536 Agricola returned to Wittenberg from Eisleben because of a cryptic invitation to consult with Luther about the upcoming meeting of the Smalcald League. The eager Agricola took this to mean that Luther had a post for him and forthwith resigned his post in Eisleben, burning his bridges behind him by sending a letter full of previously pent-up complaints about his situation to his temporal overlord and employer, Albrecht of Mansfeld. When Agricola arrived in Wittenberg with his family in tow and without arrangements for housing, Luther lodged him and his family. The two old friends got along famously until Luther got wind of some of the aberrant notions about the Law that Agricola expressed in sermons while Luther was preparing for the meeting of the Smalcald League in 1537.

By the summer of 1537, a set of theses circulated in Wittenberg not only disparaging the role of the Law in the life of the Christian, but also including quotations from the works of Melanchthon and Luther as evidence of their errors in this matter. Predictably, Luther was enraged and preached pointed sermons decrying the moral laxity of the antinomian position. Luther, Melanchthon, and Agricola attempted to come to an acceptable accommodation several times, each time to be thwarted by Agricola's stubborn tenacity in holding to his own position. Each of these attempts occurred in four theological disputations.[35] The final breach between Luther and Agricola was signaled by Luther's "Against the Antinomians" published in 1540.[36] In it Luther expressed his amazement that anyone would conclude that he did not emphasize the Law or the Ten Commandments. He had produced several expositions of the Ten Commandments,[37] he had written a catechism hymn based on the Commandments, and he frequently preached on the Ten Commandments. Luther's catechisms were especially clear treatments of the Law, emphasizing its importance for the Christian.[38]

John Agricola had appropriated only part of Luther's evangelical thought. Certainly he grasped the centrality of justification by faith without works of the Law. If taken out of context, Luther's writings could be understood as recommending that the Christian *not* do good works at all. In his commentary on Galatians, for example, Luther suggested that the Christian ignore the Law.[39] Agricola had interpreted Luther's doctrine as a hard either/or: Either the church preaches the Gospel or the church preaches the Law; there cannot be both. Agricola was blind to Luther's solidly practical sense by which he perceived the Christian to be *simul justus et peccator*. Until the Christian draws her dying breath, she remains in need of both the Law and the Gospel. The Christian remains a sinner and, therefore, needs the Law *qua* sinner. The best that can be said about Agricola's distortion of Luther's doctrine is that Luther's accent changed over the years as he became aware that people were using the Gospel as an excuse for moral license, and Agricola was somehow unaware of that change in accent.[40] However, we might well share Luther's own incredulity on the point.

FORMULA OF CONCORD

Luther's death in February 1546 opened the floodgates to much theological wrangling. Previously, Luther's towering personal authority either squelched the arguments or silenced his opponents.[41] Luther himself was concerned that after he was gone others would twist his words so his own words would be used against the Gospel for which he had labored his whole life.[42] After Luther's death his prediction was fulfilled in the confused political and theological context of the twenty years before the Formula of Concord.

A resurgence of imperial military might tested German Lutheranism. The situation was so grave by 1557 that the Jesuit participants in the colloquy at Worms stated that the dissension among the Lutherans proved they had departed from their chief statement of faith, the Augsburg Confession.[43] Finally, a different process presented itself when Jacob Andreae approached the controverted issues with a clear-cut thesis and antithesis method as suggested by Martin Chemnitz and David Chytraeus.[44]

Previously, Andreae had attempted compromise and mediation, earning him abiding mistrust among the Gnesio-Lutherans.[45] He now saw that attempts to include those who held contradictory theological positions simply would not work. Thus, in 1573 Andreae published "Six Christian Sermons," which dealt with justification, good works, original sin, free will, adiaphora, Law and Gospel, and the person of Christ in relation to the Lord's Supper.[46] Chemnitz and Chytraeus prevailed upon Andreae to abandon the sermonic style and rework the material into the thesis-antithesis structure, which was to become characteristic of the future Formula of Concord. Andreae hurriedly produced what was called the Swabian Concord (1574), to which the faculty at Tuebingen and the pastors of the Stuttgart consistory affixed their signatures.[47]

The Swabian Concord was forwarded to Chemnitz through Duke Julius of Brunswick, Chemnitz's temporal overlord. Duke Julius commanded Chemnitz to round up support for the concord. David Chytraeus completely rewrote the second article, "On Free Will," and the seventh, "On the Lord's Supper," much to the chagrin of Andreae. Chemnitz edited the whole document.[48] The project received unexpected support from Elector August of Saxony, who discovered that he had been cozened by the crypto-Calvinists in Wittenberg when some incriminating correspondence was intercepted between two of the crypto-Calvinist conspirators.[49] August, enraged by the duplicity of his theologians, imprisoned four of them. One, Christian Schuetze, was released only after spending fifteen years in prison.[50] The stage was set for a concord among the Lutherans.

In May and June of 1576, theologians, including Andreae, Selnecker, Chytraeus, Chemnitz, and Andrew Musculus, met at Torgau where the Swabian Concord was edited to take on the twelve-article shape of the later Formula.[51] This edition of the Swabian Concord was now called the Torgau Book.

When Andreae tried to drum up support for this book, he faced stiff opposition. Some objected to its length. Others, such as the Hessians, objected in principle to the addition of a confessional statement beyond the previously accepted statements of Lutheran doctrine. Therefore, Elector August of Saxony invited Chemnitz, Selnecker, and Andreae[52] to edit the document once again at Bergen Abbey. They significantly shortened this edition and added stronger terms against those who had strayed from the Augsburg Confession. Andreae also added the Epitome, which summarized the document and preceded it in the manuscript. A second meeting at Bergen Abbey was arranged. More theologians were present at this meeting so their support could be counted on when subscriptions were called for. Very little was changed at this meeting, and the Bergic Book, or the Formula of Concord, was subscribed by Andreae, Chemnitz, Selnecker, Chytraeus, Musculus, and Christopher Koerner on May 29, 1577.

The Formula of Concord was circulated in German Lutheran territories for subscription by pastors and teachers. For the 16th century the requirement for subscription was gently put. Subscriptions were not said to be coerced. Those who did not subscribe were not immediately suspended from office and were given time to deliberate. However, some university professors who refused to sign were dismissed from office.[53] Nevertheless, the confession was a resounding success. Some eight thousand Lutheran pastors and teachers signed the Formula of Concord. Harmony was returned to the Lutheran church after more than thirty years of internecine warfare. It was hoped that the Formula would be the antidote to the *rabies theologorum*.

HOW THE THIRD USE OF THE LAW BECAME AN ISSUE

The history of the Formula of Concord sets the framework for Article VI, "Concerning the Third Use of the Law." Gnesio-Lutheran theologians were deeply disturbed by Melanchthon's tacit endorsement of the doctrine of justification by works evidenced by his eventual acceptance of the Leipzig Interim. Melanchthon and other members of the Wittenberg faculty defended their support of the Interim by agreeing: "For this proposition is certainly true, that no one can be saved without love and good works. Yet we are not justified by love and good works, but by grace for Christ's sake."[54] This statement touched off what came to be called the Majoristic Controversy, after George Major, the principle protagonist.[55]

THE MAJORISTIC CONTROVERSY

Already in the 1535 edition of the *Loci Communes*, Melanchthon had said that good works are the *causa sine qua non* and are necessary to salvation. At first blush this statement was nothing other than crass Romanism. However, Melanchthon's definition of *causa sine qua non* provided a feeble opportunity for an orthodox understanding of the statement: "A *causa sine qua non* works nothing, nor is it a constituent part, but is only something without which there would not be an effect, or by which, if it were not present, the agent would be impeded because this cause was not added."[56] According to this viewpoint, good works are a cause of justification, just not a meritorious cause.[57] Nonetheless, they are necessary for eternal life. Melanchthon's 1543 *Loci* put it this way: "Nevertheless good works are necessary to eternal life in such a way that they must necessarily follow reconciliation."[58] These formulations received forceful criticism in Wittenberg. Nicholas von Amsdorf, who was to play a role in the antinomian controversy, alerted Luther to the misleading formulations of his humanist friend.[59] Luther attempted to rein in Melanchthon by both private discussions and public disputations.[60] Melanchthon adjusted the wording in his 1538 edition of the *Loci*, changing "*bona opera necessaria esse ad salutem*" to "*obedientia haec nova spiritualis necessaria esse ad salutem.*" Friedrich Bente correctly notes that this was "a purely verbal rather than doctrinal change."[61] In the 1543 edition of the *Loci*, Melanchthon deleted the words *ad salutem*.

The whole matter was exhumed at the time of the Augsburg Interim (1548), but this time Luther was not present to hold Melanchthon's formulations in check. Moreover, Melanchthon's students all too zealously dug up their magister's once-buried statements. One of those students was George Major. When Major began defending the statements of Melanchthon about the necessity of good works to salvation, Melanchthon failed to support his student and friend, remembering how this issue had concluded in the 1540s. In fact, now Melanchthon advised against the use of the phrase *ad salutem* because it obscured the doctrine of grace. He continued to do so for the rest of his life.[62] Bente also reports that Melanchthon never confessed that his original formulation was inherently wrong, merely that it was a misleading phrase. For this reason the tenacious Gnesio-Lutheran Matthias Flacius kept hammering at Melanchthon, seeking a retraction of the phrase as a doctrinal error. No retraction was forthcoming.

George Major now defended the proposition that "good works are necessary for salvation." This precipitated a storm of objections by the Gnesio-Lutherans Amsdorf, Flacius, and Nicholas Gallus.[63] Major attempted to redeem the situation by taking a page from the tactics of his mentor, claiming that his opponents were taking him out of context. He admitted that the bare statement "good works are necessary for salvation" would be misleading if not for the qualifications added by him. Major added that he was not saying that good works actually cause salvation, but the doing of good works retains salvation.

In 1552 Major was appointed superintendent in Eisleben by Count Albrecht of Mansfeld, but because the parish clergy identified him with the discredited Leipzig Interim and objected to his aberrant doctrinal formulation, they refused to serve under him. Major promised a response to their objections, but before he produced it, Count Albrecht dismissed him. Major did publish an *Antwort* from Wittenberg, where he had returned after being dismissed. However, it may have been propitious that he was back in Wittenberg at the time because the clergy of Mansfeld did not take kindly to his answer, responding with their own opinion rejecting the false formulation of Major.[64] Flacius objected that "Major's proposition, taken as it reads, can be interpreted only in a papistical sense, and that no amount of explanations is able to cure it of its ingrained falsity."[65] Major's *Antwort* did not placate the Gnesio-Lutherans. The controversy continued to rage because Major continued to hold his position with only verbal variations until his death in 1574.

THE ANTINOMIAN REACTION TO MAJORISM

Major's teachings received not only appropriate responses from Flacius, Amsdorf, Gallus, and others,[66] but also responses by Andrew Poach, Anton Otto, Andrew Musculus, and Michael Neander.[67] These replies directly occasioned Article VI of the Formula of Concord. Poach and his colleagues proved to be overzealous opponents of Majorism. They accepted the political and theological uses of the Law but denied that the Law had any place in the life of the Christian. This statement was a complete repudiation of the idea that works could contribute anything to salvation. It was also something more. Eugene Klug summarized the situation this way:

> So, the excesses to which these men came in some of their statements can in large measure be explained as overreaction to the error of Major and others who insisted on good works as necessary to salvation. Their reflex action was to de-emphasize the Law to the point of denying its continuing significance or relevance in the life of a believing sinner altogether.[68]

The controversy over the third use of the Law flared up again at a meeting of theologians at Eisenach in 1556 called to clear Justus Menius, a supporter of Major, of charges of false doctrine. Menius was cleared when he subscribed to seven propositions on faith and good works.[69] However, in typical Philippistic style, he reneged on his promise and subscription, publishing from the relative safety of Leipzig, where he was now the superintendent, several polemical works defending Majorism. While in these works Menius denied that he had ever defended the proposition that "good works are necessary for salvation," he simply substituted "new obedience," "new life," and "new righteousness" for "good works," as had Melanchthon before him. When asked if he would reject the proposition that "good works are necessary for salvation," Menius denied that he could reject it "as altogether false and heretical."[70] He was also accused of confusing justification and sanctification.

Poach rejected the concept that abstractly the Law was necessary to salvation.[71] This statement, that abstractly the Law was necessary for salvation, was the first of the propositions rejected by the Eisenach synod. By this statement theologians meant that in a purely hypothetical manner a person who was completely righteous by the Law could earn salvation, a hypothesis no longer possible this side of Eden. Poach argued that even if a person were to fulfill the Law perfectly, that person would only be fulfilling duty and not accruing merit with God. Fulfillment of duty would provide freedom from guilt and punishment, not salvation. In this way, God is under no obligation to humans to reward them with salvation for fulfilling the Law.[72] Poach argued that Christ's fulfillment of the Law was meritorious for our salvation because he was not obliged to fulfill the Law.

Otto directly denied that the Law provides any motivation to the Christian to do good works, quoting again Luther's statement from the Galatians commentary that ignoring the Law was the highest art of the Christian.[73] The Lutheran historian of dogma, Reinhold Seeberg, says that Otto and Poach were not so much opposed to a third use of the Law as they were opposed to saying that the Law *per se* was the motivation for good works in the life of the Christian.[74]

Musculus, who later helped draft and subscribed the Formula, was unguarded in his statements about the Law. He believed that the spiritual use of the Law as taught by the apostle Paul[75] did not apply to the now justified person, but only to the person who has yet to be justified.[76] Finally, Musculus stated that the Law is a long way from applying to those who abide in Christ. "For insofar as anyone remains in Christ they are a long way from and above every Law."[77]

Neander also denied that there is any relationship between the Christian and the Law, "insofar as he is justified or lives by the Spirit."[78] According to Neander, the Law only applied to Christians insofar as Christians were *simul peccatores*. When the Christian uses the Law properly, "all these are neither the third, nor the fourth, nor the twelfth, nor the fiftieth use of office of the Law, . . . but fruits of faith, of the Spirit, or regeneration. . . . But the Old Man, who is not yet new, or a part of him which is not as yet regenerated, has need of the Law, and he is to be commanded: 'Put on the new man; put off the old.' "[79]

CONCLUSION AND REMAINING QUESTIONS

The Formula of Concord brought to a close thirty years of theological dispute in the Lutheran church. It made the breach between Calvinism and Lutheranism decisive and complete and ushered in a period of relative theological peace among Lutherans that would last until the mid–18th century. The Formula also resolved the problem of the third use of the Law by articulating Luther's doctrine with the care and pedagogical precision of Melanchthon. First, the Law must continue to be preached because it is the immutable will of God for people.[80] Second, the Law must be preached to believers because they are not perfectly renewed in this life and they still must struggle with the lusts of the flesh.[81] Third, the Law must be preached to believers to keep them from falling into self-appointed and, therefore, idolatrous forms of worship.[82] Fourth, however, it must be borne in mind that Christians, insofar as they are born again, do everything with a cheerful heart and without the need of compulsion.[83]

The Formula leaves some tensions to be considered. First, what is the relationship between the works of the Law and the fruit of the Spirit?[84] Second, what are the practical consequences of preaching and teaching the Law in the church? Third, what doctrine of justification is presupposed by the definition of the Law employed in the Formula of Concord: "*unwandelbaren Willen Gottes*"? Fourth, how does the prohibition of self-chosen forms of worship affect the concept of authority in the church? These tensions sprang to life in the 20th-century discussion of the third use of the Law.

SOME HISTORICAL ANTECEDENTS

The foremost American Lutheran interpreter of the Law and Gospel dialectic was Carl Ferdinand Wilhelm Walther, the first president of the fledgling German Evangelical Lutheran Synod of Missouri, Ohio, and other States, which later became the LCMS. Walther, who was also president of the Synod's Concordia Seminary, St. Louis, hosted Friday evening lectures in his office at the seminary. In 1884 and 1885 the lectures were on the topic of Law and Gospel. After Walther's death, stenographic notes of the lectures were compiled into a volume[85] titled *Die Rechte Unterscheidung von Gesetz und Evangelium: 39 Abendvorträge von Dr. C. F. W. Walther*, which was published in 1897.[86] Walther expounded on the practical implications of the Lutheran doctrine of the distinction between Law and Gospel. For Walther, Law and Gospel had to be clearly distinguished in Christian preaching. Although both were divine doctrines, only the Gospel brought salvation to Christians. Therefore, the Gospel, properly speaking, had to predominate in Christian preaching. Walther was attempting to revive this classic distinction of Lutheran theology for the

American context. This volume had an enormous impact on American Lutherans.[87]

Walther's work set the agenda for discussions of Law and Gospel in America until the present. Robert C. Schultz has written, "Walther stands head and shoulders not only above almost all his contemporaries but also above many of his most orthodox successors in the depth of his understanding of the distinction between Law and Gospel and its application to the practical, systematic, and exegetical theology in the church of the Lutheran Confessions."[88] The Erlangen theologian Werner Elert remarked, "Even among the Luther interpreters of the last century, only a few, such as Theodosius Harnack and the American Lutheran, C. F. W. Walther, broke through to the Pauline-Lutheran understanding."[89] Unfortunately, Walther's work was often only repristinated by interpreters who used the Law and Gospel dialectic without Walther's theological insight.

Walther did not advance the discussion about the third use of the Law because he did not treat it directly in his lectures. This omission occurred for several reasons. First, Walther focused on the accusing nature, or the second use, of the Law. Second, Walther's interest in the Law and Gospel dialectic was uniquely pastoral.[90] Therefore, his approach was not systematic or structured. Yet Walther's published lectures thrust the Law and Gospel dialectic onto the American Lutheran theological stage as it had never been before.

Before 1940 few other American interpreters of Lutheran theology took a Law and Gospel approach to Christian theology. Law and Gospel were treated atomistically, as mere parts of Christian doctrine, rather than as an overarching theme. Law and Gospel and the third use of the Law were merely mentioned in tomes dealing with Lutheran confessional theology.[91] Thus, except for Walther's pastoral approach, American Lutheranism before 1940 virtually ignored Law and Gospel and, therefore, ignored the third use of the Law.

The debate about the meaning of the Law and Gospel dialectic heated up after the publication of Karl Barth's *Evangelium und Gesetz* in 1935. In this work Barth inverted the traditional Lutheran order of Law then Gospel, and this awoke many Lutherans, including Edmund Schlink, Werner Elert, Hermann Sasse, and Paul Althaus, to participate in the discussion.[92] Now Law and Gospel was a burning concern for Lutheran theologians.

Werner Elert[93] flatly denied that the concept of the third use of the Law should be retained in Lutheran theology. First, Elert contended that Luther did not teach a third use at all. This conclusion is based on criticism of the extant texts of Luther's "Second Disputation Against the Antinomians" of 1538.[94] Here, Luther putatively teaches a third use of the Law, which "is to be retained so that the saints may know which works God requires."[95] However, Elert contended that this three-use schema was an interpolation from Philip Melanchthon's *Loci Communes* of 1535.[96] While many scholars have accepted the three-use schema in Luther's "Second Disputation" as forgery, Luther scholars are by no means unanimous about this. Helmut Thielicke is of the opinion that the three-use schema is not a forgery and that there are many other places where Luther actually gives evidence of a threefold use of the Law.[97] Despite this, some scholars argue that because Luther may not have used the express term "third use of the Law," he did not teach the concept.[98] Second, Elert criticized Melanchthon's treatment of the third use. According to Elert, Melanchthon proposed a twofold purpose for the third use of the Law. The third use both condemned the "remnants of sin still present within us [Christians]" and also informed the Christian about which works are pleasing to God.[99] For Elert the condemning use is the second, or theological, use of the Law. Elert categorically denied the informatory use of the Law. Thus, if there is a "third use," it is merely the second use for the regenerate.

Elert was guided by the insight that "the Law always accuses,"[100] as Melanchthon declared in the Apology of the Augsburg Confession. For Elert there was no way to tame this accusing voice of the Law or to prevent it from speaking a verdict of guilty over us. If the Law really is God's Law, God never assumes the attitude of a human legislator merely waiting to see whether or how man will fulfill it. Rather, God is always the judge who simultaneously renders a verdict and, without making any exceptions, passes sentence. No amount of thoughtful reflection can eliminate this accusatory function from the Law.[101]

The Law cannot be merely didactic or directive in the thought of Elert. "There is no situation imaginable, so long as the Law reigns over us, where it would not exercise this accusatory function."[102] But given its juridical accusation against sinners, can the Law, then, be in any sense valid for Christians? Elert restricted the usefulness of the Law to this accusatory power or work. The Law, therefore, is totally without any constructive power in the life of the Christian. Construction is the realm of the Gospel. Elert maintained: "Here the Law has its necessary and abiding place in the preaching of the church as well as in the lives of its members. It serves not in the construction of the new man but in the destruction of the old."[103] Thus the security and strength of the church and her children must always be the Gospel message firmly anchored in the work of Christ through which he renders the world not guilty of its sin. There will never be any security for the church in the Law because it always accuses.

There is no need for "casuistry" under such a view.[104] The Law does not have as its goal to teach the good or how to achieve it. The Law provides neither rules nor guides, only accusations. In Elert's view, then, the Old Testament legislation with its rules and exceptions is abrogated with the exception of the Decalogue. Casuistry cannot take up the church's ethical energy:

> When now the church, in continuity with Christ and his apostles, confines Sinai's enduring validity to the decalogue, one must ask whether the decalogue alone can provide the Christians with that which the Torah provides the Jews, namely, casuistic answers for all the practical questions of domestic, social, and political life. The answer can only be negative. Neither the little questions of our earthly life—whether and whom we should marry, which vocation we should select—nor the practical questions of social policy in the realm of labor, taxation, or inheritance, nor the great political questions of communism, socialism, or liberal democracy can be answered from the decalogue. In reducing the Old Testament Law to the decalogue, Christ and his apostles demonstrate that this reduced Law cannot possibly be as Calvin thought, the "one everlasting and unchangeable rule" for our life.[105]

Even Jesus' own interpretation of the Decalogue had as its goal to make clear the killing power of the Law and to slay every human pretense of spiritual righteousness. The Formula of Concord testifies:

> For since the mere preaching of the Law, without Christ, either makes presumptuous men, who imagine that they can fulfill the Law by outward works, or forces them utterly to despair, Christ takes the Law into His hands and explains it spiritually, Matt. 5, 21 ff.; Rom. 7, 14 and 1, 18, and thus reveals His wrath from heaven upon all sinners, and shows how great it is; whereby they are directed to the Law, and from it first learn to know their sins aright—a knowledge which Moses could never extort from them.[106]

According to Elert, since the Law always accuses, the Law does not provide a third use, a didactic use. The Law can never be *only* didactic.

Here is the crux of the argument about the third use of the Law for Lutherans. Elert set up a false alternative: Either the Law accuses or it is only didactic.[107] The Formula of Concord does not present such an alternative. Certainly Christians are still accused by the Law insofar as they are still sinners:

> So, too, the doctrine of the Law, in and with [the exercise of] the good works of believers, is necessary for the reason that otherwise man can easily imagine that his work and life are entirely pure and perfect. But the Law of God prescribes to believers good works in this way, that it shows and indicates at the same time, as in a mirror, that in this life they are still imperfect and impure in us.[108]

Elert is on the verge of dissolving the dilemma faced by the Christian in concrete circumstances, namely, that as a regenerate Christian he delights in the Law of the Lord and as a sinner he is accused and condemned by the Law. The Formula of Concord lets the tension stand in the application of Law in the life of the Christian. Elert was correct, however, in rejecting the view that the Law is primarily or properly didactic, as Calvin taught.[109] Elert's theory had a great impact on American Lutheranism. He sent scholars scurrying back to Luther in search of a third use and forced theologians to define the third use and its relationship to the first and second uses of the Law.

Paul Althaus promoted the discussion of the third use of the Law by distinguishing between command and Law.[110] For Althaus the term *Gesetz* was irretrievably connected to the Law and Gospel polarity and thus must be the polar opposite of *Evangelium*. Althaus was led to conclude that "if the Law is clearly understood and strictly defined as the contrary of the Gospel, then it is no longer possible to speak of a third function of the Law, or to endorse the formula 'Gospel and Law.' "[111] What Lutheran theology traditionally understood as a bipolarity, Law and Gospel, for Althaus becomes a tripolarity: command, Law, and Gospel. In this scheme, command is God's will for Christians and Law God's accusing word. Thus, *command* is a term of sanctification and *Law* is a term threatening God's wrath against sin and sinners. Finally, if Althaus's distinction is maintained, it is impossible to retain a third use of the Law. From a Lutheran perspective, Althaus's proposal was daring and provoked thoughtful responses in both America and Germany.

After World War II, American Lutheran theologians flocked to German universities, especially Erlangen and Heidelberg, where they absorbed the results of this resurgence of the Law and Gospel dialectic.

Through these students, Law and Gospel became increasingly studied in America.

Edward H. Schroeder was among the first 20th-century American scholars to explore the meaning of the third use of the Law in Lutheran theology.[112] Schroeder treated the third use in the section of his doctoral dissertation dealing with Werner Elert. Even then, this section only amounted to eight pages. Schroeder introduced two points to interpret Elert's denial of the third use. First, the Christian needs no third use because the Christian has the Holy Spirit to guide ethical life.[113] Second, according to Schroeder, Elert also introduced the concepts of "life in faith" and "grace-imperatives." These Gospel imperatives are not demands, but invitations. The Christian is invited to venture great things in freedom from the Law under the canopy of forgiveness in the Gospel.[114] Elert's concept of grace-imperatives catalyzed a great deal of discussion in American Lutheranism on the topic of the relationship between Gospel and New Testament parenesis.[115]

NOTES

[1] "*Hic iterum videmus legem et evangelium, quae inter se longissime distincta, et plus quam contradictoria separata sunt, et affectu conjunctissima esse*" (WA 40/1:20). "Here again we see that the Law and the Gospel, which are utterly distinct from each other and are separated as more than mutually contradictory, are nevertheless very closely joined in experience" (LW 26:337).

[2] "*Dis ist nu der rechte unterscheid; Und ligt zwar die ganze Macht dran, das man in recht tresse. Predigen lest es sich wol oder mit worten scheiden, zum Brauch aber und in die Practica zu bringen ist hohe Kunst und ubel zu tressen. Die Papisten und Schwermer wissens gar nicht; So sehe ichs auch an mir und andern, Die auffs beste davon wissen zu reden, wie schweer dieser Unterscheid sei. Die Kunst ist gemein: Bald ists geredt, wie das Gesetz ein ander wort und lere sei denn das Evangelium; Aber Practice zu unterscheiden und die kunst ins Werk zusetzen ist mühe und erbeit*" (WA 36:24–31).

[3] Rom 10:4.

[4] 1 Tim 1:9–11.

[5] Rom 3:20. *BS* 437; SA III, 2, 4–5.

[6] Gal 5:22–26. Ep; *BS* 793; *Trig* 805. The three-use schema is characteristic of Philip Melanchthon and the Formula of Concord. See Philip Melanchthon, "The Use of the Law," in *Loci Theologici*, by Martin Chemnitz, vol. 2 (trans. J. A. O. Preus; St. Louis: Concordia, 1989), 437–38. For more on how Law and Gospel function in Lutheran theology, see Scott Murray, "Law and Gospel: The Lutheran Ethic," *Logia* 4 (July 1995): 15–24.

[7] American theologians are those theologians who have resided and worked in the United States or Canada. "Lutheran theologian" will be broadly defined as a person who has contributed to the body of published literature that is identifiable as Lutheran theology. This would not exclude parish pastors or others who would not

be considered theologians in a more technical sense. The term "American Lutheran theologians" includes those from the predecessor bodies of the ELCA, such as George W. Forell, Gerhard O. Forde, William Lazareth, Robert C. Schultz, William Hordern, and David S. Yeago, and the theologians of the LCMS, such as Edward H. Schroeder, Robert W. Bertram, Richard R. Caemmerer, Jaroslav Pelikan, Martin E. Marty, Robert D. Preus, J. A. O. Preus, Ralph Bohlmann, Richard Klann, John W. Montgomery, and David P. Scaer. All are outstanding American Lutheran theologians, each having made important contributions to the discussion of the third use of the Law.

[8] These historical periods are not established arbitrarily. The year 1940 marked the approach of a world war and the entry of Neo-Lutheranism on the American scene. The war, with its significant impact on ethics, destroyed the remnants of liberal theology in America. The year 1960 was significant because of the milestone Luther Congress and studies commemorating the four-hundredth anniversary of the death of Philip Melanchthon. See, for example, Vilmos Vajta, ed., *Luther and Melanchthon in the History and Theology of the Reformation* (Philadelphia: Muhlenberg, 1961). The terminus ad quem of 1977 is marked by the four-hundredth anniversary of the Formula of Concord and the end of the struggle for political control within the LCMS.

[9] The LCA, the ALC, and the AELC merged in 1988 to create the ELCA. The theologians of the predecessor church bodies held similar views on the third use of the Law. Therefore, when referring to the position held by these theologians as a group, they will be referred to as ELCA theologians. However, when greater precision is called for by the advancing argument, greater precision will be used.

[10] So called because of their general affiliation with Valparaiso University, Valparaiso, Indiana, and the similarity of their positions on the third use of the Law. Theologians from both the ELCA and LCMS are part of the Valparaiso school. While some in the LCMS used the term "Valparaiso theologians" in a pejorative sense during the 1970s, it is not intended negatively in this book. Instead, the term is meant to designate a theological approach, similar to employing the term "Erlangen theologians."

[11] The Epitome of the Formula of Concord stated: "*Wir glauben, lehren und bekennen, daß der Unterschied des Gesetzes und Evangelii als ein besonder herrlich Licht mit großem fleiß in der Kirchen zu erhalten, dadurch das Wort Gottes (nach der Vormahnung S. Pauli) recht geteilet wird*" (Ep V, 2; *BS* 790). "We believe, teach, and confess that the distinction between the Law and the Gospel is to be maintained in the Church with great diligence as an especially brilliant light, by which according to the admonition of St. Paul, the Word of God is rightly divided" (*Trig* 801).

[12] For more on these controversies, see subsequent discussion.

[13] *BS* 793–95, 962–69; *Trig* 805–7, 963–71.

[14] SD IV and SD V; *BS* 936–61; *Trig* 939–61.

[15] SD VI; *BS* 962–69; *Trig* 963–71.

[16] Gerhard O. Forde, "The Formula of Concord Article V: End or New Beginning?" *Di* 15 (Summer 1975): 184–91.

[17] One of the significant salvos of this battle was Edward H. Schroeder, "Law-Gospel Reductionism in the History of The Lutheran Church—Missouri Synod," *CTM* 43 (April 1972): 232–47.

[18] Jeffrey Silcock, "Luther and the Third Use of the Law, with Special Reference to His Great *Galatians Commentary*" (S.T.M. thesis, Concordia Seminary, 1993), 43–44, suggested that Luther's view of justification was clarified by his clearer understanding

of the distinction between Law and Gospel. Luther abandoned the Augustinian doctrine of progressive justification for the forensic model. For a more subtle view of Luther's relationship to Augustinianism, see Alister E. McGrath, *Iustitia Dei*, vol. 1 (New York: Cambridge University Press, 1986), 172–87; McGrath, *Iustitia Dei*, vol. 2 (New York: Cambridge University Press, 1986), 10–20; and McGrath, *Luther's Theology of the Cross* (Oxford: Basil Blackwell, 1985), 133–36. For more on Luther's discovery of the Gospel, also see Lowell C. Green, *How Melanchthon Helped Luther Discover the Gospel* (Fallbrook: Verdict Publications, 1980); and Uuras Saarnivaara, *Luther Discovers the Gospel* (St. Louis: Concordia, 1951), 9–18. Lutheranism centers the whole theological enterprise on justification, but the relationship between justification and the other loci of theology is close. F. E. Mayer described that relationship this way: "As the various facets of the diamond catch, refract, reflect the light, so the phrase 'justification by faith alone' gives brilliance to every phase of Christian revelation, and in turn each facet of Christian truth sheds new brilliance on this so-called central doctrine, whether it is viewed as justification by faith, or as the work of Christ, or as the distinction between Law and Gospel, or as faith in Christ, or as the doctrine of 'righteousness before God' " (F. E. Mayer, *The Religious Bodies of America* [4th ed.; rev. by Arthur Carl Piepkorn; St. Louis: Concordia, 1961], 143–44).

[19] Melanchthon opens his discussion of justification in the Apology of the Augsburg Confession with the distinction between Law and promises: "*Universa Scriptura in hos duos locos praecipuos distribui debet: in legem et promissiones. Alias enim legem tradit, alias tradit promissionem de Christo, videlicet quum aut promittit Christum venturum esse, et pollicetur propter eum remissionem peccatorum, justificationem et vitam aeternam, aut in evangelio Christus, postquam apparuit promittit remissionem peccatorum, justificationem et vitam aeternam*" (Ap IV, 5; *BS* 159). "All Scripture ought to be distributed into these two principal topics, the Law and the promises. For in some places it presents the Law, and in others the promise concerning Christ, namely, either when [in the Old Testament] it promises that Christ will come, and offers, for His sake, the remission of sins, justification, and life eternal, or when, in the Gospel [in the New Testament], Christ Himself, since He has appeared, promises the remission of sins, justification, and life eternal" (*Trig* 121).

[20] LW 26:88. "*Est autem veritas evangelii, quod justitia nostra est ex sola fide, sine operibus legis. Falsitas seu depravatio evangelii est, quod fide justificemur, sed non sine operibus legis*" (WA 40/1:163–64, 28–14).

[21] "*Darumb, welcher diese Kunst, das Gesetz vom Evangelio zu scheiden wohl kan, Den setze oben an und heisse in einen Doktor der heiligen Schrift*" (WA 36:29, 32–34).

[22] See Luther's "Smalcald Articles" (*BS* 415–16; *Trig* 461–63), where the work of Christ is the *Hauptartikel*, which norms the practice of the church (SA II, 1, 1; II, 2, 1; II, 2, 25). For more on the meaning of the *Hauptartikel*, see Robert Kolb, "Luther's Smalcald Articles: Agenda for Testimony and Confession," *CJ* 14 (April 1988): 119–20. See also Ap IV, 183–85; *BS* 196; *Trig* 173 for an example of the function of Christology in relation to justification.

[23] LW 26:117. "*Is locus de discrimine legis et evangelii scitu necessarius est, quia continet summam totius christianae doctrinae*" (WA 40/1:209, 16–17).

[24] See, for example, Charles P. Arand and James W. Voelz, "The Lutheran Confessions as Normative Guides for Reading Scripture," *CJ* 21 (October 1995): 373–74.

[25] Franz Pieper reflected the centrality of the Law and Gospel dialectic when he wrote: "*Weil die Schrift sich inhaltlich in Gesetz und Evangelium teilt, so kann es gar nicht*

anders sein, als daß eine Lehrdarstellung, die der Schrift entspricht, durchweg von Gesetz und Evangelium und von ihrem Verhältnis zueinander handelt" (Pieper, *Christliche Dogmatik*, vol. 3 [St. Louis: Concordia, 1924], 259). "Because Scripture divides doctrinally into Law and Gospel, one cannot but treat constantly of Law and Gospel and their mutual relation in presenting the Christian doctrine on the basis of Scripture" (Francis Pieper, *Christian Dogmatics*, vol. 3 [trans. Walter W. F. Albrecht; St. Louis: Concordia, 1953], 220). Pieper outlined how the Law and Gospel dialectic functioned in the doctrinal approach already taken by his dogmatics. See Pieper, *Christliche Dogmatik*, 3:259–60.

[26] Thus, following Luther, Walther said: "There is not a doctrine that does not call upon us rightly to divide Law and Gospel" (C. F. W. Walther, *The Proper Distinction between Law and Gospel* [trans. W. H. T. Dau; St. Louis: Concordia, 1986], 37). "*Es gibt keine Lehre, wo man nicht zugleich aufgefordert wird, Gesetz und Evangelium recht zu scheiden*" (C. F. W. Walther, *Die Rechte Unterscheidung von Gesetz und Evangelium* [St. Louis: Concordia, 1897], 35). Of the Lutheran Confessions (except the Formula of Concord), Holsten Fagerberg can say: "One can find no basic limitation to questions directly connected with the distinction between Law and Gospel" (Fagerberg, *A New Look at the Lutheran Confessions* [trans. Gene J. Lund; St. Louis: Concordia, 1972], 38). For another view of Fagerberg's interpretation, see Robert C. Schultz, "An Alternative to the Formula of Concord," *The Cresset* 36 (March 1973): 11, who says, "[Fagerberg] would respond to Walther that there are a number of doctrines that do not involve the distinction between Law and Gospel."

[27] The second antinomian controversy raged after Luther's death and was a direct antecedent to and a cause of the Formula of Concord (Articles V and VI). See pp. 23–24.

[28] Joachim Rogge, *Johann Agricolas Lutherverständnis: Unter besonderer Berücksichtigung des Antinomismus* (Berlin: Evangelische Verlaganstalt, 1960), 98–101. Cf. Timothy J. Wengert, *Law and Gospel* (Grand Rapids: Baker, 1997), 23.

[29] *Trig* 162–63.

[30] *Articuli, de quibus Egerunt per Visitores in Regione Saxoniae, 1527.*

[31] CR 26:9–10, quoted in *Trig* 163.

[32] Agricola's polemical context was different from that of the Wittenbergers. In Eisleben he had carried on an acrimonious debate with George Witzel, an old believer, who was a staunch defender of the positive role of works in justification. See Martin Brecht, *Martin Luther: The Preservation of the Church, 1532–1546* (trans. James L. Schaaf; Minneapolis: Fortress, 1993), 158.

[33] "*Decalogus gehort auff das Ratthaus, nicht auff Predigstuel*" "The decalogue belongs in the town hall, not in the pulpit" (WA 39/1:344, 30). While this statement cannot be located in the extant writings of Agricola, he was said to have made the remark to Melanchthon.

[34] Heinrich Bornkamm, *Luther in Mid-Career, 1521–1530* (ed. Karin Bornkamm; trans. E. Theodore Bachmann; Philadelphia: Fortress, 1983), 492–96; and Brecht, *Preservation of the Church*, 156–58. For more on the controversy with Agricola, see Franklin Sherman's introduction to Luther's "Against the Antinomians," in LW 47:101–6.

[35] See WA 39/1:360–584. The text of the last thesis in the second disputation has been rejected as a forgery by Werner Elert. This point will be discussed in some detail when Elert's position on the third use is examined later. See Werner Elert, *Law*

and Gospel (trans. Edward H. Schroeder; Philadelphia: Fortress, 1967), 38–40.

[36] WA 50:468–77.

[37] For example, LC, "Ten Commandments," 333; *BS* 645; *Trig* 677.

[38] See J. A. O. Preus, "Translator's Preface" to Philip Melanchthon, *Loci Communes* (trans. J. A. O. Preus; St. Louis: Concordia, 1992), 11.

[39] "*Summa igitur ars et sapientia Christianorum est, nescire legem, ignorare opera et totam justitiam activam, praesertim cum conscientia luctatur cum judicio Dei, sicut extra populum Dei summa sapientia est, nosse, inspicere et urgere legem, opera et activam justitiam*" (WA 40/1:43). "Therefore the highest art and wisdom of Christians is not to know the Law, to ignore works and all active righteousness, just as outside the people of God the highest wisdom is to know and study the Law, works, and active righteousness" (LW 26:6). In 1557 Nicholas von Amsdorf reported that the first phrase of this quotation was used at a theological colloquy in Nordhausen to defend the antinomian position (*Trig* 124).

[40] James Mackinnon, *Luther and the Reformation*, vol. 4 (New York: Russell & Russell, 1962), 169. Here Mackinnon also makes the shocking observation that "in this respect he [Luther] has come into line with Calvin." This idea is completely refuted by Hermann Sasse, *Here We Stand* (trans. Theodore G. Tappert; Minneapolis: Augsburg, 1946), 118–30.

[41] Melanchthon, on the day after Luther's death, acknowledged the authority of Luther when he announced to the students of the University of Wittenberg: "Alas, gone is the horseman and the chariot of Israel! It was he who guided the church in the recent era of the world. It was not human brilliance that discovered the doctrine of the forgiveness of sin and of faith in the Son of God, but God who raised him up before our very eyes, who has revealed these truths through him. Let us then hold dear the memory of this man and the doctrine in the very manner in which he delivered it to us. Let us then live more virtuously and remain alert to the grievous afflictions which are bound to follow in the wake of this loss. I beseech you, Son of God, O Immanuel, crucified and risen for us, to save, preserve and protect your church!" Quoted in Eugene F. Klug and Otto F. Stahlke, *Getting into the Formula of Concord* (St. Louis: Concordia, 1977), 9.

[42] These concerns surface in Luther's commentaries on Galatians (1531) and Genesis (completed in 1545).

[43] Klug and Stahlke, *Getting into the Formula*, 17.

[44] Theodore R. Jungkuntz, *Formulators of the Formula of Concord* (St. Louis: Concordia, 1977), 38.

[45] In Andreae's previous work, the "differences with Calvin were so subtly phrased that he could hope that Lutherans and Calvinists alike would approve of the writing" (Jungkuntz, *Formulators*, 27).

[46] Jungkuntz, *Formulators*, 37. Jungkuntz includes in an appendix a preface from a sermon on Matthew 24 dealing with controverted articles of faith. See Jungkuntz, *Formulators*, 135–41.

[47] Andreae was the rector of the university.

[48] Jungkuntz, *Formulators*, 38.

[49] *Trig* 190.

[50] *Trig* 190.

[51] For the other documents considered at the time, see *Trig* 244–45.

[52] David Chytraeus called these "the big three." See Jungkuntz, *Formulators*, 83.

[53] *Trig* 248.

[54] CR 7:22.

[55] George Major (1502–74) was a member of the Wittenberg faculty from 1537 to 1574, with some interruptions.

[56] "*Causa sine qua non nihil agit, ne est pars constituens, sed tantum est quiddam, sine quo non fit effectus, seu quo, si non adesset, impediretur agens, ideo quia illud non accessisset*" (CR 21:429).

[57] This is certainly one of the obvious cases where Aristotelian terminology obscures the truth, perhaps foreshadowing ominous developments to come.

[58] "*Et tamen bona opera ita necessaria sunt ad vitam aeternam, quia sequi reconciliationem necessario debent*" (CR 21:775).

[59] WABr 7:540.

[60] *Trig* 114.

[61] *Trig* 114.

[62] *Trig* 114.

[63] Nicholas von Amsdorf, *Ein Kurzer Unterricht auf Dr. Majoris Antwort, dass er nicht unschuldig sei, wie er sich rühmet* (1552); Matthias Flacius, *Wider den Evangelisten des Heiligen Chorrocks, Dr. Geitz Major* (1552); and Nicholas Gallus, *Erklärung und Antwort auf die neue subtile Verfälschung des Evangelii Christi* (1554).

[64] *Trig* 118. The clergy of Lübeck, Hamburg, Lueneburg, and Magdeburg united in this opinion.

[65] *Trig* 119.

[66] These included Chemnitz, Judex Wigand, and Moerlin. See *Trig* 118.

[67] Here it may be mentioned that Amsdorf taught that "*bona opera perniciosa esse ad salutem.*" This succeeded in muddying the theological waters still further. However, the Formula of Concord, as a testimony to its evenhandedness, rejected Amsdorf's absurd formulation along with Major's error. See *Trig* 122–23.

[68] Klug and Stahlke, *Getting into the Formula*, 47.

[69] "(1) Although this proposition, Good works are necessary to salvation, may be tolerated in the doctrine of the Law abstractly and ideally (*in doctrina legis abstractive et de idea tolerari potest*), nevertheless there are many weighty reasons why it should be avoided and shunned no less than the other: Christ is a creature. (2) In the forum of justification and salvation this proposition, good works are necessary to salvation, is not at all to be tolerated. (3) In the forum of new obedience, after reconciliation, good works are not at all necessary to salvation, but for other causes. (4) Faith alone justifies and saves in the beginning, middle, and end. (5) Good works are not necessary to retain salvation (*ad retinendam salutem*). (6) Justification and salvation are synonyms and equipollent or convertible terms, and neither can nor must be separated in any way (*nec ulla ratione distrahi aut possunt aut debent*). (7) May therefore the papistical buskin be banished from our church on account of its manifold offenses and innumerable dissensions and other causes of which the apostles speak Acts 15" (*Trig* 117–18).

[70] *Trig* 118.

[71] At the Eisenach synod, Nicholas von Amsdorf suggested that it was dangerous to say that works were necessary even abstractly. "*Etsi haec oratio, bona opera necessaria sunt ad salutem in doctrina legis abstractive et de idea tolerari potest, tamen multae sunt graves causae, propter quas vitanda et fugienda est*" (Reinhold Seeberg, *Lehrbuch der Dogmengeschichte*, vol. 4/1 [Basel: Benno Schwabe, 1960], 488). "Although the proposition, Good works are necessary to salvation, may be tolerated hypothetically and in an abstract way in the doctrine of the Law, nevertheless there are many weighty reasons why it ought and should be avoided" (*Trig* 170).

[72] This would seem to defend the freedom of God to grant salvation as a free gift, that is, free on his part.

[73] WA 40/1:43, 25–28.

[74] Seeberg, *Lehrbuch der Dogmengeschichte*, 4/1:488–90; *Trig* 171.

[75] Rom 7:14.

[76] "*De justificandis, non de justificatis*" (*Trig* 171).

[77] "*Hi, enim, quatenus in Christo manent, longe extra et supra omnem legem sunt*" (*Trig* 171).

[78] "*Quatenus est justus seu spiritu vivit*" (*Trig* 171).

[79] *Trig* 171.

[80] SD VI, 15; *BS* 966; *Trig* 967.

[81] SD VI, 7; *BS* 961; *Trig* 965.

[82] SD VI, 20; *BS* 968; *Trig* 969.

[83] SD VI, 17; *BS* 967; *Trig* 967.

[84] Especially in view of the insight "*Also, da Paulus die Neugebornen zu guten Werken vermahnent, hält er ihnen austrücklich für die Zeben Gebot, Rom. 13*" (SD VI, 21; *BS* 968). "Thus Paul, when exhorting the regenerate to good works, presents to them expressly the Ten Commandments, Rom. 13:9" (*Trig* 969).

[85] W. H. T. Dau, preface and introduction to Walther, *Proper Distinction*, viii.

[86] Walther, *Die Rechte Unterscheidung*.

[87] Robert C. Schultz, "The Distinction between Law and Gospel," *CTM* 32 (October 1961): 593.

[88] Schultz, "Distinction between Law and Gospel," 597.

[89] Elert, *Law and Gospel*, 2. See also Lowell C. Green, "The Relationship of Werner Elert and America," *Concordia Historical Institute Quarterly* 70 (Summer 1997): 82. In his summary of the Bad Boll conferences of 1948–49 (theological discussions held at Bad Boll, Swabia, among representatives of the LCMS, the German Lutheran free churches, and the *Landeskirchen*), F. E. Mayer remarked, "The proper distinction between Law and Gospel is one of the burning theological questions in Europe today. Walther's Law and Gospel has been of no little assistance in helping to solve this question" (Mayer, *The Story of Bad Boll* [St. Louis: Concordia, 1949], 28).

[90] At the outset of his lectures, Walther himself warned his hearers that he would not present a systematic treatment of the distinction between Law and Gospel. He was more deeply interested in the pastoral implications of an improper distinction between Law and Gospel. "My aim is rather to show you how easy it is to work a great damage upon your hearers by confounding Law and Gospel spite [sic] of their fundamental difference and thus to frustrate the aim of both doctrines" (Walther,

Proper Distinction, 6). David P. Scaer and Robert C. Schultz at least concur that Walther's work was essentially a work of pastoral theology and that his renewed concern for the Law and Gospel dialectic failed to make an impact upon either systematic or exegetical theology. See Scaer, "The Law Gospel Debate in the Missouri Synod," *Springfielder* 36 (December 1972): 156–71. In his *Gesetz und Evangelium*, Schultz suggested that applying Law and Gospel to systematic and exegetical theology is essential to American Lutheran theology: "*Damit ist eine der wichtigsten Aufgaben der lutherischen Theologie in Amerika gegeben: Gesetz und Evangelium ebenso zum Grundprinzip ihrer exegetischen und ihrer systematischen Theologie zu machen, wie es durch Walther zum Grundprinzip der praktischen Theologie erhoben worden ist.*" "With this is given one of the most important tasks of Lutheran theology in America: to make Law and Gospel the basic principle of its exegetical and systematic theology, as it has been elevated by Walther to be the basic principle of the practical theology" (Schultz, *Gesetz und Evangelium in der lutherischen Theologie des 19. Jahrhunderts* [Arbeiten zur Geschichte und Theologie des Luthertums 4; eds. Wilhelm Maurer, Karl H. Rengstorf, and Ernst Sommerlath; Berlin: Lutherisches Verlaghaus, 1958], 168).

[91] See, for example, Theodore E. Schmauk and C. Theodore Benze, *The Confessional Principle and the Confessions of the Lutheran Church* (Philadelphia: General Council Publication Board, 1911); or Charles P. Krauth, *The Conservative Reformation and Its Theology* (Philadelphia: The United Lutheran Publication House, 1913).

[92] Karl Barth, *Evangelium und Gesetz* (Theologische Existenz Heute 32; eds. Karl Barth and Eduard Thurneysen; Munich: Chr. Kaiser, 1935). For Barth's scorching response to Emil Brunner, see Karl Barth, *Nein! Antwort an Emil Brunner* (Theologische Existenz Heute 14; eds. Karl Barth and Eduard Thurneysen; Munich: Chr. Kaiser, 1934). For more on Karl Barth's *Evangelium und Gesetz*, see Murray, "Law and Gospel," 17–18. For the Lutheran reaction to Barth, see Edmund Schlink, "*Die Verborgenheit Gottes des Schöpfers nach lutherischer Lehre,*" in *Theologische Aufsätze, Karl Barth zum 50. Geburtstag* (Munich: Chr. Kaiser, 1936); Schlink, *Gesetz und Evangelium* (Theologische Existenz Heute 53; eds. Karl Barth and Eduard Thurneysen; Munich: Chr. Kaiser, 1937); Elert, *Law and Gospel*; Hermann Sasse, *Was Heisst Lutherisch?* (Munich: Chr. Kaiser, 1934), available in English as *Here We Stand*, 161–78; and Paul Althaus, *Gebot und Gesetz Zum Gesetz und Evangelium* (BFCT 46; eds. Paul Althaus and Joachim Jeremias; Gütersloh: C. Bertelsmann, 1952), available in English as *The Divine Command* (trans. Franklin Sherman; Philadelphia: Fortress, 1966).

[93] Werner Elert (1895–1954) taught at Erlangen University (1923–54). His most important works are *The Structure of Lutheranism* and *The Christian Ethos*.

[94] WA 39/1:426–485.

[95] WA 39/1:485.

[96] See Elert, *Law and Gospel*, 38–40.

[97] Helmut Thielicke, *Theological Ethics*, vol. 1 (ed. William H. Lazareth; Philadelphia: Fortress, 1966), 134. In a note on this subject, Thielicke offered support from various 19th-century sources including Gustav Kawerau, Friedrich Loofs, Franz Frank, and Reinhold Seeberg. William Lazareth appended an editorial comment to the note indicating that most 20th-century German and Scandinavian scholars deny a third use of the Law in Luther. For Lazareth, Thielicke's views are gravely flawed at this point. Lazareth had accepted Elert's view rather than Thielicke's.

[98] Holsten Fagerberg pointed out that Luther and Melanchthon never disagreed in public about the third use of the Law. "As far as Luther and Melanchthon are concerned, there is no recorded difference of opinion between them concerning the use

of the Law; if they engaged in any polemical exchange on the subject, it has not been preserved" (Fagerberg, *New Look*, 83).

[99] Elert, *Law and Gospel*, 40.

[100] Ap IV, 285; *BS* 217; *Trig* 201.

[101] See Elert, *Law and Gospel*, 11.

[102] Elert, *Law and Gospel*, 13.

[103] Elert, *Law and Gospel*, 36.

[104] James M. Childs Jr., "The Third Use of the Law and Constructive Ethics," *CurTM* 2 (February 1975): 35–40, attempted to place the Formula of Concord's ethical direction in the context of modern ethical paradigms, in which he claimed that the Formula's view would lead to treating rules as "general absolutes. They are absolutes that lay claim on me as definitions of how love behaves in various circumstances of life. This makes them more than just guides; that is, they are not subject to subjective reinterpretation or dismissal. They are, however, general. They do not prescribe in the sense of defining my specific behavior in every situation of life; that is, they are not subject to casuistic extension."

[105] Elert, *Law and Gospel*, 35. Lutheranism tends to view the "good" of external righteousness as a good only in a synecdochic sense. Lutheranism ascribes to humans the freedom to act prudently or foolishly in these externals. Thus the Augsburg Confession said: "*Von Polizei und weltlichem Regiment wird gelehrt, daß alle Obrigkeit in der Welt und geordente Regimente und Gesetze, gute Ordnung, von Gott geschaffen und eingesetzt seind; und daß Christen mögen in Obrigkeit, Fürsten- und Richteramt ohne Sünde sein, nach kaiserlichen und andern üblichen Rechten Urteil und Recht sprechen, Übeltäter mit dem Schwert strafen, rechte Kriege führen, streiten, kaufen und verkaufen, aufgelegte Eide tun, Eigenes haben, ehelich sein etc. Hier werden verdammt die Wiedertäufer, so lehren, daß der Obangezeigten keines christlich sei*" (AC XVI, 1–3; *BS* 70–71). "Of Civil Affairs they teach that Lawful civil ordinances are good works of God, and that it is right for Christians to bear civil office, to sit as judges, to judge matters by the Imperial and other existing Laws, to award just punishments, to engage in just wars, to serve as soldiers, to make legal contracts, to hold property, to make oath when required by the magistrates, to marry a wife, to be given in marriage. They condemn the Anabaptists who forbid these civil offices to Christians" (*Trig* 51). In Article XVIII, the Augsburg Confession ascribed a limited kind of free will to humans in civil matters. See AC XVIII, 1–7; *BS* 73–74; *Trig* 51–53.

[106] SD V, 10; *BS* 954–55; *Trig* 955.

[107] Elert, *Law and Gospel*, 40.

[108] SD VI, 21; see also SD VI, 24: "For the old Adam, as an intractable, refractory ass, is still a part of them, which must be coerced."

[109] Here we see why Lutheranism avoids defining faith as obedience. Elert said: "The Lutheran confessions understand faith as *fiducia*, trust, and by 'new obedience' they mean the good works risked in faith, though not therefore identical with faith. One can test this matter for oneself. When Jesus addresses the Canaanite woman, 'Woman, great is your faith' (Matt. 15:28), can he possibly be praising her obedience? . . . Can one substitute the term 'obedience' for faith in Heb. 11:1? In I John 3:23, faith, to be sure appears together with love as the content of the divine commandment. But to conclude from this that faith is obedience makes no more sense than to say that love is obedience. What would one gain thereby for an understanding of the nature of love? By the same token what does one gain thereby for understanding the

nature of faith? Additional legalistic interpretations of the Gospel can be seen when the kingdom of Christ is viewed as an *imperium* exercised by him by virtue of his authority to give commands, or when correspondingly, the Reformed confessions refer to Christ as a Lawgiver" (Elert, *Law and Gospel*, 47).

[110] Althaus, *Gebot und Gesetz.*

[111] Althaus, *Gebot und Gesetz*, 2.

[112] Edward H. Schroeder, "The Relationship between Dogmatics and Ethics: An Investigation into the Theologies of Elert, Barth *und* [*sic*] Troeltsch" (Th.D. diss., The University of Hamburg, 1963).

[113] Schroeder, "Relationship between Dogmatics and Ethics: An Investigation," 65.

[114] Schroeder, "Relationship between Dogmatics and Ethics: An Investigation," 67.

[115] See, for example, Walter J. Bartling, "Hermeneutics and Pauline Parenesis," in *A Project in Biblical Hermeneutics* (ed. Richard Jungkuntz; St. Louis: The Commission on Theology and Church Relations of The Lutheran Church—Missouri Synod, 1969), 57–83.

2

AMERICAN LUTHERANISM 1940–60

A PERIOD OF REDISCOVERY

SETTING THE CONTEMPORARY THEOLOGICAL CONTEXT

The period from 1940 to 1960 was a time of rediscovery among American theologians in general and American Lutheran theologians in particular. The liberalism so firmly repudiated after the First World War by European theologians was now likewise rejected by American theologians.[1]

EUROPEAN THEOLOGY

After World War I, following the lead of Karl Barth, European theologians abandoned the liberal program in which Jesus was a great ethical teacher who taught a totally immanental kingdom of the fatherhood of God and the brotherhood of man. The carnage of Flanders' fields betrayed the weakness of the ethical optimism of the liberals. Barth returned to a Reformation emphasis on the Word of God as the source for theology and espoused the abandonment of recourse to reason, philosophy, and culture as sources of theology. His 1919 *Die Römerbrief*[2] trumpeted a clarion call to return to the authority of the Word, a call that Barth refined and modified over the succeeding years. Dialectical theology sparked renewed interest in Reformation theology, creeds, and orthodoxy.[3] European theologians rediscovered the central doctrines of the Christian faith.

This trend only slowly seeped into the American theological context beginning in the 1930s. Many Americans, with notable exceptions such as Reinhold and H. Richard Niebuhr,[4] perceived the rise of dialectical theology under Barth as a loss of nerve by European theologians. However, the optimistic immanental theology of the old American liberals died a rapid

41

death at the outbreak of the Second World War with its specter of unspeakable evil.[5] American Christian theologians then began to study central doctrinal topics—man, God, Trinity, and Christ—from consciously foundational perspectives.[6]

Dialectical theology both sparked and mediated an interest in the philosophy of the Danish Lutheran Søren Kierkegaard. The melancholy Dane was the father of what came to be called existentialism.[7] Kierkegaardian existentialism influenced theology in this period in several identifiable ways,[8] the most important of which was the insight that faith was not just a matter of knowing certain orthodox formulations. T. A. Kantonen expressed the impact made by existentialism on Christianity in the term *encounter*, a term brought into vogue in the 20th century by Karl Barth. "Christianity is not a matter of belief or opinion, nor does it rest on the facts of science or the speculations of philosophy. It is a matter of faith, and faith is 'existential communication,' something that happens to a man when he encounters God."[9] Existentialism offered a model for portraying the relationship between God and humans. The notion of the existential encounter kept God from being held at arm's length by doctrinal formulations through which God became an "It" rather than a "Thou"[10] who addresses humans in Law and Gospel. This existentialism affected the theology of the period both directly and indirectly. This is the stage on which American Lutherans rediscovered Luther and his perennial theology.

THE LUTHER RENAISSANCE

The Luther renaissance of the early 20th century affected the rediscovery of Reformation theology among American Lutherans. Luther's influence on Lutheran theology cannot be overestimated.[11] However, this "Luther-orientation" immediately raises the question of which Luther is the legitimate Luther. In the early 20th century, this problem was put into sharp relief when the Roman Catholic scholars Heinrich Denifle and Hartmann Grisar produced scholarly, but uncomplimentary, biographies of Luther.[12] In his influential study *The Social Teachings of the Christian Churches*, Ernst Troeltsch portrayed Luther as a "medieval man" who offered to the church nothing but doctrinal authoritarianism.[13] This interpretation of Luther was supported by Troeltsch's tendency to lump Luther with Melanchthon and the later orthodox interpretation of Luther.[14] Luther research made positive strides forward under the pressure of these interpretations. Karl Holl was in the vanguard of the Luther renaissance that has continued to the present. Holl sharply divided Luther from

Melanchthon and his followers. Holl's influence on Luther studies was vast.

KARL HOLL

Karl Holl (1866–1926) was professor of church history at the University of Berlin. By the time of his death, he was considered the leading Luther scholar of his day. Adolf von Harnack, Holl's friend and colleague, said that Holl's Luther studies "will remain as long as there is a theological discipline and an evangelical faith, and their author will retain the glory of having become a renewer of Lutheranism."[15] In Holl's interpretation, Luther was a religious genius who, in the agonized struggle of his own conscience, rediscovered the Gospel. Thus, for Holl the locus of the rediscovered Gospel was the conscience of Luther. In this way, Holl both agreed with and differed from his predecessor, Albrecht Ritschl, who had summarized the Christian religion as a moral code in which the person participates by heartfelt obedience. Holl followed Ritschl in that Ritschl had centered the Christian religion in the human heart or conscience.[16] Yet Ritschl had also strongly emphasized the role of Jesus in the religion of Luther.[17] This was lacking in the view of Holl,[18] who ultimately denigrated the authority of Jesus and the role of Scripture in Luther's discovery of the Gospel. Holl's focus was on the genius of Luther's personal experience.

According to Holl, faith in the divine monergism was not a piece of doctrine that Luther had simply taken over from Paul; it grew out of his personal experience. But what Luther had observed in himself now became a universal insight that changed his whole view of the world. The world now no longer appeared to him as the static order that it had been for the Greeks and the Scholastics. Luther saw it as in the process of never-ceasing movement and its order as being created anew at every moment.[19]

Given this orientation, a Law that is defined as God's unchanging will is impossible, even unthinkable. Holl argued that the Christian would actually not be bound by the Law at all. For if God is alive and working, always opening up new possibilities and making new things necessary, and if the believer may act consciously as an instrument of God, then there may be instances where duty will be perceived to require actions that according to the standard of the "Law" are wrong. But woe to whoever presumes to do this with wicked intent![20] In fact, any apparently static doctrinal concept would be suspect as unLutheran and unevangelical.[21]

Holl emphasized the difference between Luther and the Lutheran Confessions. To Holl, the Lutheran Confessions betray Luther's powerful evangelical insight. The impact of Holl upon Lutheran theological dialogues was significant, as F. E. Mayer of the LCMS testified about the presentation of Werner Elert given at the Bad Boll conference in 1948.[22]

> Dr. Elert maintained furthermore that the recent Luther studies, especially those of Karl Holl, have shown that Lutheran Confessions show a deviation from Luther. German Lutheran scholars therefore are interested more in the study of Luther than of the Confessions. In a meeting of Lutherans from two continents the common ground must first be established. For the American Lutherans the common ground is the Lutheran Confessions; for the German Lutherans the person and writings of Luther.[23]

The German Lutherans were desperately seeking to distinguish themselves from Calvinism,[24] and, therefore, anything that had the slightest hint of Geneva was suspect. The sharp distinction between Luther and later confessional Lutheranism helped distinguish Lutherans from Calvinists. The result was inevitable for the third use of the Law, as has been shown already in the work of Elert. Holl's impact upon Lutheran theology was considerable.

Wilhelm Pauck

Wilhelm Pauck, a student of Holl, taught Holl's view of Luther to American students at Union Theological Seminary in New York and at the University of Chicago.[25] Pauck denied that the Word of God included prescriptions by which the church was to live out its life in the world.

> [Luther] did not conceive of the word as a legalistic and prescriptive norm, as many Protestants were to do later. For just as he did not regard Christ as "another Moses," but as the "mirror of God's paternal goodness" and as "the revealed God" who gives forgiveness and new life, so he read the Bible not as a book of rules and laws but as the written Gospel of Christ.[26]

Pauck corrects Holl by being more Christ-centered in his interpretation of Luther, but he still discounts the importance of the Law and the rule of God through the Law. Indeed, Pauck, by his greater Christocentricity, more strongly leaned toward rejecting an objective and eternally valid legal code.

This view of Luther dovetails with the existentialistic mood of dialectical theology. In this scheme Luther himself was the first existentialist.[27] T. A. Kantonen described this view of Luther in 1947: "Like Pascal and Kierkegaard after him, he was one of the greatest 'existential' thinkers of all history."[28] On this basis, Luther's reformation was betrayed by the static, intellectual, and dogmatic approach of the orthodox theologians trained in Aristotelianism by Melanchthon or the Melanchthonians.[29] This intellectualistic rewriting of the "existentialistic" Luther began already with the Augsburg Confession of 1530, in which essentialist language ("*einigen gottlichen Wesen*") was used.[30] According to Kantonen, this was "not [Luther's] handwriting."[31]

IMPACT ON AMERICAN LUTHERAN THEOLOGY

Luther studies and European theology made a great impact on American Lutheran theology between 1940 and 1960. The results were both salutary and detrimental. First, the rediscovery of perennial theology returned American Lutheranism to its Reformation roots. Second, central doctrinal topics, such as God, Christ, anthropology, justification, and Law and Gospel, received detailed treatment and restatement by American Lutherans. Third, American Lutherans became aware that the mediation of Luther through 17th-century literature provided a woefully inadequate view of the Wittenberg reformer.[32] Fourth, a rediscovery of Luther's dynamic faith in a life-changing Gospel rescued the teaching of the church from a one-sided emphasis on "pure doctrine" for its own sake. Fifth, the Gospel was now a good in itself, rather than an attempt to satisfy a legal code. Sixth, the rediscovery of the dynamic inherent in the Law-Gospel dialectic stimulated theological growth and Gospel-centered teaching.

The detrimental results were also important. The view of Luther adopted by many Lutheran theologians was existentialistic. While the interpretive vehicle of existentialism provided a dynamic view of Luther's faith, theologians failed to recognize that this view was itself a philosophical point of view like any other, subject to its own weaknesses and misapplied emphases.[33] Since the time of Kantonen, the view of Luther as a religious genius whose anxiety-filled soul conceived an existentialistic conversion had been flawed.[34] On the most basic level, it was flawed by its commitment to existentialism itself. There was the real danger that Luther would become more like Kierkegaard than like Luther.[35] Thus, existentialism blinded interpreters to Luther's support of and use of essentialist categories of thought. Finally, Holl and Pauck overinflated the difference between Luther and Melanchthon, so they ignored their close relationship and essential agreement.

Both the strengths and weaknesses inherent in the introduction of dialectical theology and the results of the Luther renaissance on American Lutheran theological thought affected American Lutheran theologians' views on the third use of the Law.[36] Three different responses occurred among American Lutheran theologians.

VALPARAISO THEOLOGIANS

"Valparaiso theology" is a term of convenience for the theological tendencies associated with some members of the theological faculty at Valparaiso University during the period 1940 to 1960. While some in the LCMS used the term "Valparaiso theology" in a pejorative sense in the 1970s, it is not intended negatively here. David P. Scaer used the term in a 1972 article on "The Law Gospel Debate in the Missouri Synod."[37] Scaer pointed out that this usage was equivalent to designating the theological approach that originated at Erlangen University in the 19th century as the "Erlangen theology" or the "Erlangen school." Scaer explicitly mentioned Robert C. Schultz, Paul G. Bretscher, and Edward H. Schroeder as members of the "Valparaiso school of theology."[38] At that time Bretscher and Schultz were members of Valparaiso University's theology department. Schroeder, a former member of the department, had joined the department of systematic theology at Concordia Seminary, St. Louis.

Other Lutheran theologians in America shared the tendencies of these theologians. Because of their decisive influence or shared theological outlook, they are identified as Valparaiso theologians, even if they never taught at the university. These theologians included Richard R. Caemmerer and Martin E. Marty. All came from the LCMS and, except for Caemmerer, graduated from Concordia Seminary, St. Louis, between 1940 and 1965.[39]

Jaroslav Pelikan and Caemmerer were the most influential members of the Valparaiso school during the period of 1940 to 1960. They communicated European theology and the renaissance in Luther studies into the American Lutheran theological context. These influences had decisive effects on the development of the Valparaiso school's doctrine of the third use of the Law.

RICHARD CAEMMERER

Richard Caemmerer was professor of homiletics at Concordia Seminary, St. Louis, from 1940 until 1974.[40] His most significant contribution to the theology of the Valparaiso school was his influential 1947 article, "The Melanchthonian Blight."[41] In it Caemmerer traced what he described as the wane of vitality in Lutheranism, attributing it to a "Melanchthonian" approach to theology. The Melanchthonian blight was the intellectualization of the Christian religion. "This point of view was that the supernatural ingredient in the Christian religion was information of divine content and origin, but that the mind apprehending it was not substantially changed by it, and hence the life actuated by that mind was substantially the same as that of natural man."[42] Caemmerer thought that Melanchthon vitiated the genuinely Lutheran emphasis on the reality of the personal relationship of the sinner with God through Law and Gospel. According to Caemmerer, this loss in vitality occurred already in Luther's lifetime, even as early as 1525. The evidence for the intellectualization of Christian theology was the reintroduction of Aristotelianism into Lutheran theology, an emphasis on the human intellect in conversion, the use of natural law in shaping theological ethics, and the abandonment of Luther's doctrine of vocation.

The Influence of Aristotelianism. At the beginning of the Reformation, both Melanchthon and Luther had harsh things to say about the influence of Aristotle upon Christian theology.[43] Luther and Melanchthon abolished the academic theological disputations at the University of Wittenberg in the heady days of the early 1520s because they smacked of scholasticism tainted by philosophy, especially Aristotelian philosophy.[44] However, by 1525 Melanchthon was again using Aristotelian concepts. The 1533 edition of the *Loci Communes* no longer included the disparaging remarks about Aristotelian philosophy found in the 1521 *Loci*.[45] In 1533 Luther reinstituted theological disputations at the University of Wittenberg.[46] Luther and Melanchthon realized that the emerging evangelical church now needed well-trained professors to teach in the universities. The disputations were the vehicle to that goal.[47] This apparent retreat back to scholasticism deviated from the original Reformation insight of the existential confrontation of the sinner before God in Law and Gospel.[48] In Caemmerer's interpretation, the reality of the relationship between God and persons was muted, and even silenced, by later developments in Lutheran orthodoxy.[49]

Conversion. Caemmerer thought that this intellectualization of the faith became most obvious in Melanchthon's doctrine of conversion. Melanchthon has been severely criticized by Lutherans for his synergistic doctrine of conversion.[50] For Caemmerer this synergism was positive proof of Melanchthon's intellectualization of the faith.[51] The pattern of conversion was still Law and Gospel, but Law and Gospel as they made an impact on the human mind. Caemmerer summarized Melanchthon's purely mental approach to the use of the Law.

> Natural man cannot keep the Law since his heart does not have the impulse for it. Hence he must hear the revealed Law. That has the power through the Holy Spirit to awaken the conscience to terror. The revealed Law accomplishes that because it revives the statutes of the will of God and informs man regarding the penalties of sin. Conscience is natural reason, a judgment approving actions in accord with revealed or natural law or condemning the opposite. The terrified conscience tells man that he has no recourse and that God must do everything. Now he listens to the Gospel. This tells him that God imputes righteousness to him for Christ's sake. Now the judgment of conscience is stilled.[52]

Conversion amounted to assent to doctrinal propositions, though "the actual readiness to believe comes through the Holy Ghost."[53] Caemmerer argued that the weakness of Melanchthon's doctrine lay in the confusion of intellect and will. The human will was subsumed into the intellect, vitiating the affective domain of faith. Luther's strong emotional and personal doctrine of regeneration was being ruined.

Natural Law. Melanchthon also revived the doctrine of natural law, according to Caemmerer. In the doctrine of justification, natural law played no part.[54] Caemmerer suggested, however, that Melanchthon permitted natural law to have far too great an impact upon ethics.[55] Here is a chasm between Luther and Melanchthon.

With Luther the doctrine basic to the new life is the concept of regeneration. The man who is justified by faith is not only forensically approved in God's sight, but Christ works a totally new life, concurrently with the faith. For Melanchthon this link is characteristically limited to an operation of the mind.[56]

Melanchthon lost sight of the vitality of Luther's connection between faith and the new life in Christ.[57] The Christian life becomes a constant intellectual dialogue between the conscience and the Law. The person who has been converted "tells himself that he must not sin again, since this will make his conscience feel bad again."[58] Thus, the Gospel increasingly becomes a motivation for good works, what Caemmerer called "a deterrent rather than a dynamic."[59] Here the Gospel becomes a means to an end, and that end is defined by the Law rather than by the Gospel. Fulfillment of the Law becomes paramount at the expense of the Gospel.

Vocation. Caemmerer also argued that Melanchthon disdained Luther's doctrine of vocation. For Luther, in the social realm good works were motivated by love made free through God's verdict of "not guilty" in justification. In love each person was free to carry out the offices to which God called him or her, to be mother or father, priest or judge, student or ruler.[60] Instead of emphasizing freedom in love, Melanchthon chose to emphasize the informative power of the Law. According to Caemmerer, Melanchthon developed Luther's concept of civil righteousness to such an extent that according to the natural law any non-Christian could determine what outward works ought to be done.[61] People would do what they should when they knew what they should do.

Caemmerer's Solutions and Influence. Caemmerer prescribed two antidotes to the insidious Melanchthonian blight.[62] First, the church must strive to overcome intellectualism.

> To make clear, . . . that religious knowledge is more than information, it is the gift of the grace of God in Christ Jesus by which the Christian becomes aware of God in a fashion different from, and beyond, the scope of natural thinking (1 Cor. 1 and 2; Col. 1). . . . the new life is not simply conformity to code, but the change of the old man to be a totally new person, and one in whom Christ literally dwells (John 15; Rom. 6).[63]

Second, the church must emphasize the evangelical character of its ministry. The ministers of the church must serve the people, not drive or coerce them with the Law. For Caemmerer, the Melanchthonian blight essentially leads to "paganism in marshaling people to a conformity to code."[64] The Gospel must be the defining characteristic of the Christian ministry.

Caemmerer identified a propensity to lapse into a subtle legalism where the Law is placed at the center of the Christian message. The Gospel itself becomes nothing more than a means to an end. The goal of the Christian life is merely a moral conformity to the Law. The means to accomplish that goal is the Gospel. For Lutherans this sets theology badly out of balance.[65] If Caemmerer's diagnosis of the Melanchthonian blight is correct, the blight would cause some pernicious effects on the relationship between Law and Gospel and on the third use of the Law.[66]

One reason Caemmerer had an enduring effect on the debate on the third use of the Law was that his students at Concordia Seminary took up his viewpoint with gusto. In the 1966 *Festschrift* for his teacher, Robert C. Schultz wrote: "The work of Caemmerer is, God willing, far from finished. What is even clearer at this point, however, is that this program has in large measure been achieved."[67] The overthrowing of the intellectualistic, rationalistic theology of old Missouri was almost complete. Schultz's optimism would be in large measure disappointed in the next decade. Nevertheless, Schultz was correct about the influence wielded by his mentor, Caemmerer.

JAROSLAV PELIKAN

A much more thorough treatment of Caemmerer's thesis was taken up by Jaroslav Pelikan in his book *From Luther to Kierkegaard*.[68] Pelikan built upon the work of Karl Holl, Wilhelm Pauck,[69] and Caemmerer. Pelikan summarized Holl's position "that much Lutheranism after Luther is not really Lutheran, but Melanchthonian, and that later Lutheranism filled Luther's words with Melanchthon's meanings and then put Luther's words into Melanchthon's categories."[70] Pelikan agreed wholeheartedly with this assessment.[71] The presentation of Luther's theology in Melanchthonian terms and categories resulted in a subtle remaking of Luther. Of course, those terms and categories were the terms and categories of the once-banished Aristotelianism. Ultimately, Aristotelianism became the official philosophy of post-Reformation orthodoxy.

Aristotelianism and Later Lutheranism. The reintroduction of Aristotelian philosophy had disastrous results at the center of Lutheranism, the doctrine of justification. Pelikan stated bluntly, "The fact of the matter is that Melanchthon's view of justification was a caricature of that of Paul and Luther."[72] Pelikan charged that Melanchthon taught that justification by faith was merely acknowledging "as objectively valid the Scriptural utterances concerning the work of Christ for me."[73] Once the validity of these utterances is acknowledged, the intellect seeks to inform the human will of the content of the divine will as defined by Law, both natural and revealed. Thus, according to Pelikan, intellectualism and legalism are closely entwined. Although in Melanchthon the connection between faith and life is vague, this legalistic pattern of thought set the intellectual trajectory for later Lutheranism.

Later Lutheranism succumbed completely to the Aristotelian pattern begun by Melanchthon. This pattern was reinforced by the humanistic educational program that glorified philosophical learning and the necessity of responding to contemporary opponents in terms understood by them.[74] Under the influence of philosophy, Lutheranism developed a definition of certainty that was based on the external infallibility of the text of Scripture. Since Scripture mediates such things as are necessary for salvation and life, the mind captures the content of the faith and perceives the will of God. This intellectual desert is devoid of the living God who reveals himself in the person of his Son. The neat, logical shape of later Lutheran theology hid "the dynamic of the personal communion between God and man that is the theme of the very Scriptures from which philosophizing theologians profess to draw their systems."[75]

Moral Law and Kierkegaard. Like Caemmerer, Pelikan criticized the Melanchthonian reintroduction of natural law into Lutheran theology. Melanchthonianism "sought a comprehensive rational system"[76] of theology. This led to a legalistic misinterpretation of Luther. According to Pelikan, this misinterpretation was overcome by Kierkegaard.

In his *Fear and Trembling*,[77] Kierkegaard rejected the principle of morality based on an eternally valid moral code. In this work, Kierkegaard used the example of the relationship between God and Abraham in the Old Testament to illustrate his rejection of an eternally valid moral code. God required of Abraham the death of his son, Isaac.[78] In faith Abraham accepted this word from God without recourse to the moral code, which forbade murder. Thus, for Kierkegaard, when God is the goal or *telos* of a life of faith, there is a "teleological suspension of the ethical."[79] Pelikan summarized the point being made by Kierkegaard as a rejection of moralism in theology.

> What Kierkegaard presents here is a Lutheran denunciation of the moralism that had replaced God with a moral law. The faith of Luther and of Kierkegaard rules out any moralistic view of God's person and action. Moralism is no better than intellectualism as the basis for a Christian philosophy.80

Pelikan is correct in that Luther had rejected a "moralistic view of God's person and action." God reveals himself in the death of the Son of God for the sins of the world, not in an eternally valid legal code. However, this is not the same as saying that there is not a moral view of God. Kierkegaard himself warns against resolving the paradox between morality and God in the tension of existential relation.[81]

Existentialistic Lutherans tried to maintain the tension between Law and Gospel in the locus of the conscience. In this pattern, the Law produces the crisis of anxiety and the Gospel brings internal peace. However, where there is no objective or external moral law, that tension is dissolved.[82] Existentialistic Lutheranism defines the Law as that which produces the anxiety that is quelled by the Gospel. Where that internal anxiety is lacking, there is no opportunity for the Gospel to be effective and there is no problem to resolve. In such a situation the Law is defined by human response to the Word of God. The Law is taken out of the hands of the holy God. God's Law remains a threat to the unanxious person only where that Law is an independent and divinely wrought reality. The existentialistic interpretation of the Law only succeeds in an age where people are plagued by the tensions of life, the angst of the life of the human subject. That age has passed, and, if it ever existed, it was restricted to the cultural elite.

SUMMARY ANALYSIS AND EVALUATION

Both Luther and Melanchthon rejected Aristotelian philosophy insofar as it suggested a way of salvation that was anthropocentric. However, it is going too far to say that when Melanchthon takes up Aristotelianism as the bridge to the prevailing theological culture, the whole body of theology constructed with it is infected by a legalistic bent. William H. Lazareth expressed a balanced judgment on the Reformers' use of philosophy and reason when he wrote, "We can understand more readily the cause for Luther's lifelong polemic against any attempt to substitute reason for faith, or to combine reason with faith, in man's religious relations with God (*coram Deo*)."[83]

This relationship between faith and reason is a crucial bellwether for the third use of the Law. In his treatment of grace and reason in Luther,[84] Brian Gerrish showed that Luther was not irrationalist when he condemned the intrusion of philosophy into Christian theology. Luther championed reason and philosophy within their own spheres. For Luther, philosophy had a ministerial purpose in the teaching of theology. Philosophy could never be master and must always be servant. Gerrish identified a key point when he wrote, "In actual fact, the assaults on reason and on the Law, properly understood, arise from the same basic motive and are expressions of the same fundamental standpoint."[85] The rejection of a proper ministerial use of reason in theology is akin to a denial of the validity of the Law.

The twin concepts of reason and Law are not both to be thrown out because of Luther's polemic against the abuse of reason. "Luther's 'irrationalism' is not to be interpreted simply as a call for the theologian to abandon the demands of disciplined thought."[86] Within the proper bounds, Aristotelianism has a place in Lutheran theology. Insofar as it leads to disciplined theological thought obedient to the biblical revelation, Aristotelianism is not to be shunned.[87] No doubt, there is room to criticize the later Lutherans for the extremes to which their Aristotelian method went. Nevertheless, such extremes do not invalidate the usefulness of the whole approach.

Pelikan and other theologians associated with the Valparaiso school joined their suspicion of reason in theology with their denial of the validity of an objective and eternally valid moral law of God. This excessive suspicion of reason was based on an overemphasis on the "young" Luther's rejection of Aristotelian philosophy. Gerrish and later Luther interpreters revised this view because they researched more in the work of the later or more "mature" Luther.[88]

Ironically, both Caemmerer and Pelikan were trained in the scholastico-Melanchthonian method in the old Missouri Synod. Therefore, they criticized that method from an internal standpoint. In fact, their works read like technical treatises following an orderly, even scholastic, pattern. The Melanchthonian blight was more difficult to overcome than either Caemmerer or Pelikan admitted. If anything, their Missouri Synod forefathers were more pastoral in their approach than were the two scholastic critics of scholasticism.[89] While Caemmerer did not provide a substitute method for scholasticism beyond his two assertions advocating Gospel-centered ministry, Pelikan, swept up by the prevailing winds of Luther scholarship, strongly suggested a wholesale acceptance of his own version of Kierkegaardian philosophy. Pelikan's acceptance of Kierkegaardian philosophy called into question the validity of the third use of the Law, as all Law. All that remained of the Law was the existential angst that took the place of the *semper accusat* of the Apology of the Augsburg Confession. The approach was far too subjective to give theological space to an informing and directing use of the Law. Caemmerer and Pelikan had set the stage for later denials of the third use of the Law that were more aggressive.

LCA and ALC Theologians

The LCA and the ALC came into being as united church bodies in 1962 and 1960, respectively. Their constituent bodies were closely related in theology and practice and moved through the period of 1940 to 1960 with something approaching uniformity.

Background and Influences

The church bodies that came to make up the ALC and the LCA experienced a clear shift in their theological orientations at this time. Like all American Lutherans they responded to dialectical theology and the Luther renaissance. In the view of E. Clifford Nelson, American Lutherans during the 1930s and early 1940s still maintained the teaching of the Reformation themes reemphasized by European theologians. However, they were expressed in forms inherited from orthodox Lutheranism, "the earthen vessels of an unhistorical confessionalism and an intellectualistic orthodoxy."[90]

Nelson described a shift among American Lutherans as this period advanced. Increasingly, there were Lutherans who attempted to understand Reformation theology in contemporary terms and to relate that theology to dialectical theology. They were called Neo-Lutherans. Those who were repristinators of the orthodoxy of the past were called Old Lutherans. The shift to Neo-Lutheranism was experienced primarily in the church bodies that made up the LCA and the ALC.[91] The LCMS maintained the Old Lutheran position.[92]

GEORGE W. FORELL

George W. Forell's *Ethics of Decision*[93] represented a Neo-Lutheran approach to the doctrine of the Law. Forell set his study within the context of contemporary efforts to understand the meaning of ethical life.[94] The moral character of life is epitomized by decision. There is no time when a human being is able to suspend the need to make decisions. Even the choice "not to decide" is a decision.[95] The dilemma of decision is a characteristic of existentialism.[96] Ethical life entails finding a value system that will make it possible to deal with the dilemmas caused by the ubiquity of decision. This search for a value system is different in Christian ethics than in philosophical ethics. "Christian ethics . . . is the description of man's situation *after* he has 'jumped'—into the arms of God."[97] Christian ethics is intimately bound up with the faith "in God's invasion into human history, the incarnation of Jesus Christ as promised and proclaimed in the Old Testament and fulfilled and proclaimed in the New."[98] The unique perspective of God on man is that man is "incurably ill."[99] An anthropocentric ethic simply multiplies the illness; it is a deviant consideration of deviation from God. In Forell's interpretation of Christian morality, only a theocentric ethic is acceptable.

Forell found a theocentric ethical perspective in a neo-orthodox doctrine of revelation as divine communication to humans.[100] Since humans have been created to receive communication from God, they must hear that "in the light of revelation, man is incurably ill."[101] Revelation contains the dire diagnosis against humans. This is revelation as threat and accusation.

Natural Law. Unlike some Lutheran theologians, Forell accepted a doctrine of "divine natural law."[102] He carefully distinguished natural law from a "Law of nature."[103] The Law of nature is a principle of order that applies to the world completely apart from God and his ordering of creation. The Law of nature has more in common with deism than with Christianity.[104]

According to Forell, the moral law inherent in God's creation keeps human rebellion in check by placing boundaries on human action. "The God who created men has a purpose for them in spite of their unbelief. Disobedience established 'orders of preservation' which keep men from following completely their revolutionary tendencies and destroying the world and themselves."[105] Divine natural law exists apart from any external legal code. Natural law describes how things are.[106] "The divine Law simply exists, quite apart from our knowledge or approval, and anybody who consistently breaks it discovers that it eventually breaks him."[107] In reality, the natural law is not easy to define. In fact, humans have not accurately perceived its content because of the depth of sin in human hearts. Despite differences among actual legal codes,[108] such codes are attempts to codify the Law of God as it confronts humans "in the very structure of the world."[109] The Law was given only as a temporary solution to the problem of human rebellion in the world.

Two Uses. Forell moved from natural law to its purposes within the context of Christian theology. The question was, Why has God given a Law that throws such an ambiguous light on human life? Forell had come to the question of the "use of the Law." Following the answer given by European Lutheran theologians, he restricted the Law to a twofold use. "The divine natural law has two uses, a theological use and a political use."[110] So far Forell had followed a Lutheran pattern in describing the Law. However, he began his discussion of the uses of the Law without mentioning the Ten Commandments. This is a significant deviation from the usual pattern of Lutheran thought, which sees the Christian use of the moral law to be defined based on the Decalogue.[111]

The theological use is the basic use of the Law. The Law accuses man *coram Deo*. The Law can never be used to justify humans before God. God uses the Law to show us that we are sinners, and we can use the Law that we might see our hopeless situation before the throne of God. Whereas the legalist believes that the Law is a means by which man can justify himself before God, that it is a means to force God to accept us into his kingdom, the New Testament sees in the Law a means to reveal man's situation in the judgment of God—to show man in revolt. The primary task of the Law is entirely negative.[112]

This is a traditional interpretation of the second use of the Law. Like Werner Elert, Forell took his cue from Philip Melanchthon's much-quoted aphorism from the Apology of the Augsburg Confession, "*Lex semper accusat*."[113] However, Forell stopped short of the legal pessimism that Elert displayed by denying to the Law any purpose other than an "entirely negative" one. Forell calls the "entirely negative" purpose of the Law its "primary task," not its *only* task.

This accusing function of the Law became definitive of the content of the Law in the thought of Forell. The Law always accuses, and whatever accuses must be Law. While it may be true that whatever accuses must be Law, that does not disclose what the Law is. This purely functional definition of the Law fits the existentialistic framework that was prevalent in the theology of the late 1940s and 1950s.[114] Its existential impact has here defined the Law, not its divine content. The Law works its accusing function precisely because of the tension that exists within its ambiguity. That is why the Law *in concreto* cannot be completely or successfully codified. "[All attempts to codify the Law] are merely more or less adequate attempts to describe the way in which the world in fact operates. Divine natural law is part of this world as it confronts us."[115] In this thinking, even the Decalogue would be one of those more or less adequate attempts. The lack of human obedience shows the inadequacy of the Law.

Forell presented the Decalogue as a description of the life of faith.

> Through faith these commandments are changed from the accusing Law to a description of the possibilities of the Christian life. They are no longer the terrifying study of what we must do for God, and cannot do, but rather, when looked at from the point of view of the Gospel, they become a description of what God can make out of our life if we let him.[116]

This quotation is virtually a definition of the third use of the Law. The third use is the description of how the Law functions under the Gospel. Interestingly, Forell never used that term in his book, though he uses the terms "first use" and "second use." He had attempted to describe the function of the Law in the life of the Christian without using the classic terminology of the Formula of Concord. Forell accepted the existentialistic criticism of Melanchthon. But he did not want to deny the importance of the Law to the process of conversion. Thus, he accepted a purely functional definition of the Law.

Legalism is one of the grave dangers confronting theologians, especially within the context of Lutheran theology. For that reason Forell also attempted to "de-legalize" the Law in the life of the Christian. While his goal was laudable, he overshot his goal by trying to do the impossible, that is, trying to make the Law less legal. He attempted this by shifting from forensic terminology to descriptive terminology. "The Christian faith is life, and only true as it is lived. For the Christian life under the Gospel, the commandments are changed from 'the Law' into a description of the 'good works' which must of necessity flow from faith in Jesus Christ."[117] Here the Law is "changed" from "Law" into "a description of good works." The descriptive language fails to hide the fact that the commandments remain, even for a Christian. The commandments remain to accuse and to describe the life of good works that God expects. This is none other than the third use of the Law.

While it is true to say that "the Christian faith is lived,"[118] it is not true to say that the life of Christian faith validates the content of the faith. There is nothing theoretical about the living Word of God as it is presented in Law and Gospel. The paradigm must remain Law and Gospel, not Law, Gospel, and a *tertium quid*. The Christian still faces the Law as a converted sinner, and any attempt to deny that this is what the convert faces is tantamount to dissolving the very tension that existentialistic Lutherans claim to uphold.

WILLIAM H. LAZARETH

William H. Lazareth produced a book summarizing Luther's theology as applied to his doctrine of the Christian home. This book, *Luther on the Christian Home*, published in 1960, was a revision of Lazareth's doctoral dissertation written under Wilhelm Pauck at Columbia University and Union Theological Seminary.[119] Lazareth's work was addressed to the need for a theology of social action.[120] Lutheranism had been, and still is, accused of supporting quietistic social ethics.[121] Lazareth sought to defend the idea that within the Law and Gospel dialectic there was opportunity for ethical life in the kingdom of this world. Lutheranism, if following Luther, should be anything but socially quietistic and otherworldly.

In support of this thesis Lazareth made a series of careful distinctions in which he emphasized the "dualistic" nature of Luther's theology, of which the Law and Gospel distinction is the paradigmatic case. Luther distinguished works from faith in the article of justification but never separated works from faith in the Christian life.

Luther's only insistence is that we properly distinguish them [works and faith] so that they are neither falsely equated nor falsely separated. *Religiously*, it is always a matter of "either-or." We are either saved by the righteousness of Christ or damned by our own self-righteousness. *Ethically*, it is always a matter of "both-and." We serve others both by reason-obeying civil righteousness and by faith-activated Christian righteousness, since the Christian is always at once both sinner and saint.[122]

Lazareth strove to show the relationship between the religious and the ethical in Luther's theology. These two were always to be held in tension.

Luther's theology began with the righteousness of the Christian expressed in what Lazareth called the "divine indicative."[123] God has done all for the salvation of humans. Thus, "an ethic of grace always places the 'divine imperative' of God's demands subservient to the 'divine indicative' of God's deeds."[124] The Christian knows what ought to be done because God has already done it. This work of God is radically different from the doctrine of Rome in which grace is merely completing what nature has begun.[125] The Christian life is not merely a qualitative improvement of what is inherent in human nature, but a quantitative transformation into an entirely new person.

Lazareth astutely pointed out that Luther sought to "take the middle course" between legalism and license. According to Lazareth, this was Luther's considered position from 1520 until his death. In his 1520 treatise "*Tractatus de libertate christiana*,"[126] Luther set the theme for his "both-and" approach to Christian ethics. "A Christian is a perfectly free lord of all, subject to none. A Christian is a perfectly dutiful servant of all, subject to all."[127] According to the work of God in Christ, the Christian is redeemed and, therefore, exalted above all persons, institutions, laws, or requirements. This is a Christian's status "*coram Deo*." However, as a person in the world of flesh and blood, the Christian's freedom constrains him to service of all. This is the Christian's status "*coram hominibus*."

Simul Justus et Peccator. These states are held together in the expression "*simul justus et peccator*." Christians living *in concreto* live as whole persons, never one or the other, never as "just" or "sinner," but as "just" and "sinner" all the time. Lazareth adeptly described this relation.

This distinctively biblical view of the whole man (*totus homo*) as being both of the flesh and life of the Spirit is vital for Luther's understanding of the Christian life. There is absolutely no possibility here of some kind of spiritual "inwardness" as a Christian alternative to carnal "outwardness."

The lines are drawn horizontally, so to speak, rather than vertically: That is, both flesh and Spirit have both inner and outer expressions since it is the whole man—both religiously and ethically—for which God and Satan are contending.[128]

Thus, the flesh-spirit dichotomy runs through all of life. There is none of the artificiality that equates sins of the flesh and concupiscence with sexuality, as in Augustine and the Augustinian synthesis of medieval thought. For Luther, concupiscence is the description of human nature's total corruption expressed in the desire to possess or control others. The abuse of human sexuality would provide only one case of such desire.[129]

Like Forell and Pelikan, existentialistic colors tint Lazareth's interpretation of Luther's social ethic.[130] "Luther's approach to ethical problems is existential, not legal."[131] The influence of Pauck and Holl is evident here. This influence keeps Lazareth from affirming the need for a third use of the Law and leads him to suggest a situationalistic ethic for the Christian life:[132] "A Christian ethic based upon the 'divine indicative' of God's grace preserves the freedom of the believer under the guidance of the Holy Spirit through the Bible, the church, and prayer, to discover anew in each concrete situation what the will of God permits or requires of him then and there."[133] The centrality of freedom under the Gospel does justice to the "*justus*" side of the equation, but Lazareth's situationalism leaves the "*peccator*" unconnected to a concrete Law. "Concrete situations" need a concrete word of Law. Because humans after conversion remain corrupted in heart, mind, and body, they are incapable of discovering anew what the will of God permits or forbids, apart from a word of God. Lazareth hints at this word by suggesting the importance of external norms—that is, "the Bible, the church, and prayer"[134]—in the process of determining the will of God. He seems, however, to dissolve the tension between Law and Gospel by presenting the concrete situation of the *simul justus et peccator* as an either-or.

> As liberated by the Gospel, he serves others voluntarily; as goaded by the Law, he serves others begrudgingly and unwillingly. In either case, God sees to it that man's pride is checked and his neighbors served, as good works contribute to the general welfare of the community no matter what the motive of the actor.[135]

Unfortunately, the human situation never presents such a simple ethical construct. Humans are never moved by a single motive. The Gospel must motivate Christians, but the Gospel is not alone in producing ethical action. Just as faith is never alone, so also the Gospel is never alone. Law and Gospel must never be separated, as faith and works must never be separated. In ethics a concrete word of God in both Law and Gospel must direct action—the Gospel to motivate, the Law to inform.

Two Uses. In the last analysis, however, Lazareth offered only a twofold use of the Law, the "*usus theologicus*" and the "*usus politicus.*"[136] No third use was possible. Lazareth carefully followed Elert on this point.[137] First, Lazareth assumed that because Luther might not have used the precise term "third use," he did not teach the concept. Lazareth criticized contemporary American Lutheran catechisms for having included a third use of the Law.[138] This inclusion identified such catechisms with the Melanchthonian scholasticism so roundly criticized by the existentialistic Lutherans. Second, Lazareth also followed Elert's attempt to rescue the Formula of Concord from the charge of teaching a third use of the Law. For Elert,[139] as for Lazareth, the third use of the Law is nothing more than the second use for the Christian. A true third use of the Law, as an *usus didacticus*, would be "unevangelical and pietistic," though Lazareth fails to defend that assertion.[140] Apparently, he accepted at face value Elert's criticism of the third use.

Summary Analysis and Evaluation

The study of Christian ethics received an enormous gift from the Luther renaissance, which restored to American Lutheran theologians the centrality of grace in Lutheran ethics. Lazareth and Forell both provide evidence of this gift. Yet their approaches to the Law in general and the third use of the Law in particular were set by the modern European theologians, not by Luther. Forell and Lazareth reflected the shift to Neo-Lutheranism in American Lutheran theology of the early postwar period.

Forell accepted a theocentric element in his approach to theology. That element was the centrality of divine revelation in dialectical theology. Divine revelation was experienced as Law and Gospel by the human subject of God's speaking. While affected by existentialism and dialectical theology to this significant degree, Lazareth and Forell still accepted natural law in the theological matrix. This represented a clear deviation from the trend set by Caemmerer and Pelikan, who identified the doctrine of an objective natural law as a significant threat to Christ-centered Christian theology. Despite their acceptance of an objective moral law, both Forell and Lazareth denied the third use of the Law. According to Forell and Lazareth, the moral law is not susceptible to correct or complete human perception. All actual legal codes, including the Decalogue, remain inadequate attempts to reflect the moral law. This leads, though by a route quite different from the one traveled by those theologians of the Valparaiso school, to a purely functional use of the Law. Thus, for these Neo-Lutherans, the moral law has an independent existence, but when it comes to proclaiming it, it is defined by the angst it produces. Whatever threatens is Law, and Law is whatever threatens.

Forell's approach is most troubling at the point where he attempts to denature the Law. The locus of the change cannot be the Law itself, which must remain the Law, but the response of the Christian individual. If this pattern is followed, there remains an existentialistic tension between the threatenings and the blessings of the Law. In Forell's approach, Law and Gospel are joined by a *tertium quid*, which is neither Law nor Gospel. This is characteristic not of orthodoxy, but of orthodoxy's rival, pietism.

Both Lazareth and Forell denied the third use as unevangelical and unLutheran. Here they followed Elert. Lazareth in particular presumed that the *usus legis* were independent and distinguishable. Thus, if the Law accused, it could not likewise instruct. The Law can threaten and instruct but will never save. That keeps the Law separated from the Gospel. The doctrine of justification is defended not where the third use is denied, but where the Law's powers are not confused with the Gospel's or where the Gospel is not used as an instructive tool. Instruction in good works remains a work of the Law if the Gospel is truly about what God has done rather than about what humans have done.

THE OLD MISSOURIANS

The Missouri Synod was most definitely an "Old Lutheran" church body in the period discussed here (1940–60). Missouri defended old-line orthodoxy. However, already by 1944 there were cracks in the once seamless orthodoxy of Missouri.[141] These cracks were covered up in time for the 1947 celebration of the centennial of the Synod so the Synod could "affirm loyalty to Missouri's repristination theology."[142]

BACKGROUND AND INFLUENCES

Missouri had a reputation for repristinating, that is, thoughtlessly and mechanically repeating the theology of the past, especially 17th-century orthodoxy. The repristinating methodology was inherited from C. F. W. Walther, who used quotations from the Lutheran Confessions, Luther, and the orthodox dogmaticians to settle controverted issues in the late 19th century.[143] In the opinion of the Missouri Synod historian Carl S. Meyer, "[Walther] showed himself to a not inconsiderable extent a

Zeitentheolog, a theologian who quoted authorities."[144] This methodology "shaped the thinking of Missouri Synod clergy for two generations."[145] Walther's method continued to have an impact in the 20th century.

The German theologians at Bad Boll in 1948 presumed before meeting with the Missourians that they would be repristination theologians in the worst sense.[146] F. E. Mayer recounted that "the vast majority of German theologians had an altogether false impression of our Synod's theology. Some thought that we were steeped in traditionalism, dead orthodoxy, and obscurantism."[147] Despite the vibrancy of these Missourians, in 1960, President A. O. Fuerbringer of Concordia Seminary, St. Louis, criticized the Missouri Synod's theological approach because it was still too heavily weighted toward systematic theology and dogmatics. In his judgment this led to a self-righteous certainty. "We have simply concluded that we have the answers or sufficient basis for the answers."[148] To fully understand Missouri's repristinating tendencies, we first look at Francis Pieper, who adopted the repristinating method of Walther and transmitted it to the 20th century.[149]

FRANCIS PIEPER

Francis Pieper was professor of systematic theology at Concordia Seminary, St. Louis, from 1878 to 1931. During that time he was the school's president (1887–1931) and also the president of the LCMS (1899–1911). Pieper lectured to three generations of Missouri Synod theological students. Those lectures were drawn together into a three-volume work entitled *Christliche Dogmatik*, published from 1917–24. This is the only complete original dogmatics work produced in the Missouri Synod in the entire 150 years of its history.[150] In an English translation it is still the standard dogmatics textbook used at LCMS seminaries.[151] This textbook has extended Pieper's enormous influence into the present[152] and is most significant in the area of theological method.[153]

Pieper's methodology followed the path trod by Walther, his forerunner. Pieper was deeply respectful of the inheritance of orthodoxy. His *Dogmatik* is filled with quotations of Luther, the Lutheran Confessions, and the 17th-century dogmaticians.[154] Despite his respect for the theologians of the 17th century, Pieper was also critical of their theology when it conflicted with his own doctrinal views.[155]

Theologians are divided on the value of the Pieper legacy. Pieper has been severely criticized for skewing the presentation of Lutheran doctrine in favor of an orthodoxist interest in the doctrine of the inerrancy and inspiration of Scripture and this doctrine's impact on the *corpus doctrinae*.

For example, Richard Koenig charged that "so important had the Holy Scriptures become for Pieper that he frequently sounds as if the doctrine of verbal inspiration, rather than justification by faith, was the article by which the Church stands or falls."[156] As far as the critics of Pieper are concerned, his interest in inerrancy and inspiration caused him to shortchange justification and, by extension, Law and Gospel.

Theologians more sympathetic to Pieper's work have a different perspective. David P. Scaer, professor of systematic theology at Concordia Theological Seminary, Fort Wayne, Indiana, pointed out that Pieper saw the doctrine of justification as an extension of Christology. Pieper devoted more than a third of his *Dogmatik* to Christology, and thus to the doctrine of justification.[157] Pieper often settled difficult theological problems by arguing from the centrality of grace, rather than from a doctrine of inerrancy, following Luther in the former argument. *Christliche Dogmatik* begins with a lengthy discussion of the character of the Christian religion as a religion of grace. In this discussion Pieper judges that any religion that does not serve and teach the doctrine of grace is a false religion, denies the doctrine of justification by faith, and affects Christology by diminishing the significance of the death of Christ.[158]

Law and Gospel was an indispensable aspect of Pieper's theological construct. He censured 19th-century liberal theologians for their disregard of the distinction because this disregard in essence attacked the vicarious satisfaction of Christ.[159] Pieper discussed the three uses of the Law following a practical order: theological use first, didactic use next, and political use last. This order reflected their relative importance for Christian dogmatics.

For Pieper the third use of the Law teaches the Christian theologian what good works are. "The Law is the only source from which the Christian theologian teaches what good works are, even as Christ Himself pointed to the Law when He answered the questions which works are commanded by God and are therefore God-pleasing."[160] For Pieper it was self-evident that there was a third use because Jesus himself had employed the third use in Matt 15:1–20; 22:35–40; and 19:16–22,[161] in which he repeated the commandments. The commandments remained the word revealing God's unchanging will, which even Jesus repeats for the church in the New Testament. Pieper follows the pattern set by orthodoxy before him. However, he is clear that the Gospel alone, never the Law, gives the power to do good works.

According to Pieper, the Law remains the rule and norm of good works. "Secondly, since the Christian because of his flesh is inclined to err in regard to the good works desired of him by God, he must daily learn from the Law, as the unchanging norm of God-pleasing life, what God would have him do."[162] This norm is unchanging. However, an unchanging divine Law, and thus a third use of the Law, would come under fierce attack after Pieper's death.

THE ABIDING WORD

The 1947 centennial of the Missouri Synod's founding saw a restatement of the position of Pieper in a collection of convention essays published in two volumes called *The Abiding Word*. The essays were consciously "based on the writings of our fathers."[163] By this phrase the editor intended to include all the preeminent teachers of the Lutheran church in the 16th and 17th centuries, as well as the leading lights of the LCMS, including and especially Walther and Pieper.[164]

In *The Abiding Word* the Scriptures are the source of the Christian knowledge of the ever-binding Law of God. The Decalogue reveals God's unchanging will for his people. Walter Geihsler expressed this position in his article "The Law and the Gospel": "From the Law of the Holy God as revealed in the Scriptures the child of God must learn day by day to know and understand more thoroughly the will of his heavenly Father, his own sinfulness and helplessness, the need of daily whipping his old Adam into submission and of keeping under his body [sic] and bringing it into subjection (I Cor. 9:26–27)."[165] Note the strong emphasis on knowing and understanding. The Christian needs a clear external Law by which he may learn the will of his heavenly Father for growth in sanctification. Clearly, this is the third use of the Law. Here the third use of the Law presupposes an objective expression of the eternal legal will of God.

Despite this penchant for supporting an objective Law of God, Geihsler did not presuppose that Christians could simply carry out this will of God once they were made aware of it. The objectivity of the will of God in the Law did not make it possible for humans to carry it out. It was not just a matter of knowing and, therefore, doing God's will. The person had to be different at heart. That difference had to be effected by the Gospel.

> The strength of this daily putting off of the old man and of putting on the new man [the Christian] receives not from his study of the Law. With this power and willingness the Holy Spirit endows him by holding before his eyes in the Gospel the Redeemer who, for the love

of man and in obedience to His holy Father, took upon Himself the enormous guilt amassed by the Christian, suffered the torment of hell which the Christian has deserved a thousandfold. . . . The glad news of what Christ has done for him, still is doing, and will do fills the Christian's heart and soul with gratitude and the unwavering determination to be and remain the loyal servant of his Lord and Redeemer. Thine I am, O my Savior! For me to live is Christ! (Phil. 3:4–14; Col. 3:1–4).[166]

The language of heart and will was restricted to the work of the Gospel. The locus of the Law was the mind. The locus of the Gospel was the human heart and will.

The Decalogue was intimately connected to the concept of natural law in *The Abiding Word*. The Ten Commandments had their source in natural law, which was defined as God's will. R. Herrmann stated that "the Decalog originated not on Mount Sinai, but in the Garden of Eden";[167] that is, the Law originally had its source in God. God placed this Law in the hearts of humans in what is called conscience. Only later at Sinai did God codify this Law in the Ten Commandments. "In order to make it convenient for [God's children] to know His will, He has kindly summarized it in a brief code, the Ten Commandments."[168] The Ten Commandments are the written expression of the natural law, which is God's unchanging will. However, the language of convenience leads to the question whether this view of the Law might be far too tame, removing the thought of threat from the Law of God. There is little that is "convenient" about the threat of God's wrath against sinners expressed by the Law, according to Lutheran theology. Herrmann reduced the Ten Commandments to information for humans about the will of God. This approach to the Law mutes the sinner's confrontation before the holy God *(coram Deo)*. Thus, Herrmann recommends that "there is only one remedy for the erring conscience: it must be corrected according to the Word of God."[169] The Law of God must be much more than an external standard by which the erring conscience is adjusted. The Law of God must threaten the human conscience because of its perverse and constant straying from God. The Law must slay the human *(totus homo)*, not merely provide a moral course correction to the person with better information. The Law as information alone emasculates the real threat of the majesty and holiness of God against the whole person.

Herrmann followed the traditional order of the threefold division of the Law, the *usus politicus* first, the *usus theologicus* next, and the *usus tertius*

last, rather than following Pieper's practical order. Herrmann's interpretation of the threefold use of the Law was guided not by the Formula of
Concord, but by the synodical catechism of the Missouri Synod.[170] The
synodical catechism described the three uses as curb, mirror, and rule,
respectively. While this might be a helpful description for children being
taught the three uses of the Law, it does not reflect the language of the
Formula of Concord. The Formula of Concord never describes the first
use of the Law as a "curb"; in fact, none of the Lutheran Confessions do.
The Law is called a "mirror" twice in the Formula of Concord. The first
mention of the Law as a mirror is a reference to the third use of the Law,
not the second use. "For the Law is a mirror in which the will of God, and
what pleases Him, are exactly portrayed, and which should [therefore] be
constantly held up to the believers and be diligently urged upon them
without ceasing."[171] Here the mirror is a clear looking glass that represents
the will of God, whereas the synodical catechism takes the mirror to be the
instrument that shows humans their radical sinfulness. The second mention of the Law as a mirror in the Formula of Concord is more clearly a
reference to the second use.[172] Thus, the language of the Formula is not
fixed, but quite flexible. The Formula of Concord reflects a certain
ambivalence when it calls the third use of the Law a "*Regel*"[173] in the
Epitome but calls the entire Word of God a "*Regel*" in the Solid
Declaration.[174] Herrmann reproduced Missouri Synod orthodoxy, but he
failed to reflect the rich nuances of the Lutheran Confessions.

Two points are worth considering in Herrmann's treatment of the
third use of the Law. First, he presumed that the three uses of the Law are
susceptible to human manipulation. "Now we make another use of the
Law, adopting it as a rule and norm of our life, of our good works, to which
also the Psalmist's words apply: Lord, 'Thy Word is a lamp unto my feet
and a light unto my path' (Ps 119:105)."[175] Herrmann wrote as if the Law
would be ours to use or not to use, adopt or not to adopt, as a rule and
norm of life. He took the Law out of the hands of the holy God and set it
in the hands of unholy humans. However, the Lutheran Confessions clearly state that this word of God speaks to sinful humans. God uses it to
accomplish his ends and goals, when and where it pleases him.[176] Humans
proclaim the Law. God uses it. Second, Herrmann dissolved the tension
between the Christian as *justus* and the Christian as *peccator*. The Law loses
its accusing voice where the third use is described as "a pleasant path to
follow through the dreary desert of this loveless world, with the mild sun-
shine of divine blessings smiling down upon us, with the oases of mutual

love, which is hallowed and sanctified by the Holy Spirit."[177] Again, the Law was altogether too friendly.

BAD BOLL AND NEO-ORTHODOXY

Pieper's influence was mitigated because of the Missouri Synod's discovery of German Lutheranism and neo-orthodoxy.[178] The conference arranged by the Missouri Synod in 1948–49 and held at the Bad Boll spa in Swabia was the Missouri Synod's ecumenical debut. The Missouri Synod came out into the Lutheran mainstream when its commissioners met personally with the giants of German Lutheran scholarship, such as Werner Elert, Helmut Thielicke, Peter Brunner, Heinrich Bornkamm, Edmund Schlink, and Adolf Köberle.

These meetings had three important results for this discussion. First, the Missouri Synod commissioners returned to the United States with an altered view of the place of Scripture in theological prolegomena.[179] This has affected the course of Missouri Synod history to the present. Second, the commissioners encountered an ambivalence about the significance of the Formula of Concord for which they were unprepared. Third, the commissioners returned to their teaching posts eager to recommend these great Lutheran scholars to their students for graduate studies.[180]

The Formula of Concord. The confessional basis for the conference was limited to the Augsburg Confession. The major reason for this was that the Augsburg Confession still served as the legal basis for the existence of the Lutheran church in Germany.[181] Since the 16th century the Lutheran churches had legal status based only on a formal adherence to the Augsburg Confession.[182] Thus, the Formula of Concord was easily set in the background of German Lutheran research into Lutheran doctrine. The Formula of Concord was given status as doxology, "having the character of hymns."[183] This was something less than the high view of the *Book of Concord* accepted by the Missouri Synod. The second reason for the German tendency to devalue the Formula of Concord was the influence of the Luther renaissance that made a sharp division between Luther and later Lutheranism, including, and especially, the Formula of Concord.

Shifting Tendencies. The Missouri Synod commissioners came away from Bad Boll externally convinced that "the so-called repristination theology of the Missouri Synod, which was described as obscurantism, traditionalism, dead orthodoxy, is in reality its strength and driving force."[184] This evaluation was undoubtedly correct. The commissioners themselves showed signs of deviating from this putative source of strength, however, by shifting away from Pieper's emphasis on the Word as an *a priori* of Christian theology. David Scaer suggested that "Dr. F. E. Mayer seems to have been impressed by the arguments of the German theologians and began to integrate certain accents into his theology."[185] Edward H. Schroeder, a commentator more sympathetic to Mayer's shift, also noted the same changed accents in the work of Mayer.[186] Those accents included an altered place for the doctrine of the inspiration and inerrancy of Scripture. Mayer himself thought of this change in his thinking as nothing less than a breakthrough.[187] Scaer theorized that Mayer was led by influences he himself did not fully understand and had not evaluated.

What Mayer had imbibed without knowing it was the last remnant of the Erlangen theology of the 19th century, which Dr. Pieper in his *Christian Dogmatics* treated vigorously. The Erlangen theology had adopted Lutheran doctrine but with Schleiermacher's underpinnings—"theology of feeling." Pieper and the Erlangen theologians could agree on many facets of the "what" of theology, but they did not agree on how they got there. Paul Tillich's criticisms of the Erlangen theology are even more pointed than Pieper's.[188]

Thus, Pieper and the Erlangen school disagreed over theological prolegomena. At many points their results converged, but they disagreed about the foundational starting point of Lutheran theology. This had definite results for the Missouri Synod view of the place of the Law in Lutheran theology. Scaer recounted the reasons for Missouri's attraction to the work of Elert.

> Werner Elert, who out of all the Bad Boll conferees on the German side would make the biggest impression on the Missourians, was part of the Erlangen tradition. He had been a pastor and professor in the Breslau Synod, a church body that has grown closer and closer to the Missouri Synod. He also appeared as a chief attacker of Karl Barth on the matter of Law and Gospel. Elert's essay *Law and Gospel* was a direct reply to Barth's *Gospel and Law*. All this endeared Elert to the Missourians. But the elevation of "*Law-Gospel*" as the controlling theological theme was the weakness of Elert's position. The Missourians did not determine that Elert had provided no basis for his theology apart from a functional use of Scriptures and Luther. Elert like Barth had a Scripture divorced from history. Elert was in fact a "Lutheran-Barthian." His "Law-Gospel" principle hung suspended in theological thin air, almost in the same fashion as the Erlangen theology a century before.[189]

For Elert, the Law functioned to accuse the sinner, the Gospel to liberate the sinner from his sin. However, this bypassed entirely the question of truth. Was it true that the Law accused and the Gospel liberated? Was it true that they should? Without a definite doctrine of authority, there could be no certainty in the Law and Gospel construct besides a purely existential certainty. This existentialistic view of certainty was a wide deviation from the orthodox position evinced by Pieper and his followers. This deviation had a great impact on the Missouri Synod's theology in the next period, 1961–76.

F. E. MAYER

Frederick E. Mayer was professor of dogmatics at Concordia Seminary, St. Louis, from 1937 until his death in 1954.[190] His influence spread through his active role as an ambassador of the Missouri Synod to ecumenical gatherings such as the Bad Boll conferences and the Lutheran World Federation meeting at Lund in 1947 and through his editorship of *Concordia Theological Monthly* from 1940 to 1954.[191]

Balance between Existentialism and Orthodoxy. F. E. Mayer approached theology by attempting to strike a balance between existentialism and orthodoxy. In Mayer's 1949 review of T. A. Kantonen's *Resurgence of the Gospel*, he criticized Kantonen for allowing the pendulum "to swing all the way to Barthian dynamics and existentialism."[192] However, Mayer also perceived the salutary effects of existentialism in Lutheran theology.

> Existential theology has indeed made a tremendous contribution to modern thinking, inasmuch as it vehemently attacked the barrenness of liberal theology and of dead orthodoxy and insists that theology must be personal and dynamic. The author [Kantonen] shows that Luther was an "existential" thinker in the sense that for him religious facts were not only objectively true, but actually implied "encounter."[193]

For Mayer a dynamic faith did not necessarily lead to a denigration of objective "religious facts." Purely existentialistic interpretations of religion denied the distinction between the objective and the subjective. Existentialism taught that only the subjective was real. Mayer believed that the subjective encounter was based on "an 'objective' truth."[194] He wanted to maintain the best of orthodoxy along with the insights of existentialism, maintaining that "the issue [of subjective and objective] is not an either/or but both/and."[195] Mayer's definitive *The Religious Bodies of America* included the same perception about Luther's view of the Gospel: "The Christ in the Gospel became an objective reality for Luther and the Gospel promises a 'given,' a 'constant,' a *datum*, which remains ever the same regardless of his own personal experiences."[196] Mayer was definitely trying to head off a purely existentialistic interpretation of Luther by emphasizing the "given-ness" of the Gospel. Nevertheless, the *datum* of the Gospel still had existential results in Mayer's thinking.[197]

Mayer reflected this balanced approach in a study of Ernst Kinder's *Gottes Gebote und Gottes Gnade in Wort vom Kreuz*.[198] The twofold danger to Christian preaching was the "false emphasis on subjectivism," on the one hand, and antinomianism, on the other.[199] Subjectivism led to the attempt to gauge the state of grace on the basis of sanctification and a servile relationship to the Law. Antinomianism was born of an overemphasis on the objectivity of the Gospel.

> This occurs when Christians, on the basis of the false application of *sola gratia*, ignore the earnest admonitions to crucify the old man. It is true that man can neither add to nor detract from the promises of God's grace, for they are and remain an objective reality regardless of man's attitude. But the objectivity of the Gospel dare never be made the basis for a kind of quietism which sees in the Gospel primarily a soft pillow on which the lazy Christian can slumber securely.[200]

The Gospel is an objective given, but it may never be taken for granted by the Christian. The Gospel must result in an active ethical life. Balance between the subjective and the objective remains the watchword.

A Third Use. The balance sought by Mayer applied to the third use of the Law, which Mayer denominated *"usus normativus."*[201] The great danger that Mayer thought Lutherans needed to avoid in the third use was putting the third use of the Law at the center of the theological enterprise. Mayer identified this approach with Calvin and Calvinism. Calvin considered the *usus normativus legis* to be the *usus praecipuus*, whereas Lutheranism considered the *usus elenchticus legis* to be the *usus praecipuus*.[202] The latter conclusion can only be reached when the theologian holds the *semper accusat* of the Lutheran Confessions. Therefore, the third use remained for Mayer a "negative factor in the Christian's new obedience."[203] Mayer avoided dissolving the tension in Law and Gospel by taking into account the accusing function of the Law.

Mayer also understood the applicability of the whole Law to the whole person in Christian preaching, though he approached this from the perspective of the preacher. "Since it is, of course, impossible to dissect the Christian biologically into the old and the new man, the pastor will constantly preach the Law to the Christian's total personality in its so-called three uses."[204] Mayer was accounting for the freedom of God to accuse the person before the standard of the Law as well as direct the good works of the Christian with the Law. The Law and its use is in the hands of the sovereign God. The Word is for the preacher to speak and for God to use. Thus, the Law placed in the hands of the preacher is an objective message. Subjectively, God uses the word of Law in the existential life context of the Christian in accordance with his will to both accuse and direct. The preacher does not control the hearing. God's Word reaches the hearer and works God's way upon the Christian, often in ways hidden and unsuspected by the preacher.[205] Thus, the Law has a both/and character that can never be separated, any more than Law and Gospel can be separated in practical application. Following the emphasis of Elert, Mayer summarized, "Even for the Christian the Law is never merely informative, but always retains its condemnatory character."[206] Wrath will never be quelled this side of heaven.[207] Therefore, the Gospel must continue to be preached in the church. The third use cannot become a way for the Christian to tame the accusations of the Law because this will sideline the Gospel by dissolving the tension between Law and Gospel. A proper understanding of the third use of the Law will safeguard the use and continuing significance of the Gospel in the church.

The importance of defending the Gospel from legalism attracted Mayer to Elert's rejection of Calvinism's acceptance of the third use as the *usus praecipuus*.[208] Identifying the third use as the *usus praecipuus* skews Calvinism's theological approach toward the Law, so the Law is the ruling principle in Calvinism. "Calvin holds that even the Gospel does not introduce a new way of salvation, but ratifies what the Law has already promised us. The Gospel differs from the Law only in the clarity with which it is manifested."[209] For Calvin, Law and Gospel differ only in the way they are communicated, not in their content.[210] This anti-Calvinistic concern, though entirely legitimate, led Elert to deny the third use entirely. Mayer did not go that far, but Mayer did share with Elert the concern to avoid legalism. "The dogmatic term 'third use of the Law' has sometimes been used as a guise to cover a legalistic theology, as though the Law were some sort of a helpmeet for salvation. The typical legalist actually makes the third use of the Law its primary function."[211]

Although less of a scholar than Elert, Mayer's concern for the practical training of Lutheran preachers[212] kept him from drawing the radical conclusions about the third use of the Law advocated by Elert.

While Mayer continued to refuse to deny the third use of the Law, he began to advocate some of Elert's views on the third use. In a 1951 article in *Concordia Theological Monthly* titled "Human Will in Bondage and Freedom," Mayer suggested that Lutheran theology's doctrine of the Christian life lacked a specific legal code. "[The Christian life] is not controlled by a codified system of laws. The Christian has no set standard of rules and regulations according to which he lives, but in every moment, in every situation, there is before him the highest of all standards: *to be active in pleasing God.*"[213] If there are no rules, how can the Christian know what does please God?

In Lutheranism the Gospel must shape the Christian life. Otherwise, there is the peril of lapsing into bondage to the Law again.[214] However, the Gospel shape of the Christian life must be restricted to the *motivation* for good works. The Gospel itself makes no demands, gives no directions; it must never become Law. The Gospel makes the person new in heart, mind, and will. The specific direction of the Spirit-led life remains to be given by the word of the Law. Thus, Law and Gospel remain in tension.[215]

The tension created by the meeting of Law and Gospel in the Christian's life also correlates to a tension among the uses of the Law. The Law accuses, but it also directs and informs. Under the life-giving word of holy absolution in the Gospel, the word of accusation also guides. The reality of this tension always brings the Christian back to the Gospel. The Christian must never flee the shadow of the cross because the Law always accuses. Thus, the Christian life occurs under the hiddenness of God in Christ. However, Mayer overstated the situation in favor of the second use when he said, "The Law has only one function, namely, to accuse man."[216] Mayer followed the influence of Elert here, admitting his dependence on Elert's *Christian Ethos* in the notes.[217] The second use remains the primary and controlling use of the Law for Mayer.

> The Law must indeed be preached to the Christian, who because of his old Adam sometimes has foolish notions as to what are good works, invents his own works, and esteems these much higher than the good works which God has prescribed. Because of the old Adam, who is identical with the world, the Law must be preached to the Christians as a curb, as a mirror, and as a rule. But in this threefold function the Law remains plaintiff and judge (cp. Formula of Concord, Art. VI, pars. 18–24). *Lex semper accusat.*[218]

Mayer followed Elert while also using the terminology of the synodical catechism, "curb, mirror, and rule."[219] The Law's primary function is to accuse, but it does not only accuse.

The third use of the Law increasingly received less emphasis in Mayer, whom Elert deeply affected. The existential confrontation of the sinner by God became more important, though Mayer denied that he had been converted to existentialistic Lutheranism. The trajectory of Mayer's approach inspired later students to take a more radical angle on the third use of the Law.

SUMMARY ANALYSIS AND EVALUATION

LCMS theologians took varied approaches to the third use of the Law. The theologians who provided articles for *The Abiding Word* were deeply affected by the orthodoxy they inherited from Walther and Pieper. They emphasized the Law as an objective standard that provides instruction for Christian holiness. Unfortunately, their viewpoint tended to accept a tamed Law. They also made a sharp division between the heart and the mind of the Christian. The Gospel affected the heart; the Law affected the mind. These old Missourians emphasized the third use so strongly that they tended detrimentally to de-emphasize the second use. They also presumed that the Law was susceptible to human manipulation so the preacher controlled the uses of the Law. Later critics of these positions had ample room to chide the old Missourians.

The participation of LCMS theologians at the Bad Boll conferences affected LCMS theology. This was especially evident in the work of F. E. Mayer. He tried to meld orthodoxy and existentialism. He tried to strike a balance between the subjective and the objective. One did not rule out the other. He followed the lead of Werner Elert in de-emphasizing the third use of the Law. Mayer picked up the anti-Calvinistic concerns of German Lutherans and warned against legalism in the doctrine of the third use of the Law. The rejection of ethical rules in the later works of Mayer shows this concern. Mayer is significant because of the influence he wielded with the generation of students who drove his insights to more radical conclusions in the next period to be considered.

INTERPRETATION AND CRITICISM

Three different approaches to the third use of the Law developed in this first period discussed (1940–60). Theologians of the Valparaiso school denied the third use of the Law because they determined that it had its roots in the legalism of later Lutheran orthodoxy. This evaluation, based on contemporary Luther studies, went too far. First, a ministerial use of reason must remain part of theological deliberation. Second, Brian Gerrish showed that Luther did not deny reason a rightful, though limited, place in the theological enterprise.

The LCA-ALC approach still accepted natural law but denied the third use of the Law. Forell and Lazareth subscribed to the idea that the third use was simply the second use for Christians. Lazareth suggested that for Christians the Law becomes a description of good works rather than a threat against sinners. He thus introduced a *tertium quid*, which is neither Law nor Gospel, but a mingling of Law and Gospel.

The LCMS still gave lip service to Lutheran orthodoxy, but in reality it tended to deviate from orthodoxy. The theologians who contributed to *The Abiding Word* were more legalistic in their doctrine of the third use of the Law, suggesting that the Law was susceptible to human manipulation. They also introduced a tendency to distinguish the Law and Gospel in an anthropological fashion, with the Law making an impact on the mind, the Gospel on the heart. Mayer also deviated from orthodoxy by a tendency toward Neo-Lutheranism. This tendency bore more obvious fruit in the period to follow. The third use of the Law was in trouble in American Lutheran theology.

NOTES

[1] Liberalism in Protestantism had roots in the early 19th century. Liberal theologians emphasized that the basic religious truths are the fatherhood of God, the brotherhood of man, and the perfectibility of man. Liberalism incorporated modern discoveries in science, psychology, philosophy, and ethics. It was a method of inquiry rather than a body of knowledge. Its main proponents were Friedrich D. E. Schleiermacher, Albrecht Ritschl, and Ernst P. W. Troeltsch.

[2] Karl Barth, *Epistle to the Romans* (6th ed.; trans. Edwyn Hoskyns; London: Oxford University Press, 1933).

[3] Kenneth Hagen, "Changes in the Understanding of Luther: The Development of the Young Luther," *TS* 28 (September 1968): 477.

[4] T. A. Kantonen, *Resurgence of the Gospel* (Philadelphia: Muhlenberg, 1948), 26.

[5] Kantonen, *Resurgence of the Gospel*, 24.

[6] Kantonen, *Resurgence of the Gospel*, 22–33. For another compact summary of the American theological scene in this period, see Carl E. Braaten, *No Other Gospel* (Minneapolis: Fortress, 1992), 16–17.

[7] For a clear summary of the varieties of existentialism, see Alasdair MacIntyre, "Existentialism," in *The Encyclopedia of Philosophy* (repr. ed.; ed. Paul Edwards; New York: Macmillan, 1972).

[8] In summarizing the theological problems identified by the conferees, F. E. Mayer, one of the LCMS commissioners to the Bad Boll conferences of 1948–49, stated, "The German theologians are under the impact of an 'encounter,' an 'event' theology" (F. E. Mayer, *The Story of Bad Boll* [St. Louis: Concordia, 1949], 20).

[9] Kantonen, *Resurgence of the Gospel*, 20.

[10] Martin Buber, *I and Thou* (trans. Ronald Gregor Smith; New York: Scribner, 1957).

[11] In almost any controversy among Lutheran theologians, Luther's imprimatur was eagerly sought by the controversialists. This is hardly surprising because three writings of Luther came to have normative confessional status in the *Book of Concord*: the Small and Large Catechisms and the Smalcald Articles. The Formula of Concord sought to resolve Lutheran battles about doctrine in part by quoting Luther. Lutheran systematic theologies are often full of citations of the Wittenberg reformer. Jaroslav Pelikan understated Luther's influence on Lutheran theology by saying, "One cannot understand Lutheranism unless one sees, for example, that the person and experience of Martin Luther have assumed a paradigmatic role in the history of Lutheran piety" (Jaroslav Pelikan, foreword to *The Structure of Lutheranism*, by Werner Elert [trans. Walter A. Hansen; St. Louis: Concordia, 1962], ix). David S. Yeago pointed out the interdependence of Luther studies and Lutheran systematic theology. "Few of the influential German Protestant theologians whose thought was formed in that era (post World War I)—the theologians who dominated the academic scene until the 1960s—escaped the influence of powerful new currents in Luther-research, which became a significant scholarly industry in its own right at just that time. Indeed, given Luther's symbolic status as the greatest of the Protestant founder-figures, and that theological generation's widely shared intention to recover the authentic spirit of the Reformation, it is not surprising that for some theologians, the prolegomena to systematic theology became almost identical with Luther-interpretation" (David S. Yeago, "Gnosticism, Antinomianism, and Reformation Theology," *ProEccl* 2 [Winter 1993]: 37).

[12] Hartmann Grisar, *Luther*, 3 vols. (Freiburg im Breisgau: Herder, 1911–12); and Heinrich Denifle, *Luther und Luthertum in der Ersten Entwicklung* (Mainz: Kirchheim, 1904).

[13] Troeltsch placed Luther in the category of the church type in his now famous threefold typology of Christian communities. The three types are the church type, the sect type, and the mystical type. For purposes of this book, a description of the church type and the sect type will suffice: "In religious social ethics a sect is understood to be a particular type of religious organization which, by combining and applying in a distinctive way theological doctrines that in themselves may be quite orthodox, forms small, intimate, exclusive, voluntary societies based on explicit faith; resistance to compromise with 'the world'; participatory, protodemocratic, or populist leadership; and a normative metaphysical-moral vision, demanding rigorous ethical standards. This is understood to be in contrast to a church-type religious organization, which is large and based on implicit faith, adjustment to the world, hierarchical priesthood, and modulation of ethical rigor" (Max L. Stackhouse, "Sect," in *The Westminster Dictionary of Christian Ethics* [rev. ed.; eds. James F. Childress and John Macquarrie; Philadelphia: Westminster, 1986]). As far as Troeltsch was concerned, Luther had abandoned the free and freeing Gospel message by in some cases permitting and in other cases supporting the intrusion of the state into the life of the church. Luther's acceptance of the church-type led to several pernicious results. First, Luther accepted an absolute conception of truth. By teaching a universal church, Luther was led to accept a universal truth embodied in the absolute authority of the

Bible. See Ernst Troeltsch, *The Social Teaching of the Christian Churches*, vol. 2 (trans. Olive Wyon; New York: Macmillan, 1931; repr., New York: Harper Torchbooks, 1960), 484–85.

[14] Karl Holl, *What Did Luther Understand by Religion?* (eds. James Luther Adams and Walter F. Bense; trans. Fred W. Meuser and Walter R. Wietzke; Philadelphia: Fortress, 1977), 106, n. 72.

[15] Adolf von Harnack and Hans Lietzmann, *Karl Holl: Zwei Gedächtnisreden* (Berlin: Walter de Gruyter, 1926), 12–13, quoted by Walter F. Bense in the editor's introduction to *What Did Luther Understand*, 1.

[16] Heinrich Hermelink sees Holl as bringing to completion the work of Ritschl, contending that his understanding of Luther is "the culmination of the process of ethicising Luther that had been begun by Ritschl" (Hermelink, *"Ein Wendepunkt in der Lutherforschung," Die Christliche Welt* 38 [1924]: 108).

[17] See Holl, *What Did Luther Understand*, 51, n. 28.

[18] See Friedrich Gogarten, *"Theologie und Wissenschaft: Grundsätzliche Bemerkungen zu Karl Holls 'Luther,' " Die Christliche Welt* 38 (1924): 34–42, 71–80.

[19] Holl, *What Did Luther Understand*, 57.

[20] Holl, *What Did Luther Understand*, 107.

[21] In 1947, describing the contemporary scene, T. A. Kantonen scolded, "American Lutheran theology itself is still largely oriented in the seventeenth century, and, adhering to the traditional methods, continues to busy itself with old distinctions and abstractions quite removed from the present theological battlefield" (Kantonen, *Resurgence of the Gospel*, 37).

[22] For more on the organization and history of the Bad Boll conferences, see John W. Behnken, *This I Recall* (St. Louis: Concordia, 1964), 112–13.

[23] Mayer, *Story of Bad Boll*, 16.

[24] See Mayer, *Story of Bad Boll*, 13.

[25] See, for example, Wilhelm Pauck, *The Heritage of the Reformation* (rev. ed.; New York: Oxford University Press, 1968).

[26] Pauck, *Heritage of the Reformation*, 34.

[27] This was certainly evident in biographies of Luther, where the material is heavily weighted toward the young Luther. Up to the present time, the standard one-volume biography has been Roland Bainton's *Here I Stand: A Life of Martin Luther* (Nashville: Abingdon, 1950). Despite the fact that it is absorbingly written, Bainton's treatment is handicapped by the lack of attention to the later Luther. This lack of attention to the later Luther occurred because of occupation with existential concerns. Bainton's biography was organized to answer the question, "How can I find a gracious God?" This is certainly a central question to ask of the life of Luther, but it was not the only important concern for the Wittenberg reformer. James M. Kittelson, in his more recent *Luther the Reformer* (Minneapolis: Augsburg, 1986), goes beyond Bainton by asking how Luther sought to communicate the answer to that question in the life of the church. For more on the recent history of Luther research, see Helmar Junghans, "Interpreting the Old Luther (1526–1546)," *CurTM* 9 (1982): 271–81.

[28] Kantonen, *Resurgence of the Gospel*, 35.

[29] See pp. 47–51 for details on the Melanchthonian character of Lutheran orthodoxy.

[30] AC I; *BS* 50; *Trig* 43.

[31] Kantonen, *Resurgence of the Gospel*, 35. Luther used "essentialist" or philosophical language when such language became necessary to explain a theological point. For example, his treatise "That These Words of Christ, 'This Is My Body,' Still Stand Firm" (1527) uses the same terms used by Melanchthon in the Augsburg Confession (1530): "*Wesentlich*" and "*wesen*." Robert H. Fischer notes that when Luther uses "*Wesentlich*," it means " 'in essence' in the ancient philosophical sense" (LW 37:57, n. 97). Likewise, Luther uses "*wesen*" in the same philosophical sense elsewhere in the text of this treatise (LW 37:119). Speaking of the relationship between the communicant and Christ in the Sacrament of the Altar, Luther says, "*Also sei Christus durch das Sacrament, so wir essen und trinken, naturlich und wesentlich inn uns und wir inn ihm*" (WA 23:238, 8–10). "So Christ through the sacrament which we eat and drink is by nature and essence in us and we in him" (LW 37:121). Nor is this a development restricted to the so-called later Luther. The same language shows up prominently in "Against Latomus" (1521), in which Luther chides Latomus and the Louvain faculty for their ignorance of philosophy. See WA 8:43–128. "*(loquor ad morem Aristotelis, non sophistarum, qui adhuc nesciunt, quid sit per se apud Aristotelem propria passio)*" (WA 8:77, 11–13). "(I speak after the fashion of Aristotle, not of the sophists, for they still don't know what is an essential or proper attribute according to Aristotle)" (LW 32:186–87). Thus, while Luther rejected Aristotle's pernicious effects upon theology, he used Aristotelian terms or concepts if these served to clarify a point of theology. For more on Luther's use of philosophical terms, see Heinrich Bornkamm, *Luther in Mid-Career, 1521–1530* (ed. Karin Bornkamm; trans. E. Theodore Bachmann; Philadelphia: Fortress, 1983), 192–95; and Richard Klann, "Luther on Teaching Christian Ethics," in *A Lively Legacy* (eds. Kurt E. Marquart et al.; Fort Wayne: Concordia Theological Seminary Press, 1985), 96–104.

[32] For more on how this 17th-century mediation of Luther affected a non-Lutheran, John Henry Newman, in the 19th century, see Scott Murray, "Luther in Newman's 'Lectures on Justification,' " *CTQ* 54 (April–July 1990): 155–78.

[33] Frederick E. Mayer aptly said of *Resurgence of the Gospel*, "The significance of this book lies in its 'existentialist' approach. . . . To present Luther's theology as a 'dynamic' existentialist theology is, in our opinion, both the strength and weakness of this book" (Mayer, review of T. A. Kantonen, *Resurgence of the Gospel*, CTM 20 [April 1949]: 313). John W. Montgomery pointed out that existentialism is subject to the same critical analysis as any other philosophical presupposition. "Bultmann has argued, in defense of his use of existentialistic categories in interpreting biblical data, that existentialism is really not an alien philosophy, but a heuristic methodology that does not commit one to extra-biblical positions. It is almost universally agreed, however, both by professional philosophers and by lay interpreters of existentialism, that this viewpoint does indeed constitute a philosophy, and that its presuppositions (e.g., 'existence precedes essence,' 'the objective-subjective distinction must be transcended,' 'truth is found only in personal encounter,' etc.) can and must be subjected to philosophical analysis and criticism" (John W. Montgomery, *Crisis in Lutheran Theology*, vol. 1 [Grand Rapids: Baker, 1967; 2d rev. ed., Minneapolis: Bethany Fellowship, 1973], 25).

[34] In 1967, Montgomery summarized the critical evaluation of existentialism. "Such a process of critical analysis has been going on for some years now, and the results have been devastatingly negative for the existentialist position. Indeed, faced with the blistering criticism directed against existentialism by analytical philosophy in particular, contemporary thought is now beginning to move away from Albert Camus' [sic] dread city of Oran into more congenial philosophical habitats" (Montgomery, *Crisis*

in Lutheran Theology, 1:25). Even if not flawed, the existentialistic interpretation has been abandoned. Braaten stated that "the coalition that was branded neoorthodoxy is virtually dead—salvific (*Heilsgeschichte*) biblical theology, dialectical theology, Kierkegaardian and Luther studies, and the dogmatics of the various theologians of revelation" (Braaten, *No Other Gospel*, 16).

[35] Lewis Spitz Jr. pointed out that the development of existentialism from Kierkegaard to the present owed a great deal to Luther, but to paint Luther in existential colors misses the true Luther. "This total development owes much to Luther, it is true, but it offers a false image of the whole and wholesome Luther. As Katie Luther was not Regine Olsen, even so was Luther so much more than Kierkegaard. In many ways, Nikolai F. S. Grundtvig (1783–1872) was more like Luther than was Sören Kierkegaard" (Lewis W. Spitz Jr., "Images of Luther," *CJ* 11 [March 1985]: 49).

[36] Gerhard Forde aptly said, "The debate over Luther's theology has been carried out in living dialogue with the developing demands of systematic theology. This is no doubt the reason why in many Lutheran circles Luther research has been almost a substitute for systematic theology, or at least a determinative factor in it" (Gerhard Forde, *The Law-Gospel Debate* [Minneapolis: Augsburg, 1969], 198–99). Lewis W. Spitz Jr. held a similar view: "As that [20th-century] revival of interest in Luther progressed, he and his *theologia crucis et passionis*, which emerged clearly in his 1516 letters, sermons and letters prior to his 1517 theses, became increasingly adjunct to systematic theology" (Spitz, "Images of Luther," 47).

[37] David P. Scaer, "The Law Gospel Debate in the Missouri Synod," *Springfielder* 36 (December 1972): 156–71.

[38] Scaer, "Law Gospel Debate," 157–58. This group also included Jaroslav Pelikan, who had been a teacher of philosophy at Valparaiso University, Walter E. Keller, Robert J. Hoyer, Robert W. Bertram, and, later, Kenneth F. Korby and David G. Truemper.

[39] Of these theologians, only Korby and Bretscher remain on the LCMS clergy roster.

[40] Caemmerer was a member of the faculty majority that "walked out" of Concordia Seminary in February 1974.

[41] Richard R. Caemmerer, "The Melanchthonian Blight," *CTM* 18 (May 1947): 321–38.

[42] Caemmerer, "Melanchthonian Blight," 323.

[43] Melanchthon stated that the purpose of the 1521 edition of the *Loci Communes Theologici* was to help youth understand "how corrupt are all the theological hallucinations of those who have offered us the subtleties of Aristotle instead of the teachings of Christ" (Melanchthon, *Loci Communes Theologici* [ed. Wilhelm Pauck; trans. Lowell J. Satre; LCC 19; Philadelphia: Westminster, 1969], 19). Elsewhere, speaking of the doctrine of qualities in Aristotelian logic, Melanchthon says, "Those Aristotelian figments about qualities are quite tiresome" (Melanchthon, *Loci Communes Theologici*, 87). Luther's "Disputation Against Scholastic Theology" (1517) included a ringing rejection of Aristotle: "41. Virtually the entire Ethics of Aristotle is the worst enemy of grace. This is in opposition to the scholastics. . . . 43. It is an error to say that no man can become a theologian without Aristotle. This is in opposition to common opinion. . . . 44. Indeed, no one can become a theologian unless he becomes one without Aristotle. . . . 45. To state that a theologian who is not a logician is a monstrous heretic—this is a monstrous and heretical statement" (LW 31:12;

WA 1:221–28).

[44] See Kittelson, *Luther the Reformer,* 248. See also James M. Kittelson, "Luther, the Church Bureaucrat," *CJ* 13 (October 1987): 294–306.

[45] See Caemmerer, "Melanchthonian Blight," 325.

[46] For an example, see the fragment of the 1536 disputation about human nature in WA 39/1:175–80.

[47] See Kittelson, *Luther the Reformer,* 248.

[48] Carl Braaten offers a stinging criticism of an existential doctrine of justification: "The total message of God's righteousness for the world cannot be translated into the framework of an existentialistic individualizing anthropology. Existentialist soteriology is a modern form of the earlier pietistic reduction" (Braaten, *The Future of God,* [New York: Harper & Row, 1969], 99). For Braaten, existentialistic approaches to justification are far too limiting because they look at theology from an anthropological perspective rather than a theological perspective.

[49] Kurt Marquart gives this scathing assessment of the penchant for Lutheran moderates to attack Aristotelianism: "True, Aristotle, that idol of scholasticism, is generally booed—but mainly because he is out of fashion. The new Aristotles, evil geniuses like Darwin, Marx, and Freud, now set the tone" (Kurt Marquart, *Anatomy of an Explosion* [Concordia Seminary Monograph Series 3; Fort Wayne: Concordia Theological Seminary Press, 1977], 138). Nietszche and Sartre might be added to the list of geniuses here.

[50] See, for example, *Trig* 128–9: "Melanchthon must be regarded as the father of both synergism and the rationalistic methods employed in its defense, and as the true father also of the modern rationalistico-synergistic theology represented by such distinguished men as Von Hofmann, Thomasius, Kahnis, Luthardt, etc." See also Franz Pieper, *Christliche Dogmatik,* vol. 2 (St. Louis: Concordia, 1917), 583. John M. Drickamer offered this clear definition of synergism: "Synergism is any doctrine of conversion that attributes to man any ability to contribute something to his own conversion. Monergism, the Lutheran position, holds that God alone brings about the whole of conversion" (John M. Drickamer, "Did Melanchthon Become a Synergist?" *Springfielder* 40 [September 1976]: 95).

[51] The charge of intellectualization of the faith was, already in 1937, countered by Hermann Sasse of Erlangen. In the foreword to the American edition of his book *Here We Stand,* Sasse pointed out that the Lutheran church's struggle has always been over doctrine and the significance of her confessional documents. "This is not, as has sometimes been maintained, a false intellectualization of the Christian faith. It is rather a fruit of the Reformation of Martin Luther who once recalled Christendom to a renewed search for true doctrine, for the truth of the Gospel" (Sasse, *Here We Stand* [trans. Theodore G. Tappert; Minneapolis: Augsburg, 1946], 7).

[52] Caemmerer, "Melanchthonian Blight," 329.

[53] Caemmerer, "Melanchthonian Blight," 330.

[54] Philip Melanchthon, *Commentary on Romans* (trans. Fred Kramer; St. Louis: Concordia, 1992), 97.

[55] Caemmerer, "Melanchthonian Blight," 331.

[56] Caemmerer, "Melanchthonian Blight," 332.

[57] Luther expressed this dynamic relationship between faith and good works in the words quoted in the Formula of Concord (SD IV, 10–12): "*Aber Glaube ist ein göttlich*

Werk in uns, das uns mandelt und neu gebiert aus Gott, Joh. 1. und tödtet den alten Adam, machet uns ganz ander Manschen, von Herzen, Muth, Sin und allen Kräften, und bringet den Heiligen Geist mit sich. Des ist ein lebendig, schäftig, thätig, mächtig, Ding unb ben Glauben, daß ummüglich ist, daß er nicht ohn Unterlaß sollte Guts wirken Er fraget auch nicht, ob gute Werk zu thun sind, sondern ehe man fraget, hat er sie gethan, und ist immer im Thun. Were aber nicht solche Werk thut, der ist ein glaubloser Mensch, tappet und stehet umb sich nach dem Glauben und guten Werken, und weiß weder was Glaube oder gute Werk sind, wäschet und schwäßet doch viel Wort vom Glauben und guten Werken.

"Glaube ist ein lebendige, erwegene Zuversicht auf Gottes Gnade, so gewiß, daß er tausend mal drüber stürbe. Und solche Zuversicht und Erkenntniß göttlicher Gnade machet frölich, troßig und lüstig gegen Gott und alle Creaturn: welchs der Heilige Geist thut im Glauben. Daher ohn Zwang willig und lüstig wird Federmann guts zu thun, Federmann zu dienen, allerlei zu leiden, Gott zu Liebe und zu Lob, der ihm solche Gnade erzeiget hat, also daß ummüglich, als Brennen und Leuchten vom Feur mag gescheiden werden" (WADB 7:10).
"Thus faith is a divine work in us, that changes us and regenerates us of God, and puts to death the old Adam, makes us entirely different men in heart, spirit, mind, and all powers, and brings with it [confers] the Holy Ghost. Oh, it is a living, busy, active, powerful thing that we have in faith, so that it is impossible for it not to do good without ceasing. Nor does it ask whether good works are to be done; but before the question is asked, it has wrought them, and is always engaged in doing them. But he who does not do such works is void of faith, and gropes and looks about after faith and good works, and knows neither what faith nor what good works are, yet babbles and prates with many words concerning faith and good works. [Justifying] faith is a living, bold [firm] trust in God's grace, so certain that a man would die a thousand times for it [rather than suffer this trust to be wrested from him]. And this trust and knowledge of divine grace renders joyful, fearless, and cheerful towards God and all creatures, which [joy and cheerfulness] the Holy Ghost works through faith; and on account of this, man becomes ready and cheerful, without coercion, to do good to every one, to serve every one, and to suffer everything for love and praise to God, who has conferred this grace on him, so that it is impossible to separate works from faith, yea, just as impossible as it is for heat and light to be separated from fire" (*Trig* 941).

[58] Caemmerer, "Melanchthonian Blight," 332.

[59] Caemmerer, "Melanchthonian Blight," 332.

[60] For more on the Lutheran doctrine of vocation, see Werner Elert, *The Christian Ethos* (trans. Carl J. Schindler; Philadelphia: Muhlenberg, 1957), 131–35; Helmut Thielicke, *Theological Ethics*, vol. 1 (ed. William H. Lazareth; Philadelphia: Fortress, 1966); and Gustaf Wingren, *The Christian's Calling: Luther on Vocation* (trans. Carl C. Rasmussen; Edinburgh: Oliver & Boyd, 1958).

[61] See Caemmerer, "Melanchthonian Blight," 334. Interpreters who share Caemmerer's presuppositions would ascribe also to Luther a doctrine of civil righteousness that aimed at a high degree of external righteousness, lessening the divide between Luther and Melanchthon on this point. See, for example, William H. Lazareth, *Luther on the Christian Home* (Philadelphia: Muhlenberg, 1960), 117: "Luther was convinced that all God's rational creatures—despite sin—are still capable of a high degree of civil righteousness by virtue of the divine Law which God has written 'with his own finger' into their hearts at creation." See WA 10/3:373.

[62] See Caemmerer, "Melanchthonian Blight," 337–38.

[63] Caemmerer, "Melanchthonian Blight," 337.

[64] Caemmerer, "Melanchthonian Blight," 337.

[65] The last thesis of Walther's *Gesetz und Evangelium* is "*Das Wort Gottes wird ein-undzwanzigstens nicht recht getheilt, wenn man in seiner Lehre nicht das Evangelium im Allgemeinen vorherrschen läßt*" (C. F. W. Walther, *Die Rechte Unterscheidung von Gesetz und Evangelium* [St. Louis: Concordia, 1897], 391). "The Word of God is not rightly divided when the person teaching it does not allow the Gospel to have a general predominance in his teaching" (C. F. W. Walther, *The Proper Distinction between Law and Gospel* [trans. W. H. T Dau; St. Louis: Concordia, 1986], 403).

[66] For more on the Melanchthonian blight's impact and basis, see Ken Schurb, "Twentieth-Century Melanchthon Scholarship: With Particular Reference to 'The Melanchthonian Blight,' " *CTQ* 62 (October 1998): 287–307.

[67] Robert C. Schultz, "Pastoral Theology," in *The Lively Function of the Gospel* (ed. Robert W. Bertram; St. Louis: Concordia, 1966), 15.

[68] Jaroslav Pelikan, *From Luther to Kierkegaard* (St. Louis: Concordia, 1950).

[69] Pelikan admitted that "in my method I have been particularly influenced by the work of Werner Elert and of Karl Holl, the latter through Wilhelm Pauck, who was Holl's pupil and, in turn, my teacher" (Pelikan, *From Luther to Kierkegaard*, vi).

[70] Pelikan, *From Luther to Kierkegaard*, 26.

[71] See Jaroslav Pelikan, *Fools for Christ* (Philadelphia: Muhlenberg, 1955), 5.

[72] Pelikan, *Fools for Christ*, 42. Pelikan based this judgment on the work of Holl, "*Die Rechtfertigungslehre in Luthers Vorlesung über den Römerbrief*," in *Gesammelte Aufsätze sur Kirchengeschichte*, vol. 1 (Tübingen: J. C. B. Mohr, 1948), 126–29.

[73] Pelikan, *From Luther to Kierkegaard*, 42.

[74] Pelikan, *From Luther to Kierkegaard*, 52–55. For more on the relationship between philosophy and theology in later Lutheranism, see Robert D. Preus, *The Theology of Post-Reformation Lutheranism*, vol. 1 (St. Louis: Concordia, 1970), 128–40.

[75] Pelikan, *From Luther to Kierkegaard*, 59.

[76] Pelikan, *From Luther to Kierkegaard*, 115.

[77] Søren Kierkegaard, *Fear and Trembling* (trans. Walter Lowrie; Princeton: Princeton University Press, 1941; repr., Garden City: Doubleday Anchor, 1954).

[78] Genesis 22.

[79] Kierkegaard, *Fear and Trembling*, 64.

[80] Pelikan, *From Luther to Kierkegaard*, 116.

[81] Kierkegaard, *Fear and Trembling*, 77.

[82] In fact, Wolfhart Pannenberg has stated that the Lutheran doctrine of justification is no longer a valid doctrine for contemporary preaching because modern man no longer suffers from the internal anxiety over sin. See Wolfhart Pannenberg, "Protestant Piety and Guilt Consciousness," in *Christian Spirituality* (Philadelphia: Westminster, 1983), 13–30. Peter Sedgwick summarized: "Common to modern existentialist writing is the meaninglessness of the Reformation formulas of forensic judgement and imputed righteousness in describing our human plight" (Sedgwick, " 'Justification by Faith': One Doctrine, Many Debates?" *Theology* [January–February 1990]: 11). This was especially true at the end of the Second World War, when German clergy concluded that "in spite of the emphasis on the guilt question, there is, however, no genuine consciousness of guilt" (Mayer, *Story of Bad Boll*, 20).

[83] Lazareth, *Luther on the Christian Home*, 74.

[84] Brian A. Gerrish, *Grace and Reason* (Oxford: Clarendon Press, 1962).

[85] Gerrish, *Grace and Reason*, vii

[86] Gerrish, *Grace and Reason*, vii.

[87] See Gerrish, *Grace and Reason*, 73.

[88] Gerrish did the bulk of his research in Luther's familiar "Lectures on Galatians" of 1535. See Gerrish, *Grace and Reason*, viii.

[89] See p. 88, n. 212.

[90] E. Clifford Nelson, "The New Shape of Lutheranism 1930–" in *The Lutherans in North America* (ed. E. Clifford Nelson; Philadelphia: Fortress, 1975), 497.

[91] Nelson documents how this shift affected Lutheran colleges and seminaries in this period: "A discernable change appeared about 1947 when some professors began to approach the Scriptures theologically and historically rather than with the a priori of inerrancy and verbal inspiration. What was a small voice in 1947 became a large noise within a decade" (Nelson, "New Shape of Lutheranism," 497). See also E. Clifford Nelson, *Lutheranism in North America: 1914–1970* (Minneapolis: Augsburg, 1972), 163–66. Generally, this shift was uniformly accepted in LCA and ALC circles. However, there were still notable exceptions, such as E. C. Fendt, "The Theology of the 'Common Confession,' " *LQ* 2 (August 1950): 308–23; and E. C. Fendt, ed., *What Lutherans Are Thinking* (Columbus: Wartburg, 1947).

[92] In the LCMS, Robert W. Bertram, ed., *Theology in the Life of the Church* (Philadelphia: Fortress, 1963), represented a Neo-Lutheran perspective in a church body committed to Old Lutheranism.

[93] George W. Forell, *Ethics of Decision* (Philadelphia: Muhlenberg, 1955).

[94] The contemporary context was dominated by the situation ethics debate. See James F. Childress, "Situation Ethics," in Childress and Macquarrie, eds., *Dictionary of Christian Ethics*. Situational ethics and existentialist ethics hold in common one essential characteristic, namely, the rejection of objective standards of moral action. Joseph Fletcher, the popularizer of situational ethics, wrote, "Situationism, then, is the crystal precipitated in Christian ethics by our era's widespread reaction against legalism" (Joseph Fletcher, *Moral Responsibility* [Philadelphia: Westminster, 1967], 27). Legalism was defined as the imposition of an external and trans-temporally valid legal code. Both situationism and existentialism denied such a code because it was legalistic and constricting.

[95] See Forell, *Ethics of Decision*, 4.

[96] Edwards, *Encyclopedia of Philosophy*, 3:149.

[97] Forell, *Ethics of Decision*, 65; emphasis in the original.

[98] Forell, *Ethics of Decision*, 65–66.

[99] Forell, *Ethics of Decision*, 78.

[100] See Forell, *Ethics of Decision*, 68–69. Here Forell included a lengthy quotation from Emil Brunner, *Man in Revolt* (trans. Olive Wyon; Philadelphia: Westminster, 1947), 97–98.

[101] Forell, *Ethics of Decision*, 78.

[102] Forell, *Ethics of Decision*, 80.

[103] Forell, *Ethics of Decision*, 81.

[104] Cf. Gustaf Aulén, *The Faith of the Christian Church* (trans. Eric H. Wahlstrom and G. Everett Arden; Philadelphia: Muhlenberg, 1948), 189: "The idea lex naturae has often appeared as a substitute for the lex creationis, or lex creatoris, of Christian faith. Lex naturae, the Law of nature, could be described as a rationalized and secularized variety of lex creationis. The foundation of both is a universal Law. The difference between them can be defined in this way, that lex naturae is a metaphysical conception, while lex creationis is a religious concept, originating in the relation to God and inseparably connected with faith in God as 'Creator.' "

[105] Forell, *Ethics of Decision*, 81.

[106] G. E. Moore described this as the so-called naturalistic fallacy, namely, a definition of goodness "in terms of natural properties and thus implying that it itself is a natural property" (Jonathan Harrison, "Ethical Naturalism," in Edwards, ed., *Encyclopedia of Philosophy*). For a discussion of how the naturalistic fallacy has been treated in Christian theology, see Paul R. Sponheim, "The Knowledge of God," in *Christian Dogmatics* (eds. Carl E. Braaten and Robert W. Jenson; Philadelphia: Fortress, 1984), 233–35. Joseph Sittler also taught a natural law that conformed to the shape of creation. In a more philosophical treatment of Christian ethics than Lazareth's, Sittler wrote, "The Ten Commandments, as the Law of God, are a verbalization of the given structures of creation. They stand above all men, believers and non-believers alike, as an accurate transcript of the facts—that the world is of God, that ultimate relations among men and things are grounded in him. The Stoic-immanental concept of natural law with which many systems of philosophical ethics operate is not introduced here because it is not needed" (Joseph Sittler, *The Structure of Christian Ethics* [Baton Rouge: Louisiana State University Press, 1958], 70).

[107] Forell, *Ethics of Decision*, 85.

[108] According to Forell, these differences are mainly differences in degree. For example, "Of course, there is a tremendous difference between Pennsylvania Quakers and New Guinea headhunters—but the difference is rather in the scope of the prohibition than in the prohibition. Even the headhunters have Laws that prevent them from taking the lives of their fellows in the same tribe or village" (Forell, *Ethics of Decision*, 86–87).

[109] Forell, *Ethics of Decision*, 87.

[110] Forell, *Ethics of Decision*, 87.

[111] Luther taught a close connection between the Ten Commandments and the natural law. The Ten Commandments provided a valid testimony to the binding contents of the moral law. For Luther the question remained, Which word of Moses applied to Christians? How far and in what particulars did the Decalogue extend to Christians? *"Also halt ich nu die gepot, die Moses geben hat, nicht darümb, das sie Moses geboten hat, sondern das sie mir von natur eingepflanket sind und Moses alhie gleich mit der natur ubereinstummet etc"* (WA 16:380, 23–25). In fact, Forell could not altogether avoid the Ten Commandments. The final third of Forell's book includes an exposition of the Ten Commandments. See Forell, *Ethics of Decision*, 104–50.

[112] See Forell, *Ethics of Decision*, 88.

[113] Ap IV, 38; 4, 128; *BS* 167, 185; *Trig* 165–67, 191.

[114] Laudably, Forell was attempting to reach a broader community with Christian ethics by using the then-familiar and popular philosophy of existentialism. He concluded the chapter "The Life of Man under the Law" with a section headed, "Modern Man and the Law of God." He concluded that section with a quotation

from Blaise Pascal's *Pensees*.

[115] Forell, *Ethics of Decision*, 91.

[116] Forell, *Ethics of Decision*, 104.

[117] Forell, *Ethics of Decision*, 120.

[118] Forell, *Ethics of Decision*, 120.

[119] See Lazareth, *Luther on the Christian Home*, ix.

[120] See Lazareth, *Luther on the Christian Home*, 8–9.

[121] See Lazareth, *Luther on the Christian Home*, 119.

[122] Lazareth, *Luther on the Christian Home*, 61; emphasis in the original.

[123] Lazareth, *Luther on the Christian Home*, 83.

[124] Lazareth, *Luther on the Christian Home*, 84.

[125] See Lazareth, *Luther on the Christian Home*, 85.

[126] WA 31:372–77.

[127] LW 31:344. "*Christianus homo omnium dominus est liberrimus, nulli subiectus. Christianus homo omnium servus est officiossimus, omnibus subiectus*" (WA 7:49, 22–25).

[128] See Lazareth, *Luther on the Christian Home*, 98.

[129] Elert, *Christian Ethos*, 148.

[130] See Lazareth, *Luther on the Christian Home*, 98.

[131] George W. Forell, *Faith Active in Love* (Minneapolis: Augsburg, 1954), 187.

[132] Situation ethics has a strong flavoring of existentialism, so ethicists consider existentialistic ethics a subspecies of situation ethics. See Childress, "Situation Ethics," in Childress and Macquarrie, eds., *Dictionary of Christian Ethics*.

[133] Lazareth, *Luther on the Christian Home*, 100.

[134] Lazareth, *Luther on the Christian Home*, 100.

[135] Lazareth, *Luther on the Christian Home*, 99.

[136] Lazareth, *Luther on the Christian Home*, 115.

[137] "Recent Luther research has proved conclusively that Luther taught no third use of the Law (*usus didacticus*) in the Calvinistic-Melanchthonian sense of 'guiding rule of life for the regenerate' " (Lazareth, *Luther on the Christian Home*, 125, n. 56).

[138] See Lazareth, *Luther on the Christian Home*, 125, n. 56.

[139] See Elert, *Christian Ethos*, 294–303; and Werner Elert, *Law and Gospel* (trans. Edward H. Schroeder; Philadelphia: Fortress, 1967), 38–43.

[140] Lazareth, *Luther on the Christian Home*, 125, n. 56.

[141] The famous "A Statement" of 1945 showed a deep theological unrest mainly among younger pastors and theologians. See Nelson, *Lutheranism in North America*, 244. See also Ralph A. Bohlmann, "Missouri Lutheranism, 1945 and 1995," *Lutheran Forum* 30 (February 1996): 12–17.

[142] Bohlmann, "Missouri Lutheranism," 12–17.

[143] Walther produced an edition of John William Baier, *Compendium Theologiae Positivae*, 2 vols. (St. Louis: Concordia, 1879), which was a list of passages from 17th-century theologians on the various topics of theology. This book was used as a textbook at Concordia Seminary in St. Louis into the 20th century. Already in 1862

Walther was defending himself and his church body from the charge of a lack of creativity because of the repristinating tendency. See August Suelflow, ed., *Editorials from "Lehre und Wehre"* (trans. Herbert J. A. Bouman; vol. in *Selected Writings of C. F. W. Walther*; St. Louis: Concordia, 1981), 102–14.

[144] Carl S. Meyer, *Log Cabin to Luther Tower* (St. Louis: Concordia, 1965), 78.

[145] Meyer, *Log Cabin to Luther Tower*, 78.

[146] Martin H. Franzmann, *Bad Boll 1949* (St. Louis: The Lutheran Church—Missouri Synod, 1950), 62. Franzmann, the great Missouri Synod exegete, returned from Bad Boll embarrassed by the lack of scholarship shown by the Missouri Synod commissioners in comparison to the prodigious learning of the German Lutherans. See also Mayer, *Story of Bad Boll*, 18.

[147] Mayer, *Story of Bad Boll*, 8.

[148] A. O. Fuerbringer, quoted in "Counselors and Fiscal Conference Majors in Theological Study," *The Lutheran Witness* (4 October 1960): 522.

[149] This reputation for "repristination theology" in the worst sense of the word has dogged the Missouri Synod into the present, a reputation that is not always well deserved. Leonard Klein, a theologian of the ELCA, was surprised by the theological acumen and congeniality of the younger Missouri Synod pastors and theologians whom he met at the annual Symposium on the Lutheran Confessions in 1992, which meets in Fort Wayne, Indiana, at Concordia Theological Seminary. See Leonard Klein, "Back Home Again in Indiana," *Forum Letter* 21 (4 March 1992): 2. Klein expected to meet narrow-minded and dead orthodox theologians, but he found a vibrant group of thoughtful, confessional Lutherans. Klein recalled the mood of the Fort Wayne gathering: "Twenty years after the explosion of the seventies, some of Missouri's most important theological leadership is anything but ghettoized in spite of what some might have predicted or wished. Indeed, criticism of Missouri's tendency to converse only with its own tradition was common. Professor Kurt Marquart reminded a consenting crowd that theology is not 'the mantra-like recitation of misunderstood formulas' " (Klein, "Back Home Again," 2).

[150] Two systematic theologies are now in progress in the LCMS, one under the editorship of Ralph Bohlmann, the other, *Confessional Lutheran Dogmatics*, was under the editorship of the late Robert Preus. The latter has already issued three volumes, one each by David P. Scaer, Kurt E. Marquart, and John R. Stephenson.

[151] Francis Pieper, *Christian Dogmatics*, 3 vols. (trans. Walter W. F. Albrecht; St. Louis: Concordia, 1950–53).

[152] For more on how the repristination theology fared at Concordia Seminary in the Pieper period, see Meyer, *Log Cabin to Luther Tower*, 89–95.

[153] Pieper's theological work was already eclipsed by dialectical theology when it was put into print because it primarily repudiated 19th-century liberal theology. See David P. Scaer, "Francis Pieper," in *Handbook of Evangelical Theologians* (ed. Walter A. Elwell; Grand Rapids: Baker, 1993), 42.

[154] See Scaer, "Francis Pieper," in Elwell, ed., *Handbook of Evangelical Theologians*, 43.

[155] See Pieper's criticism of the 17th-century doctrine of *intuitu fidei*, which, according to Pieper, ascribed to humans merit in conversion (Pieper, *Christliche Dogmatik*, 3:566–68).

[156] Richard E. Koenig, "What's behind the Showdown in the LCMS? Church and Tradition in Collision," *Lutheran Forum* (November 1972): 18.

[157] See Pieper, *Christliche Dogmatik*, vol. 2. Scaer pointed out that "Pieper regarded justification as a subsidiary article of Christology, to which he devoted over three hundred pages, and that the discussion of election is really about justification" (Scaer, "Francis Pieper," in Elwell, ed., *Handbook of Evangelical Theologians*, 47).

[158] See Pieper, *Christliche Dogmatik*, 1:6–19.

[159] See Pieper, *Christliche Dogmatik*, 1:84–85.

[160] Pieper, *Christian Dogmatics*, 1:79. "*In bezug auf gute Werke soll der Theologe aus dem Gesetz lehren, was gute, das ist, Gott wohlgefällige, von Gott gebotene Werke sind, wie Christus die Frage nach guten Werken aus dem Gesetz beantwortet*" (Pieper, *Christliche Dogmatik*, 1:88).

[161] Pieper, *Christliche Dogmatik*, 1:88. Of these passages listed by Pieper, only the first strongly implies a second use of the Law by Jesus. The other two are better seen as third use because of the outcome of this preaching of the Law by Jesus.

[162] Pieper, *Christian Dogmatics*, 3:239. "*Zum andern, weil der Christ dem Fleische nach geneigt ist, sich in bezug aud die guten Werke, die Gott von ihm haben will, zu irren, so hat er noch fortgehend aus dem Gesetz Gottes, als der unveränderlichen Norm eines gottgefälligen Lebens, zu lernen, was Gottes Wille an ihn sei*" (Pieper, *Christliche Dogmatik*, 3:282).

[163] Theodore Laetsch, ed., preface to *The Abiding Word*, vol. 1 (St. Louis: Concordia, 1946), v.

[164] Some of the essays in the collection are merely strings of quotations from district convention essays and "*Lehre und Wehre*" articles. See, for example, Walter Geihsler, "The Law and the Gospel," in *The Abiding Word*, vol. 1 (ed. Theodore Laetsch; St. Louis: Concordia, 1946), 121–22.

[165] Geihsler, "The Law and the Gospel," 1:120.

[166] Geihsler, "The Law and the Gospel," 1:120.

[167] R. Herrmann, "The Decalog and the Close of the Commandments," in *The Abiding Word*, vol 1 (ed. Theodore Laetsch; St. Louis: Concordia, 1946), 124.

[168] Herrmann, "The Decalog," 1:124.

[169] Herrmann, "The Decalog," 1:126.

[170] *A Short Explanation of Dr. Martin Luther's Small Catechism* (St. Louis: Concordia, 1943), 85–86.

[171] SD VI, 4; *Trig* 963. "*Dann das Gesetz ist ein Spiegel, in welchem der Wille Gottes und was ihme gefällig, eigentlich abgemalet ist, das man den Gläubigen stets fürhalten, und bei ihnen ohn Unterlaß fleißig treiben soll*" (*BS* 963).

[172] SD VI, 21; *BS* 968; *Trig* 969.

[173] Ep VI, 1; *BS* 793; *Trig* 805.

[174] SD VI, 3; *BS* 963; *Trig* 963.

[175] Herrmann, "The Decalog," 1:134.

[176] AC V, 2; *BS* 58; *Trig* 45. Melanchthon knew well that the Law was not susceptible to human manipulation because human ethical action was not motivated by single, discrete causes. He astutely pointed this out in his 1543 *Loci*: "[*Pii*] *sciunt ejusdem facti multas esse causas et ordinatas. Sciunt, potius propter Deum recte faciendum esse, quam propter poenas. Sed sciunt hoc quoque, Deum velle agnosci voluntatem suam, et iram in poenis, velle metui poenas praesentes et futuras*" (Philip Melanchthon, *Loci Communes* [1543], quoted in Martin Chemnitz, *Loci Theologici*, vol. 2 [Frankfurt: Christian Henry

Schumacher, 1690], 6).

[177] Herrmann, "The Decalog," 1:134.

[178] Neo-orthodoxy was a movement of 20th-century theology that opposed liberalism. Proponents included Karl Barth, Emil Brunner, and Reinhold Niebuhr. Neo-orthodoxy emphasized encounter with the word, a dialectical approach to theology, and the importance of the subject. It was influenced by the existentialism of Kierkegaard.

[179] See Scaer, "Law Gospel Debate," 160–61; and Edward H. Schroeder, "Law-Gospel Reductionism in the History of The Lutheran Church—Missouri Synod," *CTM* 43 (April 1972): 245–47.

[180] See Scaer, "Law Gospel Debate," 165.

[181] Mayer, *Story of Bad Boll*, 17.

[182] Calvinist churches in Germany did not receive legal status until after the Thirty Years War (1618–48), at the Peace of Passau; thus, until that time, they were considered to be illegal according to imperial law.

[183] Mayer, *Story of Bad Boll*, 17.

[184] Mayer, *Story of Bad Boll*, 62.

[185] Scaer, "Law Gospel Debate," 161.

[186] See Schroeder, "Law-Gospel Reductionism," 244–45.

[187] See Schroeder, "Law-Gospel Reductionism," 246.

[188] See Scaer, "Law Gospel Debate," 161–62. For the comments of Tillich about the Erlangen attempt to Lutheranize Schleiermacher, see Paul Tillich, *Systematic Theology*, vol. 1 (Chicago: University of Chicago Press, 1951), 42.

[189] Scaer, "Law Gospel Debate," 162–63.

[190] Before coming to Concordia Seminary, St. Louis, Mayer taught at Concordia Theological Seminary, Springfield, Illinois, from 1926 to 1937.

[191] William F. Arndt, "In Memoriam," *CTM* 25 (September 1954): 641–46.

[192] Mayer, review of *Resurgence of the Gospel*, 313.

[193] Mayer, review of *Resurgence of the Gospel*, 313.

[194] Mayer, review of *Resurgence of the Gospel*, 314.

[195] Mayer, review of *Resurgence of the Gospel*, 314. Jaroslav Pelikan suggested that the "subject-object" distinction was unknown to the Lutheran Confessions but originated with the work of John Gerhard. See Jaroslav Pelikan, "The Origins of the Object-Subject Antithesis in Lutheran Dogmatics," *CTM* 21 (February 1950): 94–104.

[196] F. E. Mayer, *The Religious Bodies of America* (4th ed.; rev. by Arthur Carl Piepkorn; St. Louis: Concordia, 1961), 130.

[197] See Mayer, *Religious Bodies of America*, 130.

[198] Ernst Kinder, *Gottes Gebot und Gottes Gnade im Wort vom Kreuz* (Munich, 1949). See F. E. Mayer, "The Function of the Law in Christian Preaching," *CTM* 21 (February 1950): 123–29.

[199] Mayer, "Function of the Law," 123.

[200] Mayer, "Function of the Law," 123.

[201] Mayer, "Function of the Law," 127.

[202] In the context of the confessing church movement in the Germany of the 1930s, this question of the *praecipuus usus* of the Law was essential. After World War II, German Lutherans were anxious to distinguish themselves from the Calvinism that gave rise to the confessing church. See pp. 26–28.

[203] Mayer, "Function of the Law," 127.

[204] Mayer, "Function of the Law," 127.

[205] Rom 10:17.

[206] Mayer, "Function of the Law," 128.

[207] Mayer commented in passing that "antinomianism is in reality a false anticipation of the future glory" (Mayer, "Function of the Law," 123).

[208] See Mayer, "Function of the Law," 128. "*Tertius usus, qui et praecipuus est, et in proprium Legis finem proprius spectat, erga fideles locum habet, quorum in cordibus iam viget ac regnat Dei Spiritus*" (John Calvin, "*Institutio Christianae Religionis*," in *Opera Selecta*, vol. 3 [eds. Peter Barth and William Niesel; Munich: Christian Kaiser, 1928], 337; [2, 7, 12].

[209] Mayer, "Function of the Law," 128.

[210] Helmut Thielicke also rejected Calvin's approach, which so influenced Karl Barth. "On this whole question of Law and Gospel, Barth is undoubtedly following Calvin rather than Luther. For Calvin repeatedly takes the unity of God as the starting point in his deliberations on Law and Gospel. Consequently, he sees the two not in tension, but in harmonious and complementary relation to one another" (Thielicke, *Theological Ethics*, 1:121). See also Forde, *Law-Gospel Debate*, 140.

[211] F. E. Mayer made a distinction between dogmatics and symbolics that presents a dilemma. Dogmatics is an attempt to make a comprehensive statement of the faith for the church. Symbols are statements of the church's faith that are given birth within a temporal circumstance. That temporal circumstance limits their scope of applicability. Symbolics does not attempt to be exhaustive but applies the faith to the issues that have been raised in a specific place and time. A symbol is not, for that reason, any less binding on the church as a confession of faith, however. If Mayer is using this distinction consistently, it is curious that he should denominate the third use a "dogmatic term" when the term is sanctioned by an official symbolic statement of the Lutheran church, the Formula of Concord. This makes it a symbolic term, rather than a dogmatic term. He might be thinking primarily of its origination in the work of Melanchthon as indicated earlier. This tends to lower the value of the term to a dogmatic opinion of Melanchthon rather than a confession binding on the church. See F. E. Mayer, "Human Will in Bondage and Freedom: A Study of Luther's Distinction between Law and Gospel," *CTM* 22 (October-November 1951): 818. See also Mayer, *Religious Bodies of America*, 145.

[212] Mayer distinguished between the scholarly approach to theology taken by the Germans, who were primarily university teachers, and the practical approach to theology taken by the Americans who were seminary teachers. "The American theological method can be said to be more Scripture-oriented and more definitely integrated with the actual church life" (Mayer, *Story of Bad Boll*, 53). Mayer also attributed the rapid expansion of the Missouri Synod to successful preparation of men for the ministry at the "practical" seminary of the Synod in Springfield, Illinois. See Mayer, *Religious Bodies of America*, 186.

[213] Mayer, "Human Will in Bondage and Freedom," 811; emphasis in the original.

214 See Mayer, "Human Will in Bondage and Freedom," 816.

215 See Mayer, "Human Will in Bondage and Freedom," 816.

216 Mayer, "Human Will in Bondage and Freedom," 816.

217 See Mayer, "Human Will in Bondage and Freedom," 814 et passim.

218 Mayer, "Human Will in Bondage and Freedom," 818; emphasis in the original.

219 *A Short Explanation of Dr. Martin Luther's Small Catechism*, 85–86.

3

AMERICAN LUTHERANISM 1961–76

A PERIOD OF EXTREMES

INTRODUCTION

This period in American Lutheranism, 1961 to 1976, was marked by intra- and interchurch theological conflict. The LCMS was torn by the "battle for the Bible," which exploded around Concordia Seminary, St. Louis, in the late 1960s and early 1970s. The ALC and the LCA were heading in a trajectory that would result in an organic union of the two church bodies in the next period. The nature of the Gospel and its relationship to the Law, and especially the third use of the Law, were significant issues between 1961 and 1976. The Valparaiso theologians continued to hold the most radical position on the third use of the Law, doing so often at great disturbance to their Missouri Synod brethren. Among ALC and LCA theologians of the period there was more balance, at least on the part of Gerhard Forde. This may be attributed to the fact that they were less directly affected by the Missouri Synod wars. As the period came to a close, theologians of the Valparaiso school and the theologians of the ALC and the LCA had grown closer to one another and would ultimately join the same church body.

THE VALPARAISO THEOLOGIANS

The significant theologians of the Valparaiso school during this period were Edward H. Schroeder, Robert W. Bertram, Walter J. Bartling, Robert J. Hoyer, Paul G. Bretscher, Walter R. Bouman, and Robert C. Schultz.[1] Of these, Schroeder, Bertram, Hoyer, Bretscher, and Schultz taught at Valparaiso University during their careers.

BACKGROUND AND INFLUENCES

These theologians were deeply affected by two significant influences. First, they were indebted to the prevailing European theology because many of them studied in Europe after the Second World War. Second, they were caught up in the maelstrom of the ecclesiastical and doctrinal battles that occurred in the Lutheran churches in America, especially in the 1960s and 1970s.

EUROPEAN INFLUENCES

The Erlangen school of theology attempted to overcome the theological relativity of 19th-century liberalism.[2] The Erlangen theologians[3] responded to Pietism, the Enlightenment, Schleiermacher, and the philosophies of Hegel and Schelling. The responses were not entirely negative but included elements of these same influences on German theology. The Erlangen theologians often dialogued with the prevailing influences in the contemporary German theological scene but in such a way that those influences often modified their viewpoint.[4]

Werner Elert. Werner Elert reflected the tendencies of the Erlangen school of theology in his work. Personally and through his profound writings he affected American Lutheran theologians, especially the Valparaiso theologians.[5] Two major factors influenced his theological method. First, Elert was a determined "Old Lutheran" in the mold of the Breslau Synod, a German Lutheran free church that had experienced persecution at the hands of the anti-Lutheran Prussian government in the 19th century. The Breslau Synod[6] sought to distinguish itself from the Reformed-Lutheran melange created in the Prussian Union of 1817. This occurred by making sharp distinctions between Calvin and Luther and also between Reformed theology and Lutheran theology. Polemics provided the synod's raison d'etre. Elert's theology is filled with these sharp distinctions.[7]

Second, Elert was spawned by the Erlangen school of theology. Elert's dogmatic method allowed for the importance of ethics by centering on the Lutheran distinction between Law and Gospel. Elert organized his major dogmatics work, *Der christliche Glaube: Grundlinien der lutherischen Dogmatik*, under the principle of Law and Gospel. Lowell C. Green, a student of Elert's, wrote, "Like no one else, he developed Law and Gospel into a coherent theological system embracing both dogmatics and ethics, which he presented in eight major books and in many shorter articles."[8] The grounding of the dogmatic enterprise in Law and Gospel led Elert to reject the scriptural text as the primary ground of theology. Elert focused his theological approach on a Law-Gospel foundation. Thus, Law-Gospel as an independent theological principle actually judges Scripture.

This approach was based on Elert's strongly anti-Calvinistic bias. He lauded Melanchthon's early *Loci*, which began with the gracious promise of the forgiveness of sins, rather than the authority of the text of Scripture.[9] Elert was critical of the Calvinistic tendency to make theologically central the concept of revelation, thus smoothing out the revelation of God so the whole Bible has equal authority to faith and the church. In reaction to Karl Barth, Elert rejected the view that the Gospel could be defined by its character as revelation. If their similarity as revelation defines Law and Gospel, they are then perceived as two similar words from God. For Elert, however, the content of the Gospel, not its mode of transmission, was distinctive.

Elert criticized Calvin for receding from the fresh start made by Luther and the early Melanchthon.

> But already in Calvin the feature which distinguished the Gospel was the character it had as revelation. Certainly these two views are not mutually exclusive. But Calvin's understanding then led to the situation where the concept of revelation took a prior order. And this, in turn, resulted in a coordination of Law and Gospel, which not only is diametrically opposed to the Lutheran understanding but which also led to a reinstatement of the Scripture-principle of medieval theology.[10]

Elert gave a high premium to Christian experience. The Gospel had priority in the experience of life under the Law and the Gospel. "Our determination of the ultimate ground cannot summarily oppose the kerygma to human self-understanding."[11] This grounding of dogmatics on the Law and Gospel dialectic rather than on Scripture as the *principium cognoscendi* showed that, true to his roots, Elert was an Erlangen theologian indebted to Schleiermacher along with strong anti-Calvinistic tendencies.

Elert's anti-Calvinistic bias also led him to denigrate the Law's didactic purpose. As has been shown in previous chapters, Elert denied that Luther used the term "third use of the Law." Although this contention cannot be proven absolutely, the point might be conceded without denying that Luther employed the concept of a third use of the Law or accepted the idea as it was presented in Melanchthon's *Loci* during Luther's life.[12] Even Elert had to admit that Luther held a positive function for the Law. "In his explanations to the commandments[13] Luther elicited even from these prohibitions a positive side."[14] Nonetheless, Elert wrangles with the Formula of Concord's approach to the third use of the Law. Elert summarized the Formula of Concord's view.[15]

> The question of the need for an informatory function in the (unat-
> tainable) ideal case of a perfect saint is answered in the negative, but
> in view of the actual situation of the regenerate the answer is affirma-
> tive. However, the possibility of the Law's being *purely* informatory is
> categorically denied.[16]

The "actual situation" is the one with which the Formula of Concord was
concerned.[17] The Formula of Concord raises the hypothetical case of the
"perfect saint" only to illustrate the real need for an informatory function
of the Law.[18] This argument is a *reductio ad absurdum*: If there were any
perfect Christians (and there are not), then they would never be in need of
information from the Law on what is to be done. Since in this life the old
Adam still inheres, however, the Law is still needed both to goad and to
inform. Only perfect Christians can jettison the third use, according to the
Formula of Concord,[19] and there are no perfect Christians.

Consequently, the Law has a transitory character in the Formula. The
Formula states that both Law and Gospel will be unnecessary at the resurrection. They both meet the needs of proclamation to sinners, "until the
body of sin is entirely put off, and man is perfectly renewed in the resurrection, when he will need neither the preaching of the Law nor its threatenings and punishments, as also the Gospel any longer; these belong to
this [mortal and] imperfect life."[20] Although there is something provision-
al about the whole Law and Gospel construct according to the Formula of
Concord, Law and Gospel remain for the concrete human situation
shaped by the *simul*. The Formula also states that the doctrine of the Law
is still needed even for believers because believers can only be *simul justus
et peccator*. Because the Law still applies to the believer as a whole person,
it also and always remains a threat.

Elert reminded his readers that the Law remains a threat: "The
moment never arrives in the life of the Christian when the Law has nothing more than an informatory significance for him."[21] To state this is not
to criticize the position set forth in the Formula of Concord, but something else entirely. The Formula will have no part in a Law that only
informs. Elert's criticism of the third use of the Law[22] is actually criticizing Calvin's doctrine.

Elert's criticism of Calvin's pedagogical function of the Law is the real
target of his reservations about a Lutheran third use of the Law. The danger for the warrior of the Breslau Synod was that the Lutheran church was
succumbing to Calvinism by accepting any kind of third use of the Law
because Calvin taught a third use. Certainly, Calvin's position on the ped-

agogical function of the Law is not compatible with Lutheran theology. Calvin's third use of the Law, which he calls the principal use of the Law, remains incompatible with Lutheran theology. According to Calvin, "The third use of the Law (being also the principal use, and more closely connected with its proper end) has respect to believers in whose hearts the Spirit of God already flourishes and reigns."[23] Furthermore, Calvin contends that the Law itself gives motivation to holiness.[24] Calvin's contention that the Law itself gives motivation for Christian holiness is absolutely irreconcilable with the Lutheran structure of Law and Gospel where the Gospel is the sole motivation for good works.[25]

Elert's views on Law, the third use of the Law, and prolegomena have had significant effects upon American Lutheran theology. Edward H. Schroeder identified Elert as the force that most influenced the rediscovery of the centrality of Law and Gospel to Lutheran theology and hermeneutics. In 1972 Schroeder wrote of Elert's influence in restoring the topic of Law and Gospel to prominence in the LCMS: "Members of the current faculties of the church's schools at St. Louis, River Forest, and Valparaiso, spurred on by the work in historical and systematic theology produced by Elert, are undoubtedly the prime movers for nudging the topic back toward the center of the synod's theological agenda."[26]

Stephen Schmidt, a member of the faculty of Concordia Teachers' College, River Forest, Illinois, when rejecting the third use of the Law simply accepted the judgment of Elert as a sufficient basis. Schmidt was critical of the LCMS catechism's teaching of the third use because he presumed that any third use entailed the supposition that the Law could be understood as a friendly, nonthreatening guide to moral life.

> The third use of the Law, so significant in the Catechism's definition, has no place in Elert's theology. This accusing word of God could never become a friendly guide for morality. Elert's [sic] attributes the third use in confessional theology to Melanchthon and later scholastics.[27]

John W. Montgomery, criticizing the Valparaiso theologians, quite correctly pointed out that they relied on the work of Elert.[28] Schmidt nowhere treats Elert's conclusions on Law and Gospel with a critical eye. In fact, at one point he equates a "Lutheran" view with Elert's view.[29] Elert's theologically significant work was important to the theologians of the Valparaiso school who served on the three faculties mentioned by Schroeder.

Paul Althaus. Paul Althaus was professor of systematic theology and New Testament at Erlangen from 1925 to 1966. He exhibited an extensive knowledge of the theology of Martin Luther.[30] Althaus's *Gesetz und Gebot* had a significant influence on the American theological scene, especially through the translation that appeared in the widely read Social Ethics series published by Fortress of Philadelphia in the 1960s.

Althaus was critical of the positions of Karl Barth,[31] Werner Elert, and Emil Brunner on Law and Gospel, though his thought was closest to Elert's and was influenced by Elert. Althaus tried to resolve the problem of Law and Gospel by suggesting the creation of a *tertium quid* to account for the reality of the abiding significance of the Law in the life of the Christian.[32] Althaus began with Law (*Gesetz*) and Gospel. Following Elert, Althaus understood the Law strictly as the accusing word of God. However, he added a third element to the usually bipolar dialectic. He argued for this third element based on the presuppositions that the biblical Gospel includes imperative elements and that the ethical teachings of the Bible have enduring significance in the life of the Christian.[33] The third element added by Althaus was "command" (*Gebot*). Law becomes command in the life of the Christian. Thus, after the fall there are three distinct but related elements in the kerygma: Law, Gospel, and command.

Althaus, influenced by Elert, also rejected a specific third use of the Law. In distinction to Elert, Althaus was loath to jettison its ethical direction in the life of the Christian. Althaus questioned Elert's position. He wondered "whether the traditional doctrine of the *tertius usus* may not contain an element of truth, an element that can easily fail to receive its due if this doctrine is rejected."[34] Ethical considerations were essential to Althaus's thinking,[35] thus he could not avoid the significance of the third use for Lutheran theology and ethics. He resolved the problem of the third use by introducing the divine command as a third element together with Law and Gospel.

While Althaus argued that there is some warrant for his distinction between Law and command in the New Testament, he still had to concede that this distinction was unknown in the Lutheran confessional documents, in which *lex* and *praecepta* are used interchangeably.[36] In fact, Althaus determined that Law as used in the Pauline corpus "is not precisely the same as the eternal, unalterable will of God for man."[37]

This is not supported by Luther, who says that the Law is the eternal will of God: "the Law is the eternal, irrevocable, unchangeable will of God."[38] Althaus's view is also a contradiction of the Formula of Concord, which declares that the one Law is the unchangeable will of God: "the one Law, namely the unchangeable will of God."[39] This contradiction of Lutheran confessional theology was not unusual for a genuine Erlangen theologian such as Althaus. New Testament theology could give new insights that Erlangen theologians used to progress beyond Lutheran confessional theology. Althaus clearly did so at this point.

Althaus began with the primal situation in which humans in innocence are confronted with the divine command.[40] In this situation humans are confronted with both the command and its obverse, the offer of God's love. God's love impresses also obligation or summons on those to whom the love is expressed. But obligation remains secondary, love primary. Love implies a summons to the person to whom it is expressed.

> God cannot be my God in a saving way unless I *let* him be my God. Otherwise the nature of the personal relationship, as God himself intends it, would be contradicted. He calls me to trust him above all things. This is offer (*promissio*) and at the same time summons, command, and call.[41]

Althaus remained concerned about the need for humans to respond to the call, and in that way he reflected the Erlangen penchant for an anthropocentric theological method. The reaction of the human subject in letting God work his way takes an important place in Althaus's thought at this point.

Command is primal; it is supralapsarian. Command only becomes Law after the fall.[42] The love of God so certainly carried the command with it that the command clearly takes on characteristics that Lutheran confessional theology ascribes only to the Gospel. Althaus used terms from perennial Lutheran theology to describe the command's significance over against the Law.

> The divine command is not a strange word of God, a *verbum alienum*, but the most proper word of love, a *verbum proprium*. His call to me has the character of permission, of freedom, of an open door, of access to that life with God which is my bliss. His demand—the "shall" ("You shall love the Lord your God")—is really a permission: "You may."[43]

For Althaus God's Word is primarily a revelational encounter with humans. Like many other German theologians of the period, Althaus, too, thought of the Word of God as God's address to humans, rather than emphasizing the content of the revelation. For him the unifying factor of theology was the unique character of God's self-revelation rather than the gracious appeal of the word of the Gospel. With this presupposition it is easier for Althaus to see the Law and the Gospel drawn together into a third kind of divine revelation that has characteristics of both Law and Gospel.

Because of his strong background as a Luther scholar, Althaus himself expressed some concern about whether there was anything in his concept of command to distinguish it from the Law. "It might well be asked whether it is advisable, from the theological point of view, to designate this appeal of God which accompanies his gracious offer to man by the word 'command'—whether the connotations of this term are sufficiently distinct from those of 'Law.' "[44] Althaus's nagging reservation was derived from the influence of Luther upon all his theological studies, and rightly so, because Luther rejected such thinking as a confusion of Law and Gospel.[45]

For Althaus the difference between Law and command is purely formal; that is, Law and command are essentially identical in content, differing only in form. Human guilt is the source of the change in form by which command becomes Law. The experience of guilt causes the command to be perceived as Law, condemning and negative. The *ding an sich* is unchanged; Law and command are identical.[46] Sinful humans only perceive the command as Law. Althaus put it this way: "The imperative is drowned out by the prohibitive 'You shall not . . . !' The Law is a memorial to our sin."[47]

Althaus described this change in form from command to Law in terms of the difference between the imperative and prohibition. Before the fall, humans were led to God by the inviting imperative implied by the gracious word, "Let me be your God." For Althaus the imperative invitation of God, "Trust yourself to my love," was equivalent to the imperative command of God, "Give me your love."[48] The imperative grammatical form may not always carry the weight of a command. In Lutheran theology, certain biblical statements that are imperative in form are understood to be gracious invitations that bear in their words power to receive their gracious content in faith. The word of the Gospel is always a living and empowering word in Lutheran theology.[49] Thus, invitations might be imperative in grammatical form,[50] but they are only commands grammatically, not in their content.[51] In content and meaning they remain pure, empowering Gospel. Thus, some of the things that Althaus identified as command are properly thought of as Gospel.[52]

Althaus struggled with the infusion of command into the concept of Gospel at its point of contact with humans. That point of contact was faith. Althaus was well aware that classical Lutheranism taught that faith was *pure passive*.[53] He adapted this concern by suggesting that faith is only passive relatively speaking. In reference to salvation, faith is passive, receiving and offering nothing. But this was only half of the story for Althaus.

> There is more to faith than this. The very same faith that in the question of salvation is pure renunciation and receiving is at the same time a most lively act of rejoicing in the fact that God is love, of surrender to this love, i.e., of readiness to be moved and grasped by it, as by true life. If the matter is viewed from this perspective, then the objections to our statement that faith lives only in its concrete enactment as works fall away.[54]

Classical Lutheranism maintained a careful distinction between faith and works whereby faith produced works, naturally and normally, indeed without compulsion.[55] Such works were not of the essence of faith, but flowed from it. Althaus is correct to say that "faith lives only in its concrete enactment as works fall away."[56] But from this does not follow that there is more to faith than pure receptivity, as Althaus contended.[57] Faith and its results are not the same, just as cause and effect are not the same.

Althaus rejected the concept of the third use of the Law as taught by Melanchthon and the Formula of Concord. This rejection is to be expected because of his formulation of the *tertium quid* of command. Althaus set out three reasons why the third use is to be rejected.

First, he argued that the dichotomy between Law and Gospel is so firmly set in the history of theology as condemning and justifying, respectively, that the term *Law* might not be easily used to refer to the significance of ethics in the life of a Christian. These *dicta* are so firmly set in the concrete history of theology that they cannot carry any other linguistic freight. Thus, Althaus preferred to speak of "biblical commands and moral directives in the Christian life."[58]

Second, a reason related to the first, Althaus believed that the term *Law* necessarily carries with it "the notion of a legalistic regulation of the Christian life."[59] Legalism quenches the free exercise of the Spirit's life within Christian ethical practice. Ultimately the spiritual character of what is required of the Christian by the Lord in the present moment is destroyed by rules and regulations. *Law* becomes an unacceptable term for this confrontation between the believer and God. The term is too fraught with static and normative ideas to be useful in the existential moment before God.

Third, the third use of the Law implies that only the imperative element within Scripture gives ethical direction to the Christian. Althaus warned that this would severely limit the use of biblical personages as ethical encouragement, and not only biblical saints but all the heroes of the faith that church history has commended to us would be diminished by the insistence upon a third use of the Law. There is more to ethics than the imperative.

In the last analysis, Althaus also was deeply affected by an existential approach to the Law and its application to Christian, ethical life. "No biblical or church directive, no biblical or churchly models, can relieve me of the necessity of making my own decision."[60] The tension of decision points to an existentialistic view of the Law, which cannot tolerate the static prescriptions of an eternal and unchanging legal code. For Althaus the best that could be said about the Law is that it is the adversary of the Gospel, nothing other than a threat that drives the person to seek mercy. There can be no constructive use of the Law as direction to the Christian. While Althaus attempted to advance beyond Elert, he did so in ways that seem less satisfactory, despite their novelty. Nonetheless, Althaus had a significant impact upon North American theological thought on the third use of the Law.

AMERICAN ECCLESIASTICAL FERMENT

The years 1961 to 1976 witnessed great theological and ecclesiastical upheaval in American Lutheran circles. Both the ALC and LCA came into being at the beginning of this period through mergers of smaller church bodies. The ALC, the result of the consolidation of smaller German and Norwegian churches, came into being January 1, 1960. The LCA came into being January 1, 1962.[61]

The denominational unions that occurred during this period should have signaled a sense of strength and confidence among American Lutherans. Yet American Lutheranism suffered a period of profound self-doubt and momentous doctrinal upheaval. In this period, Lutheranism, now completely emerging from the chrysalis created by language and cultural barriers,[62] felt threatened by American denominationalism and its decidedly ecumenical character.

The attitude toward Lutheran identity in missions and doctrinal controversy serve to illustrate this self-doubt and upheaval. Lutheran church historian E. Clifford Nelson pointed out that American Lutherans were even questioning their right to exist.

Within the spectrum of American Christianity did Lutheranism have a viable future as a separate confessional church? In the face of the so-called great issues of the last third of the twentieth century, was there anything unique, and therefore worthy of preservation, about Lutheranism?[63]

This crisis of identity showed itself among LCA members and also in the Missouri Synod. For instance, Conrad Bergendoff[64] stated flatly that Lutherans had no call to Lutheranize the world.[65] In the LCMS the famous "mission affirmations" of 1965 showed the same kind of uncertainty about the existence of the Lutheran church. They affirmed that the Evangelical Lutheran Church "is chiefly a confessional movement within the total body of Christ."[66] The period's discomfort with past denominationalism and doctrinal positions led to "intricate and widespread unrest"[67] among Lutherans in North America.

Throughout this period, the LCMS was increasingly wracked by doctrinal controversy and ecclesiastical disputes, culminating in the famous "walkout" from Concordia Seminary, St. Louis, in 1974.[68] Already in 1966, John W. Montgomery stated acidly, "Only an inebriated mole would claim that the Missouri Synod is not in theological ferment."[69] Nor was the fall-out from these titanic doctrinal and political struggles within the Missouri Synod confined to the Synod alone. These struggles touched all American Lutherans and indeed many American Protestants.

The symptoms of a leftward move within the LCMS have already been touched upon in the previous chapter.[70] The 1960s saw a profound acceleration of this movement in the LCMS as elsewhere. The faculty of Concordia Seminary, St. Louis, "was divided into two schools, the old-line Missourians and a growing minority of progressives or moderates."[71] By the early 1970s that growing minority had blossomed into a powerful majority.

Beginning in 1969 with the surprising election of J. A. O. Preus Jr., who was the conservative challenger to the hegemony of Oliver Harms, to the office of president of the LCMS at the Denver convention, the battle over Missouri was joined in earnest. The battle raged over the significance of the Bible in the life of the church, especially the meaning of its inerrancy and inspiration. When Preus was reelected in 1973, the majority at Concordia Seminary saw the handwriting on the wall. In a gesture filled with drama and significance, the faculty majority walked out of classes at Concordia Seminary on February 19, 1974, along with most of the students, to show support for the seminary's embattled president, John

Tietjen. They hoped that they would chasten the church body into calling them back to their classes at the world's largest Lutheran seminary. The conservative LCMS, including and especially Preus, did not react as expected and, instead of begging for the faculty to return, accepted the walkout as a *fait accompli*. Paul G. Bretscher, writing in support of the faculty majority, had to admit that the faculty majority had defied the Synod: "Since they were not doing their work, but were seemingly in defiance of the Synod which employed them, their jobs were terminated and their homes and offices ordered vacated."[72] The faculty minority, under the direction of interim president Martin H. Scharlemann, organized classes for the students who remained and began preparing the seminary to recover from this enormous trauma.[73]

Eventually the faculty that walked out organized Christ Seminary (Seminex), which was subsequently absorbed into the Lutheran School of Theology in Chicago. The LCMS lost about one hundred thousand communicant members, whose ranks mainly joined the ELCA when it was constituted in 1988. Those who left the Missouri Synod over the controversy included such American theological luminaries as Martin E. Marty, Jaroslav Pelikan, and Richard John Neuhaus. E. Clifford Nelson correctly measured the effect this had when he wrote about the 1973 convention of the LCMS: "The trauma of the 1973 synod produced wounds, bitterness, and deep sorrow, not only within the Lutheran Church—Missouri Synod, but throughout the ecclesiastical world."[74] Nelson's judgment is equally true of the entire doctrinal war in the LCMS. Hermann Sasse remarked in 1976 that the doctrinal crisis in the LCMS was "the crisis of the entire Lutheran Church."[75]

This was the stage upon which theological discussions took place in the period of 1961 to 1976 in American Lutheranism. More pointedly for the purposes of this book, the more prominent theologians of the Valparaiso school were for the most part LCMS professors who eventually left the Synod during those days of upheaval. One of the major issues over which American Lutherans battled in this period was the doctrine of the third use of the Law.

Summary of Views

The views of the Valparaiso theologians of this period can be summarized under the following four headings: (1) Gospel reductionism; (2) *Gesetz und Gebot*; (3) Decalogue, Law, and parenesis; and (4) doctrine, church authority, and Law. Each of these points highlights a crucial aspect of their teaching that affected or was affected by the third use of the Law.

GOSPEL REDUCTIONISM

"Gospel reductionism" was a term coined in the Missouri Synod during the 1960s.[76] The term had its birth in the battle over the normative nature and extent of the Law and Gospel principle implicit in Lutheran theology. In the 1960s some theologians began to invoke Law-Gospel as the ruling or the only hermeneutical presupposition in Lutheran theology. They adopted this hermeneutic as a replacement for the old inspiration doctrine, which they had decisively abandoned in this period. The adoption of this method spurred a critical response by John W. Montgomery and others, such as Ralph A. Bohlmann and Robert D. Preus.[77] Montgomery traveled around the Synod during the spring and fall of 1966 delivering papers opposing the doctrinal aberration, which he called "Law/Gospel reductionism," among other things.[78] Montgomery's essays were printed in book and pamphlet form and were widely disseminated in the LCMS and beyond. In time "Law/Gospel reductionism" became known by the more compact moniker "Gospel reductionism." Edward H. Schroeder responded to Montgomery's charges against "Gospel reductionism" in his 1972 article, "Law-Gospel Reductionism in the History of The Lutheran Church—Missouri Synod." It was universally agreed that Gospel reductionism could make a major impact on the doctrinal basis for the existence of the LCMS.[79]

Schroeder summarized the important contributions made to Lutheran theology by C. F. W. Walther and Werner Elert, which have been reviewed in previous chapters.[80] Their work showed the importance of the Law-Gospel principle in Lutheran theology.[81] However, Schroeder went beyond what Walther and Elert had taught about Law and Gospel. For Schroeder, Gospel reductionism became more than just a way of denominating the Lutheran habit of judging doctrine based on metatheological themes, such as justification, which is the obverse of the Law and Gospel coin.[82] Law and Gospel was *the* biblical hermeneutic of the Lutheran church for Schroeder. This approach generated a firestorm of opposition.

How could such an apparently Lutheran approach to theology generate such significant opposition? The principle of Gospel reductionism itself was not the problem. The problem of Gospel reductionism revolved around its meaning, extent, and relationship to other significant Lutheran principles of theology. Schroeder, among others, was using Gospel reductionism as a principle of biblical interpretation, a hermeneutic, indeed, as the only Lutheran hermeneutic.

Schroeder's form of Gospel reductionism was criticized because it functioned as a hermeneutical presupposition rather than strictly as a theological principle. For Schroeder Law and Gospel had become "*the* hermeneutical touchstone"[83] of the Lutheran Confessions.[84] Schroeder even defended his position as consistent with a *quia* subscription to the Lutheran Confessions.[85] "Thus anyone concerned with his *quia* subscription to the Lutheran Symbols could hardly take umbrage at anyone using the centrality of the Gospel, even 'reducing' issues to Gospel or not-the-Gospel, as his Lutheran hermeneutical key for interpreting the Bible."[86] Schroeder believed that the theologians who wrote the classical confessional documents of the Lutheran Reformation had actually functioned with just such a hermeneutical key to Scripture.

> The distinction between Law and Gospel is the operating yardstick whereby the confessors practiced their Gospel reductionism. That distinction gave them a theological Occam's razor to keep from multiplying Gospels (or from expanding the Gospel to include more and more things that one *must* believe) and to perceive when something was Gospel and when something was not. Thus the distinction is not a doctrine itself. But it is a procedure practiced as an auxiliary theological tool in theology and proclamation to keep the Gospel "Gospel."[87]

The problem with this characterization of the function of Law and Gospel in Reformation Lutheran theology is that, though it was *a* basis, it certainly was not the *only* basis for the confessors' principled rejection of the work righteousness of the Roman Catholics.[88] For example, when Luther and Melanchthon were confronted with the need to support their views, they repaired to a grammatical-historical exegesis of the essential biblical texts. Ralph Bohlmann, who inductively drew the hermeneutical principles employed by the Lutheran confessors from the Lutheran confessional documents, has shown this.[89] Thus, this argument by Schroeder fails to convince because there is no evidence that the Lutheran confessors used the Gospel alone as their biblical hermeneutic.[90]

Moreover, a serious contention remained over whether Law and Gospel was a *hermeneutical* principle at all.[91] The Law-Gospel principle functioned as a principle of theology in the writings of the Lutheran Reformation, but it was not a hermeneutical presupposition in the sense that Schroeder used.[92] Law and Gospel was a principle that led the

Lutheran Reformers to reject certain teachings and practices because the teachings and practices were opposed to the Gospel or in conflict with the Gospel. For example, in the Augsburg Confession, Melanchthon used the Gospel to reject the imposition of human traditions upon the practice of the church:

> They are admonished also that human traditions instituted to propitiate God, to merit grace, and to make satisfaction for sins, are opposed to the Gospel and the doctrine of faith. Wherefore vows and traditions concerning meats and days, etc., instituted to merit grace and to make satisfaction for sins, are useless and contrary to the Gospel.[93]

The practice of the church was to be normed by the Gospel, so the practices that contradicted it could not be tolerated when they implied that forgiveness of sins was merited by their observance. This principle was drawn from Scripture; it was not a presupposition used in the interpretation of Scripture or imposed upon Scripture. *Stricte dictu*, it was not a biblical hermeneutic.[94]

Holsten Fagerberg, whom Schroeder criticized, pointed this out for the doctrine of justification in the Lutheran Confessions. "But this doctrine is not a general key to the Scriptures. Instead of being the sole principle for the interpretation of the Scriptures, it provides the basic rule which clarifies the Scriptural view concerning the relation between faith and good works."[95] The same can be said of the Law and Gospel theme in the Lutheran Confessions.[96] The Law and Gospel theme had extensive norming significance in Lutheran theology, but it was itself normed by the text of Scripture.[97] Fagerberg stated precisely, "The confessional statements on Law and Gospel do not contain any general orientation for the interpretation of the Bible."[98] Kurt Marquart provided a more nuanced criticism of the Gospel reductionistic approach to use the Gospel as the sole norming authority.

> Of course justification, or the Gospel in its strictest sense, is the heart and soul of, and therefore the key to, the entire Scripture. And just *because* the Gospel permeates the entire Scripture (always presupposing the Law), the Scripture-principle is Gospel-authority. Hence it is always and only actual Bible texts, that is the "certain and clear passages of Scripture," and not some "Law and Gospel" floating above them, which constitute the "*rule*" for interpretation![99]

The Gospel or Scripture choice reflected a false either/or. Therefore, Schroeder's claim that the Gospel reductionistic hermeneutic was the hermeneutic of the Lutheran Reformation was gravely flawed.[100]

The use of Gospel reductionism as a hermeneutical tool had significant effects upon the approach to the third use of the Law. This result can be seen in the essays of Robert J. Hoyer in *The Cresset*, the magazine of Valparaiso University. Hoyer stated that Law and Gospel interpreted Scripture and were used to norm preaching and teaching in the church.[101] For Hoyer, Law and Gospel are to be used to elicit meaning from the biblical text. The distinction was not just a theological filter, but a biblical hermeneutic.

As already shown Gospel reductionism reduced authentication of points of Lutheran doctrine to whether they were "Gospel or not-the-Gospel."[102] With such a sharp razor of discernment, the third use of the Law is ripe for excision. The Law immediately comes under scrutiny as "sub-Gospel."[103] Schroeder suggested that George Stöckhardt[104] critiqued the third use of the Law using the razor of Gospel reductionism already in 1887.[105] While the determination of the validity of this claim remains outside the parameters of this discussion, Schroeder definitely was leading to a decisive break from the Lutheran doctrine of the third use of the Law.[106] This use of the Law-Gospel hermeneutic is set into sharp relief by the writings of Hoyer. The Law could only judge and condemn and no more. The Law "can not really tell man what to do leading to a proper relationship with God."[107] There could be no ethical use of the Law whatsoever. In fact, to use it as an ethical tool would be rebellion against the Law itself. "The ethical use of the Law *is* that rebellion."[108] Basing his argument on Romans 1, Hoyer asserted that the only ethical causation attributable to the Law is rebellion against God.[109] The Law's only purpose is condemnation.[110] For Hoyer, not even civil or social righteousness remains for the Law. In a short 1968 article, Hoyer advocated anarchy. "Yes, anarchy is what I propose. The proposal may be folly because of human weakness. Grace is the solution to human weakness."[111] The third use of the Law has absolutely no place in this approach. Not even the first use of the Law survives these presuppositions.

The simplicity of the principle of Gospel reductionism leads to abuse. Because of its simplicity, theologians can easily use it to criticize central Christian teachings, such as the validity of the Law in the life of the Christian. There is a serious threat of a severe reduction of Christian doctrine to a bare Gospel, which is no Gospel at all.[112] A further difficulty

implied by the simplicity of the principle is that it can be radically interpreted so as to rule out significant and central Christian doctrines. One
person's Law might be another person's Gospel. The lack of an anchoring
certainty troubled the critics of these Gospel reductionistic techniques.
For Schroeder, Gospel reductionism functions without being anchored in
authoritative texts and even functions to judge the meaning and applicability of the text of Scripture. Ironically, Law-Gospel reductionism functioned to rule out the third use of the Law. Thus, in the end, Schroeder
had reduced Law-Gospel reductionism to be truly only Gospel reductionism, and that based on an extremely narrow definition of Gospel.

Gesetz und Gebot. The *Gesetz und Gebot* of Paul Althaus influenced the
theologians of the Valparaiso school.[113] Those who were concerned about
the need for ethical standards often sought to ground them in terms taken
from Althaus. For Walter Bartling *nomos* and *paraklesis* were parallel to
Gesetz und Gebot. "If *paraklesis* should still be regarded as *Gebot*, it is certainly no longer *Gesetz*."[114] This is what Edward Schroeder identified as
one of the "evangelical alternatives" to the third use of the Law. Since Law
can never be made friendly, even for the Christian, there is no possibility
of a third use of the Law.[115] The alternative must be "evangelical"; that is,
the Gospel must be the source for the action of the Christian life. The Law
must remain only an accuser.

Decalogue, Law, and Parenesis. The theologians of the Valparaiso school
exhibited various approaches to the significance of the Ten
Commandments in the life of the Christian. The structure of the Lutheran
Confessions requires Lutheran theology to account for the Ten
Commandments. Luther makes the Ten Commandments the first of the
six chief parts in his catechism. Yet Stephen Schmidt contended that the
commandments are no guide to Lutheran morality: "Lutheran morality,
then, could be no code of ethical responses to given rules or new stipula-
tions. The Ten Commandments can serve as no guide for Lutheran morality: The Law does not serve a Gospel function; it can only accuse."[116]
Schmidt accepted uncritically the Elertian position that if the Law always
accuses, it only accuses. While Schmidt was interested in social ethics, he
made a sharp division between theological ethics and social ethics.
"Christians are under the Law in every sense by virtue of their creatureli-
ness and their citizenship. Such ethical instruction is not the focus of theological instruction. In theological terms, the Law serves only to
accuse."[117]

Could an argument be made that theological ethics would make no impact upon society, family, or government, or even that theological ethics is not social ethics as well?[118] A short tour through Martin Luther's "Table of Duties" answers the question decisively in favor of the strong relationship between social and theological ethics in Lutheran theology.[119] There is no other plane on which Christian or theological morality can be played out except the social context into which God places the Christian by reason of his or her vocation.

More troubling, however, was the tendency in those who denied the third use of the Law to attribute to the Gospel a norming or exhortative function in the Christian ethical life. Schmidt stated indirectly that the Gospel is a "guide" to ethical action. "The Ten Commandments can serve as no guide for Lutheran morality. The Law does not serve a Gospel function; it can only accuse."[120] Here Schmidt confused Law and Gospel by suggesting that it is the task of the Gospel to guide the Christian in ethical action. The third use of the Law becomes subsumed under the effects of the Gospel. This is a confusion of Law and Gospel.

Robert J. Hoyer, a longtime member of the LCMS Board of Parish Education, went far beyond the position espoused by Schmidt. He denied any place for civil righteousness or social ethics. According to Hoyer, the Ten Commandments are an absolute standard but only in the sense that the Law's condemnation of the sinner is absolute: "In this sense only it is an absolute standard—not an ethical standard of what we must do, but a judgmental standard of what we are."[121] Ultimately, the Law cannot bring validity to any ethical standard but functions only to destroy any ethical pattern in the human relationship with God.[122] Martin Marty also held that the external code of the Ten Commandments has little validity in the context of Christian ethics. While discussing the prohibition of coveting at the end of his section on the Decalogue, Marty points out the importance of the involvement of the forgiven heart. "The hidden character of the Christian ethic is made evident where action is not involved. The character of the forgiven heart is called into question; the external code is unimportant by comparison."[123] While it is true that where there is a heart not made new in Christ, the external code is quite useless, it also remains true that the specific prohibition of coveting clarifies the character of the forgiven heart for the Christian. Marty seems to accept a false either/or that there must be Law or freedom. For him that freedom will not seek to be normed by any external authority; indeed, such authority is useless.

Gwen Sayler exhibited this attitude toward the Law. She denied that the Law can provide a norm for holiness. "The Law serves unceasingly to convict the new person of sinfulness and to drive the person back to Christ. Good works are done by the new person on the basis of faith; there are no objective criteria for goodness."[124] Sayler reflects strong Elertian bias and draws a radically existentialistic conclusion from the *semper* when she denies that there are any "objective criteria for goodness."[125]

While the Valparaiso theologians accepted only a narrow theological field upon which the Law could work, that is, as an accuser, they still had to account for the existence of New Testament ethical instruction, especially in the Pauline Epistles. For them, New Testament parenesis replaces the third use of the Law. Ethical direction in the life of the Christian begged for a term simply because there seemed to be such an abundance of ethical instruction in the New Testament. New Testament ethical instruction was denominated by a term taken from the New Testament, namely, parenesis. Parenesis is "a form in which general hortatory moral maxims are loosely strung together."[126]

Walter J. Bartling argued that Pauline parenesis required reinterpretation based on leading themes or motifs of Pauline theology. The Pauline *agape* ethic could be used to interpret the meaning of Pauline parenesis. An *agape* ethic consistently applied to specific ethical instructions would have a major impact on the meaning of Pauline parenesis.

> The absolutizing of the Law of love in a remorselessly situational ethic has a ring of modernity about it, but it is little more than commentary on Augustine's oft-quoted dictum: *ama et fac quod vis*. The original text for both the modern and the Augustinian elaboration of the theme is Rom. 13:10: "Therefore love is the fulfilling of the Law." The question, "What should I do?" the argument runs, is not only impossible to answer in the complexities of actual situations but is in principle needless. From moment to moment love must actualize itself within the demands of the given situation.[127]

The same could be said of the freedom granted by the Spirit. Thus, actual exhortations are only paradigmatic and certainly not universally binding. For Bartling this is an essential component in the resolution of the problem suggested by Pauline parenesis.

A further attempt to deal with the Pauline parenesis is based on the changing situation in the early church's life. The church needed to deal with the fact that the apparently imminent return of Christ had been unexpectedly delayed. What was to be done in the interim? This was the impelling force behind the construction of parenesis. Parenesis was an "in-between times" ethic. But this explanation did not account for what Bartling called the "double emphasis" of Pauline eschatology, that it is both a realized and a waiting eschatology; it lives in time awaiting the parousia. Nor did it account for the fact that even the earliest Pauline literature includes an abundance of parenetic material. Thus, even before the apparent realization of a delayed return of Christ there was strong ethical instruction included in the New Testament.

Closely related to the relationship of parenesis and eschatology was the view of Albert Schweitzer that through parenesis Paul was taking into account the disjunction between the real and the ideal in his theology.[128] The indicatives represent the ideal and the imperatives the real. This does not satisfactorily consider the fact that for Paul there is no disjunction between the indicatives showing forth the mercy of God and reality. The indicatives are real. The imperatives are more than "merely accommodation to practical necessity."[129]

For Bartling the dilemma boils down to striking an appropriate balance between the prescriptive force of Pauline parenesis and the kerygmatic motifs of Pauline theology, namely, *agape* and freedom in the Spirit. How is parenesis to be understood and used in the church if, indeed, "parenesis is not an ungainly addendum but is as central as the cross itself"?[130] Ultimately, the Gospel itself serves to shape the interpreter's understanding of the parenetic material. "The Gospel is the norm for every interpretation of parenesis and for any contemporary translation."[131] This is a variation on the theme of Gospel as hermeneutic championed by Schroeder, Schultz, and others and attacked by Montgomery. The Gospel certainly causes results in the life of the Christian, but to call it a "norm" is to risk a confusion of Law and Gospel, especially if its normative power includes making judgments of doctrine.[132] Judging remains a task of the Law. Here once again there is Gospel reductionism.

Although Bartling claimed that he intended to avoid the debate about the third use of the Law, he could not avoid the implications for the third use brought to the surface by his study. He was correct that the third use of the Law is primarily a problem of systematic theology. "This is rather a historic and systematic problem than a strictly exegetical one."[133] If systematic theology is to be biblical, however, one has to search for biblical or exegetical roots for the third use of the Law.

Bartling was willing to point out "evidence on the level of vocabulary usage and the indicative/imperative structure of Pauline parenesis." This evidence led him to see parallels between *paraklesis* and Gospel, so Law and *paraklesis* mirror the coordination of Law and Gospel. "Parenesis is *paraklesis*, and *paraklesis* is *usus practicus evangelii*."[134] Bartling verged upon a confusion of Law and Gospel by making exhortation parallel to Gospel.[135] Thus, Bartling had no problem with the phrase "*usus practicus evangelii*" to describe *paraklesis*. If Gospel includes an "*usus practicus evangelii*" then this is perilously close to Calvin's primacy of the didactic use of the Law. But for Bartling this didactic use is still called "Gospel" rather than "Law," as it was called by Calvin. Bartling's "Gospel" has ultimately become Law with a norming force. Where there is a diminishment of the Law by rejection of a third use, the Gospel inevitably is infected by Law elements such as parenesis or exhortation.[136]

Bartling also relegated the Decalogue to an inferior position by arguing that New Testament parenesis has no apparent relationship to the Decalogue. If Gospel leads only to *paraklesis* and *Gebot*, and not to the Decalogue, then the Law, *Gesetz*, is relegated to a sub-Christian status. If there is no Christian purpose to the Decalogue, in principle there can be no third use of the Law.

DOCTRINE, CHURCH AUTHORITY, AND LAW

The theologians of the Valparaiso school were suspicious of church authority, especially when that authority enforced doctrinal standards. Often the rigid application of the "Occam's razor"[137] of Gospel reductionism accompanied or was even occasioned by the rejection of any doctrinal discipline imposed by church authorities.[138] Edward H. Schroeder developed his positions in 1972, but already as early as 1966 he had championed the view that Melanchthon himself had taught that when the hermeneutic of the Gospel is applied to Scripture it would "add" things to Scripture. Ultimately this hermeneutic would adjust and correct those texts of Scripture that were themselves Law. "So in an exegetical situation which without reference to faith in Christ calls for man to do good works and to please God, faith in the righteousness of Christ *must be added* to the Bible passage *because the Bible demands it*."[139] Here is a clear description of a hermeneutic that is over the text, rather than interpreting the text. The point of this bold hermeneutic is to modify the meaning and significance of the Law in the Bible. Law ceases to be Law under such a method. The Law is simply swamped by the radical claims of the Gospel upon the text of Scripture.

In the end, having correct teaching or pure doctrine becomes unimportant under this hermeneutical assault on the text of Scripture. Scripture cannot serve to provide an objective witness to inform Christians of the truth. Schroeder remarked of the catechesis of the church: "The purpose is not that they will have the right answer for the great final examination but rather that they can have that answer happening in their own lives."[140] For Schroeder, true teaching is not as important as the existential experience of making the truth happen. Schroeder was following the pattern set by his American mentor, Richard Caemmerer, who expressed this so clearly in the previous decade and in whose *Festschrift* this viewpoint found such clear expression. Schroeder was convinced that because the Gospel was "promise" in Lutheran theology, the divine word could not be information. He gives a classic expression of this position using terms borrowed from Martin Buber:[141] "Viewing the Gospel as a promise moves it away from the 'I-it' relationship, as though it were a 'thing'—information, rules, reports, even *divine* information, *divine* rules, *divine* reports—and defines it in terms of an 'I-Thou' relationship."[142] Promise was a personal relationship rather than information.[143] Schroeder accepted completely the relational or existential character of truth.

This perspective led to a view of lawful church authority that was low indeed. For in principle there could be no church authority apart from the existential character of truth, itself a slippery notion. An existentialistic Gospel is not susceptible to codification in doctrinal standards or enforcement of those standards. Thus, doctrinal orthodoxy is not a piety to be pursued in faithful service to the Lord of the church, but a positive evil to be avoided at almost any cost.

Paul G. Bretscher commented that because Jesus accepted sinners in the kingdom he was unconcerned about Law. "Jesus must have looked like a 'liberal,' quite careless of Law and discipline."[144] Bretscher argued passionately and eloquently that the Gospel should keep Christian teachers from undergoing doctrinal discipline. Such discipline smacked of rationalism and unfaith.[145]

The ultimate conclusion for Schroeder was that the Gospel as defined as promise did not, indeed could not, forbid the use of the modern, higher-critical interpretive tools. He adds this at the end of his 1966 article for the Caemmerer *Festschrift*. After championing the hermeneutic of Luther and Melanchthon, Schroeder permits to himself these modern interpretive tools.

> Perhaps there are other operating procedures for exegesis in our time which are not identical with those the Reformers utilize. There are no *a priori* reasons why one could not use the tools of source criticism

and *Formgeschichte* and still be interpreting the Scriptures in keeping with these Lutheran hermeneutic [*sic*] principles.[146]

This acceptance of these other operating procedures for which he had not argued anywhere in the article was out of place, especially since Schroeder had argued so strenuously for the unity of Lutheranism's hermeneutic, the Gospel. Now suddenly, like a hermeneutical *deus ex machina*, Schroeder posited that the new hermeneutical methods of critical scholarship should not be rejected. Any hermeneutical tool that does not in its results contradict the Gospel was acceptable to Schroeder. The Law no longer set standards for method or results because there was no third use of the Law.[147] Therefore, there was no objective standpoint from which church authorities could criticize the methods or results of theological inquiry. If there is no third use of the Law with standards for Christian faith and practice, there could be no scrutiny of doctrine within the church or of the church practice that emanates from doctrine. For example, Paul G. Bretscher argued that the Gospel itself was the norm for faith and practice and that the Law had no place norming the practice of a Gospel-centered church. He complained of the abuse of the Synod's constitution, which enjoined unity in faith and practice in Article II.[148]

> As for the terms "faith and practice" in Article II, "faith" now has to do with holding faithfully to the doctrine of inspiration and inerrancy of the Bible apart from and larger in scope than the Gospel. "Practice," in turn, has to do not only with a life of faith, hope, and love through Christ our Lord, but in particular now with methods and exegetical persuasions in Biblical study.[149]

The Gospel alone was the norm here. The Law no longer had any norming authority for the church's practice. No theological space was left to the third use of the Law.[150]

A denial of the third use of the Law thwarted efforts toward doctrinal unity within the LCMS. The choices were set out in stark contrast: Gospel or unfaith, absolute freedom or choking discipline, realistic and loving concern or unloving perfectionism, and Gospel-normed action or legalistic church practice.[151] For the Valparaiso theologians this was portrayed in the simple terms of an either/or.[152] Paul G. Bretscher was typical in this regard, setting out a choice of either doctrine or authentic faith in his *After the Purifying*. "Is the truth and purity of God's Word fixed in a body of doctrine to be taught? Or is our structure of doctrine itself subject to continual purging and renewal through whatever testings the Lord might choose to lay upon any or all of His people?"[153] Could it not be that God's Word gives a norm by which we are always being renewed? In any case, doctrinal norms, like any other legal norms, did not fare well in this approach.

Summary Analysis and Evaluation

The theologians of the Valparaiso school evinced a new approach to biblical hermeneutics by championing Gospel reductionism. It was an attempt to clear the LCMS hermeneutical field for the freedom to operate with historical critical hermeneutics. This generated a firestorm of opposition among the Missourians. Schroeder and the others were not correct in arguing that Law and Gospel was a biblical hermeneutic in traditional Lutheran exegetical practice. The method had drastic results for the third use of the Law by relegating it to a sub-Christian status. Thus, the Gospel in this approach simply excluded it as "not-the-Gospel."

With the Occam's razor of the Gospel wielded in this way, the search was on for theological space for the application of Christian ethics. The approach suggested by Althaus found expression as parenesis in the work of Bartling. Others took a more radical approach and advocated what could be taken for moral and theological anarchy. In either case doctrinal standards were lowered in the name of the Gospel, and discipline was considered a sign of unfaith.

Finally, in varying degrees the defenders of the Valparaiso theology were prone to attribute to the Gospel parenetic purposes so the Law's work was subsumed under the Gospel. The denial of the third use of the Law leads to a redefinition of the Gospel to include legal concepts. The Gospel is no longer the gratuitous promises of God to the anxious sinner.

LCA and ALC Theologians

The theologians of the LCA and ALC[154] shared many emphases with the theologians of the Valparaiso school. As the years progressed, a growing number of these theologians joined the LCA or ultimately the ELCA, a testimony to their relative theological harmony. The LCA and ALC theologians who had the most impact on the issue of the third use of the Law were William Lazareth, Gerhard O. Forde, and William Hordern. They will be denominated "ELCA theologians."

Background and Influences

During this period the theologians of the ELCA were influenced by European theologians and European theological trends.[155] ELCA theologians were also more fully open to the most progressive trends in European theology. For example, Carl Braaten became the foremost American apologist for Jürgen Moltmann's theology of hope.[156] Among American Lutherans, Braaten reached beyond the old Erlangen synthesis. Braaten had enormous influence on the theology of the ALC and the LCA through his ecumenical journal, *Dialog*, which he launched in 1962.

Dialog set the tone for the ALC and LCA approach to the third use of the Law. In 1963 *Dialog* published an article by Lauri Haikola[157] entitled "A Comparison of Melanchthon's and Luther's Doctrine of Justification."[158] This article was a slightly abridged version of a paper delivered by Haikola at the Second International Luther Research Congress held in Münster, Germany, in 1960.[159] Following the pattern set in the Luther renaissance, Haikola saw a wide gulf between Luther and Melanchthon. That chasm was especially wide at the point of the character of the Law and its impact on the doctrine of the justification of the sinner before God. Such a division within the Wittenberg Reformation would have a considerable impact on Lutheran doctrine. This division set the stage for separating Luther and his dynamic doctrine from the dusty and legalistic revision of Lutheranism undertaken by the methodological children of Melanchthon in Lutheran orthodoxy.[160]

Haikola astutely pointed out that for Luther and Melanchthon the doctrine of the Law affected their views of the whole of Christian doctrine. "Both Luther and Melanchthon's total understanding of the Christian faith is determined by their understanding of the Law."[161] For the Wittenberg Reformation, the dichotomies of the Christian faith held a preeminence that could not be overcome by a purely Christocentric theology. Those dichotomies, all analogs of the distinction between Law and Gospel, set the framework for all Christian theology. "The Law precedes the Gospel just as the Old Testament precedes the New, as Creation precedes Redemption, and as Nature precedes Grace. These basic presuppositions are universally valid for every Christian theology."[162] In this Haikola is correct. His views on both Melanchthon's and Luther's doctrines of the Law have extensive implications.

Melanchthon held that there was a *lex aeterna*, an eternally valid expression of the will of God. Because of the eternal validity of the Law, Melanchthon held that the Law is embodied in an objective order.[163] That objective order gives understanding of both God's activity and human activity. In that sense Haikola implies that the Law is as normative for God as it is for humans in the conception of Melanchthon. God himself is not *ex legibus*, but he is constrained by his own objective construct.

Melanchthon, echoing Augustine, looked at the human condition under three states—the state of innocence, the state of corruption, and the state of grace.[164] Before the fall, humans were in a state of innocence. They both externally did the things commanded by the Law and internally agreed with and delighted in the Law. But for Melanchthon even humans in the state of innocence did not merit anything through their perfect obedience. Perfect obedience would only have been acting in accordance with what was already an accomplished fact because of their nature before the fall, which truly fears, truly loves, and truly trusts God.[165] Yet, Melanchthon suggested, at least in theory, humans could receive divine blessedness by keeping the Law. The Law provided a theoretical way of salvation, if the Law's conditions could be met. This is what Haikola called Melanchthon's "abstract understanding" of the Law.[166] It is abstract because there is no actual case where a human being has rendered such obedience, except Christ the Mediator. Furthermore, Haikola suggested that Melanchthon thought the Law could be comprehended in a few clear rules, namely, the Decalogue. Several catastrophic doctrinal consequences resulted from this foundation.

Melanchthon had to reconstruct the Gospel to fit the shape required by the eternal Law. Because the Law must be fulfilled so persons can enjoy divine blessedness, the Gospel must declare Christians to have fulfilled the Law vicariously. Another's obedience to the Law must suffice to provide gratuitous righteousness for humans. The Gospel does not confer personal righteousness, but the righteousness of another.[167] The God-Man, Jesus Christ, must offer satisfaction to God in the place of humans and bring a perfect compensation on behalf of humans. Haikola was interested in showing that Melanchthon had reduced the work of God in Christ to a transaction intended to buy humans out of their sin back to God.

> For our purposes it is enough to establish that Melanchthon actually tried to rationally demonstrate how God's righteousness really received adequate, even more than adequate, satisfaction for sin and how the last jot of the Law's demand was met. Now God actually had ground and cause enough to forgive men and declare them righteous. Christ's satisfaction and merit are so great that they even provide the adequate basis for justification in the future and in the past time (of the Old Testament).[168]

This satisfaction theory of Melanchthon is what Haikola calls the "forensic doctrine of justification."[169] The more Romanism and Osiandrianism confronted Melanchthon, the more he emphasized the objective nature of the justification and its purely legal character. Haikola made this radical conclusion about Melanchthon's doctrine:

> One must thus note that the pure logic of the thesis of adequate satisfaction (*victima sufficiens*) excludes *every* human addition and activity. As a result even faith which was demanded before the fall into sin as the condition of preserving the state of grace is now superfluous.[170]

Haikola judged that Melanchthon's doctrine renders faith "superfluous." In reality faith is not superfluous in Melanchthon's doctrine of justification. Faith is simply not meritorious. Faith remains the ὄργανον ληπτικόν, receiving the work of Christ, but not working anything.[171] This objectivity left Melanchthon open to the charge of ethical indifferentism. An objective righteousness left humans without any option for personal participation. In the main, Melanchthon had embraced a theory of justification controlled by the doctrine of the Law as outlined earlier in this section.

According to Haikola, Melanchthon treated the receptivity of faith as the condition of justification.[172] Like Luther, Melanchthon was not entirely systematic in his approach to the actual situation of the Christian life. Thus, Haikola was forced to take into account the ways in which Melanchthon actually used affective terms rather than purely forensic and declarative terms in various places. Melanchthon had a developed doctrine of the results that justification brings with it, but Haikola was critical of it because there was a logical division between justification and its results.[173] The Christian life with its changed affections only comes to be because of the declaration of acquittal in justification. Having a close unity between forgiveness of sins and the renewal of the Christian life was crucial to Haikola. He was critical of what he thought was Melanchthon's separation of the two things.[174] But for Melanchthon the distinction was one that was theological—that is, faith always brought with it renewal, but in teaching about the two, faith and renewal had to be carefully distinguished.[175] Without this careful distinction in practice, the merit and glory of Christ would be obscured and souls troubled.[176]

Melanchthon allowed for the reality of anthropology with the *simul justus et peccator* doctrine characteristic of Lutheran teaching on the Christian life. Haikola argued that Melanchthon used the *simul* doctrine to construct a doctrine of the Christian life under the rubric of mortal and venial sins. Mortal sins are intentional sins committed against conscience and result in the loss of faith. Mortal sins are the so-called gross sins. Venial sins are unintentional and are not committed against conscience. They require only the third use of the Law. "Man needs nothing except the mild discipline of the Law (*tertius usus legis*) to receive forgiveness of venial, unintentional sins."[177] Haikola contended that Melanchthon conceived of a "mild" use of the Law. This would directly contradict the "*semper accusat*" of the Apology of the Augsburg Confession. It is significant that when Melanchthon is discussing the accusatory power of the Law in the Apology he does not draw examples of the accusatory power of the Law over the unbeliever. Instead, he offers examples from the Christian life to show the accusatory power of the Law still holds sway in the life of the Christian. The fact that the Law troubles the saints insofar as they remain sinners powerfully shows the need for the justification provided by a merciful God.[178]

Haikola tried to interpret Melanchthon's doctrine of the third use of the Law through a Calvinistic filter. Because both Melanchthon and Calvin posit three uses of the Law, Haikola tends to presume that both Melanchthon's and Calvin's third use of the Law are the same. Calvin taught a friendly use of the Law, but for Melanchthon there can be no friendly Law. At the same time, the Law remains useful in the life of the Christian, even as it drives him or her repeatedly to the mercy of the Mediator in the promise of forgiveness of sins.

Haikola chided Melanchthon for this forensic construct. "In the Melanchthonian treatment of the forgiveness of sins, we thus find the same moralistic and nomistic basis that we previously found in his doctrine of the state of perfection and the Law."[179] The objectivity of the doctrine leads to legalism especially in the area of the third use of the Law. For Haikola, Melanchthon's doctrine is, at bottom, Calvinistic and, therefore, legalistic. Haikola's approach is echoed in the work of ELCA theologians.

SUMMARY OF VIEWS

The work of William Hordern and Gerhard O. Forde will serve to give a representative view of the ELCA approach to the third use of the Law. References to other ELCA theologians will appear in the notes to show the relative consistency of their ideas. Hordern's approach is simpler and less technical. Forde's work is written for a theologically trained audience. Both, however, exhibit the abiding distrust of the value of the third use of the Law in ELCA Lutheranism in this period.

William Hordern

William Hordern[180] reflected the ambivalence of ELCA theologians to the doctrine of the third use of the Law. Hordern approached the problem of the Law from the perspective of how the church's doctrine of justification is affected by church practice. Hordern's thesis was that a great deal of contemporary Lutheran church practice contradicted the doctrine of justification by grace through faith.[181] If justification is the doctrine by which the church stands and falls, nothing—no practice and no doctrine—may be permitted to crowd it out of its central place in the Lutheran church.

Hordern was critical of the way in which Protestant churches substituted lifestyle goals for spiritual goals when they attempted to reach out beyond the confines of the church. He charged that by the mid-1970s the American Protestant view of Christianity had become completely identified with middle-class values. The approach went like this: "If you become a Christian you will be happy, successful, middle class, married, and have two children."[182] If this was true of Protestant churches in this period, then Hordern is correct in charging that this is Law and not Gospel, an approach unworthy of a truly Gospel-centered church.[183]

Hordern held an existentialistic view of faith and the Christian life. He made a sharp distinction between faith as trust and faith as belief in correct doctrine. He criticized the Protestant penchant for reducing salvation to "correct belief."[184] Faith cannot merely be holding a set of correct propositions about God. That is not the trust of the heart of which the Lutheran Confessions speak.[185] Hordern pushes this distinction so far, however, that he calls into question the significance of rules in the conduct of the Christian life.[186] He identifies the use of the Law to norm conduct in the Christian life with the behaviorism of B. F. Skinner.[187] Rules giving shape to behavior is religious "behaviorism" in the thought of Hordern. According to Hordern, the 16th-century Reformers wanted to free people for ethical conduct through a righteousness from God. "It was their intention to free people for an entirely new way of righteousness, a righteousness that is not behavioristic obedience to Law, rules, or regulations."[188]

The flaw here is that obedience to the Law is not necessarily the behavioristic result of religious conditioning. Christian people might well follow rules of Law joyously and freely. Rules do not make robots. Unthinking adherence to rules characterized by joylessness and a lack of trust in God results in a behavioristic adherence to rules for their own sake. Adherence to rules for their own sake makes robots. Nevertheless, Hordern identifies rules *per se* with Skinnerian behaviorism.

Hordern begins his discussion of the new life in Christ with a rather unconventional definition of justification. "Justification means that the love of God awakens an answering love in the heart of the Christian, and where God is loved there will be the desire to do that which pleases God."[189] Formally, this is not a Lutheran definition of justification. In fact it has more in common with Osiandrianism than it does Lutheranism, confusing as it does the results of justification with justification itself.[190] Lutheranism always has the work of Christ in his death and resurrection in view when it defines justification. God is the actor. The closest historical Lutheranism can come to Hordern's definition is the battle waged mainly in the 19th century among German theologians and church historians on whether justification is a synthetic or an analytic judgment.[191] As a synthetic judgment, justification would be a purely forensic, declaratory doctrine of justification. Justification as an analytic judgment would be making the sinner righteous. An analytic judgment centers the cause of justification in the human, so inhering righteousness leads to being forgiven by God. Thus, the person is said to be made right with God, rather than accounted right before God, as in the case of the synthetic judgment. The doctrine of the synthetic judgment has had its detractors, such as Karl Holl, who criticized it because it is a "legal fiction."[192] By defining justification in terms of the believer's love of God, which is an analytic judgment, Hordern arrives at a point beyond even Holl.[193] The best that can be said for Hordern on this point is that he is attempting to define justification phenomenologically. His book is intended to be practical rather than technical. Even with this perspective Hordern's definition of justification fails to be congruent with perennial Lutheran theology.

Hordern's concept of sanctification flows from his definition of justification. He thought that this immediately raised the question of the uses of the Law.

> Christians who have come to love God because God first loved them will naturally desire to do the will of God. This means that they must seek to know God's will for them. Historically this has raised the question of the place of the Law in the life of the Christian.[194]

In his discussion of the uses of the Law, Hordern begins with Calvin's threefold use of the Law. This approach has been analyzed previously.[195] Hordern adopts the position taken by Elert and the theologians of the Valparaiso school by repeating the fact that Luther describes only two functions of the Law in the Smalcald Articles.[196] Hordern compares what the Formula of Concord says with what Calvin taught about the third use of the Law, quoting the Epitome of the Formula of Concord at what he considers the crucial point of Article VI.[197] This looks suspiciously like Calvin's doctrine because it mentions the need to coerce the old Adam that inheres in the reborn.

Hordern is correct in saying that the debate over the third use of the Law is more than just a squabble over theological theory.[198] The third use of the Law will justify legalistic preaching and church practice according to Hordern.

> A major thesis that I have been presenting is that many Protestants believe in salvation by works because the practice of Protestant churches has spoken more loudly than their preaching of justification. But if we accept the third use of the Law, we could justify many of these practices.[199]

The third use of the Law is the doctrinal Achilles' heel of Lutheranism. According to Hordern, if the third use were retained, it would lead to a restructuring of the doctrine of justification. "It is important, therefore, to examine closely whether we should restructure our doctrine of justification based on the third use of the Law or whether a proper understanding of justification precludes the third use."[200] It is appropriate to say that justification and the third use of the Law are related and will affect each other. Hordern is arguing from his view of what justification is and concludes that the Formula of Concord's doctrine of the third use of the Law is faulty, a sign of unfaith and legalism in later Lutheranism.[201]

Hordern's criticism of the third use of the Law is based on his doctrine of justification, influenced by its existentialistic tone. His doctrine of justification itself contains more than a strand of legalism and does not reflect the Formula of Concord's own view of justification as was shown previously. If nothing else, this is a major methodological flaw. Hordern is interpreting the Formula of Concord not within its own historical context, but on the basis of his existentialistic definition of justification. Carl Braaten is correct in claiming that existentialistic interpretations of justification have more in common with Pietism than with historic Lutheranism.[202] This putative strand of legalism leads Hordern to reject the Formula of Concord's doctrine of the third use of the Law.

Hordern incorporates legal concepts in his doctrine of the Gospel. Hordern states that Luther would have said that the third use of the Law was a logical impossibility.

> With Luther's use of the terms "Law" and "Gospel," the first thing
> that he would probably say about the third use of the Law is that it is
> a logical impossibility. Both Calvin and the authors of the Formula of
> Concord see two aspects under the third use of the Law. First, the
> Law is guidance as to the will of God for the Christian who has been
> filled with a desire to do God's will. For Luther this would be no
> longer "Law" at all. Inasmuch as the Christian is searching the
> Scripture to find God's will because he longs to do God's will, it
> comes under Gospel not Law.[203]

In this view, the third use of the Law is unnecessary because renewal is
affected and directed in the Christian by the Gospel. However, direction
about what to do whether for believers or unbelievers would be and remain
Law for Luther. "Everything that preaches about our sin and the wrath of
God, no matter how or when it happens, is the proclamation of the Law.
On the other hand, the Gospel is a proclamation that shows and gives
nothing but grace and forgiveness in Christ."[204] Luther would have rejected Hordern's statement as a confusion of Law and Gospel. The Gospel
does not instruct us to do or to act, but it gives and seals the forgiveness of
sins and God's grace. For Hordern what has traditionally been the Law's
guidance has become the Gospel.

Hordern was correct in seeing the close relationship between justification and the third use of the Law. When the Gospel is reduced to a new
Law, justification itself has been tainted by works righteousness. Thus, the
third use of the Law is not merely a biblicistic construct in Lutheranism,
but the third use stands related to the chief article of the faith. The third
use of the Law in Lutheran theology functions to defend the doctrine of
justification from the taint of works righteousness.[205]

Hordern is inconsistent in what he rules out of the Gospel's scope and
what he permits to remain. As we have seen, he accepts an existentialistic
doctrine of faith as trust without content.[206] The question might legiti-
mately be asked, "Trust in what?" While it is true that faith is not merely
assent to true propositions, faith as trust must repose in the promises of
God. There is a specific doctrinal content to the preaching of the Gospel,
which engenders and calls forth trust in the heart. This is trust in the
Gospel promises of the living God. Hordern's existentialistic faith eschews
content of this sort. But when it comes to doing God's will, which is certainly doctrinal content, this Hordern places "under the Gospel, not
Law."[207] Ultimately, Hordern has put himself in the same legalistic morass
from which he is attempting to extricate the church. His denial of the third

use of the Law leads to a confusion of Law and Gospel because, in fact, doing God's will is not Gospel, but Law.

Hordern displays a common feature of the theology of those who want to deny the third use of the Law a place in Lutheran teaching. Once the third use has been given the *coup de grace*, it is resurrected by injecting ethical instruction into the structure of the Gospel.[208] Hordern is just less subtle than other Lutheran theologians, who, as we have seen, have renamed the third use of the Law parenesis or *Gebot*.

GERHARD O. FORDE

Gerhard Forde made an enormous contribution to the discussion about the third use of the Law through *The Law-Gospel Debate*, a work that reviewed the 19th-century debate between orthodoxy and *Heilsgeschichte* over the doctrine of the atonement.[209] Forde maintains that this debate in the Erlangen school set the parameters for the modern discussion on the relationship between Law and Gospel. He suggests that understanding the weaknesses of both orthodoxy and *Heilsgeschichte* would clarify the modern dogmatic problem of situating the Law in Christian doctrine.[210]

When the Prussian government attempted to unite Reformed and Lutheran churches at the beginning of the 19th century, interest in Lutheran theology revived in Germany. The revival of Lutheranism was characterized by intense interest in and support for orthodoxy. E. W. Hengstenberg[211] was a prime example of someone who supported the orthodox revival. Hengstenberg worked tirelessly as a teacher and a church politician to revive the orthodox doctrine of the atonement and to repair the damage done to theology by rationalism. According to Forde, Hengstenberg and his orthodox colleagues simply substituted one form of rationalism for another. Rationalism had championed the human mind's perception of truth in all things, including theology. Rationalism sought "scientific" objectivity in the universally valid truths discernable by reason. Hengstenberg merely shifted the source of objective knowledge from the human mind's use of reason to the text of the Bible. The authority of the Bible was absolute for Hengstenberg.[212]

This is the point at which J. C. K. von Hofmann[213] entered the fray by criticizing the orthodox for objectifying the relationship between God and humans. Hofmann attacked the biblicism of orthodoxy and, therefore, the whole theological edifice built on the orthodox method. Hofmann was critical of the way in which the Law gave orthodoxy its shape, including regulating the content of the Gospel itself. He criticized orthodoxy for its doctrine of the vicarious satisfaction, excoriating it for attributing to God a system whereby God may be "bought off" through an expiatory sacrifice of Christ. Since the Law required perfection of sufficient quality and quantity, God had to provide it in Christ, who became a perfect substitute for the sins of the world, taking the world's punishment on himself. The satisfaction requires God to render a verdict of "not guilty" for the world. The transaction of the vicarious satisfaction was a prime target for Hofmann. The Law gave the whole doctrine of justification its shape and framework in the orthodox system. This was not acceptable to Hofmann.

Hofmann proposed that Christ became *the* true human instead of a substitute. "He did not suffer alongside of man, as one man instead of another, but *in* mankind. *In* him, not merely *through* him, man becomes the object of divine love."[214] Hofmann focused his atonement doctrine on the new humanity made complete in Christ. In the *Heilsgeschichtliche* method of Hofmann, Christ became the greatest manifestation of the unfolding of the plan of divine love. The *Heilsgeschichtliche* method replaced Law with the idea of the new humanity. "There is no trace of the traditional idea of the *lex aeterna*, no trace of the traditional scheme of the *usus legis* and no hint of a 'third use of the Law.' Law is displaced entirely by the reality of the new humanity."[215] The method was driven by the idealistic philosophy of history brought to its apogee by G. W. F. Hegel.[216] The Law, and especially the third use of the Law, cannot survive Hofmann's criticism.

Several proponents of orthodox theology, including Friedrich Adolph Philippi, Gottfried Thomasius, and Theodosius Andreas Harnack, seriously challenged Hofmann.[217] Philippi criticized Hofmann for supporting a doctrine of the atonement that was far too subjective and, therefore, uncertain. Philippi charged that Hofmann's doctrine had more in common with Roman Catholicism than Lutheranism because in Hofmann's doctrine the change in the atonement took place in humans. Hofmann took the criticism seriously and set about defending his doctrine from the charge of subjectivism. He recognized that the change that was affected in the atonement was not solely in humans.

> It is God's *relationship* to man which has changed in the atonement, and it is changed *objectively*, if one must use such terms, and in and through what is accomplished *by* God in Christ. In acting this way through Christ, God has not exercised his will to love mankind without at the same time exercising his hatred of sin. What has occurred is a change in dispensation, a real and "objective" change in the "times" which changes man's relationship to God. Of course, the

change has not occurred "objectively" in the sense that the old dis-pensation has been obliterated.[218]

Hofmann argued that Law was not *lex aeterna*, but only a part of the his-torical dispensation that led persons to take seriously the love that God holds for them. The debate between Hofmann and the orthodox reached a stalemate when the problem of the place of the Law in theology could not be resolved. This is the point at which Forde takes up his critical analy-sis of the place of the Law in what he calls "the theological system."

Both Hofmann and his opponents had difficulty accounting for the place of the Law in their theological systems. According to Forde, the 19th-century debate showed that the orthodox could no longer understand the Law "in a static-ontological sense, as a *lex aeterna* according to which God can be 'bought off.' "[219] In his opinion the *Heilsgeschichte* doctrine fared no better.

Clearly, the "Law could not be treated as though it were part of a his-torical dispensation superseded by a dispensation of love."[220] In either case, the radicalness of the work of God to save the world was being blunted by placing that work in a system where the outcome was assured. The ortho-dox system assured the results to be realized by the death of Christ through the Law's demands upon God's righteousness. Ultimately, both God and the cross were captured in the theological system. The *Heilsgeschichtliche* method simply substituted for the orthodox doctrine of the Law a concept of divine love progressively revealing itself through the stages of history—a view of history borrowed from Hegel, to whom Hofmann was intellectually indebted.[221] Both ways failed because the assured results "detracted from the seriousness of the cross event itself."[222] Thus, for Forde both Hofmann and the orthodox had developed theories about the cross but had failed to present the existential reality of the cross itself.

The systems generated in the 19th century made the cross anticlimac-tic. Whether it was the Jesus portrayed by the orthodox or the *Heilsgeschichtliche* method, Jesus knew the systematic details and, therefore, could face death with prosaic equanimity, knowing as he did what the assured outcome would be. For Hofmann, Jesus would have known that he was unfolding another aspect of divine love for the world. There would be nothing new and, therefore, nothing central about the cross. The cross becomes merely one way of revealing God's love in holy history. For the orthodox, Jesus easily faced the cross because the Law assured that the results would be accepted. Because the results would be accepted, there was a note of inevitability in the resurrection of Jesus. Real suffering and death are cut off in this scheme. Both *Heilsgeschichte* and orthodoxy are ultimately tainted by a docetic Christ who knows that everything will turn out nicely in the end if the theory is followed correctly. This theorizing about the cross destroys its power and meaning in the life of the church, according to Forde.[223]

Ultimately, Hofmann did not repair the problem of the static-onto-logical view of the Law. Forde stated that Hofmann simply replaced the orthodox view with the idealistic view of historical progress, that is, another equally certain systematic framework in which to capture the work of God in Christ and ultimately to destroy its existential freshness. "In the shift from the legalistic scheme of orthodoxy to a scheme based on histor-ical process, the continuity or idea of progress accomplishes the same function as Law in the system of orthodoxy—it provides the structure for understanding the Christ event."[224] For Forde, Hofmann missed the radi-cal break with the old era that the cross represented. The key to the prob-lem of understanding the cross was the eschatological newness of the Christ event, something obscured by both orthodoxy and *Heilsgeschichte*.

Forde attempted to resolve the problem he identified through his analysis of the atonement debate of the 19th century by suggesting that eschatology holds the key. Forde claimed that Lutheranism's placement of the cross at the center of the faith dwarfs the Law. The cross stands astride all of time and calls a halt to the Law's work. The cross is the eschatolog-ical sign of temporal discontinuity. The Law belongs to the old time. The Gospel belongs to the eschaton. The temporal order is central: Law comes and then Gospel.[225]

For Forde there is nothing rationalistically self-evident about the function of Law and Gospel. The distinction between Law and Gospel is apparent only to faith. "There is no possibility of speaking about Law *and* Gospel prior to faith. At the same time, however, it is apparent that it is precisely faith which grasps the Gospel as God's *final* Word and that from this standpoint Law must be ordered *before* Gospel."[226] The cross's division of time into two radically different ages shapes the whole Law-Gospel dialectic by giving temporal order to it.

> Quite obviously it is only by faith in God's eschatological act that the believer sees that his existence must be understood in terms of the two ages, where being in Adam under the Law is always before being in Christ under the Gospel. Faith grasps the Gospel as God's "last Word"; thus it places Law before Gospel.[227]

For Forde the eschatological character of God's self-revelation provides a limit to the action of the Law in the world. The limit is theological. Therefore, it is an insight that can be reached only in faith. The limit is also temporal. Therefore, it is indicative of the eschatological discontinuity introduced by the cross. Since this eschatological approach is only known "by faith,"[228] it should not have any of the systematic flaws that Forde identified in orthodoxy and *Heilsgeschichte*.

At this point, Forde presented the theoretical possibility of a third use of the Law to evaluate its impact on Christian doctrine. A reintroduction of the Law at the point of the cross results in a blurring of the sharp division between the times and of the distinction between Law and Gospel. "It might be objected, however, that if one does grasp the eschatological dialectic of the ages and all that that means, then it is a relatively harmless thing to speak of another use of Law *after* the Gospel, perhaps a 'third use' of the Law."[229] The problem here is that after the cross, Law would require such radical redefinition that it would no longer be recognizable as Law. Law might be understood as the "admonitions *of the Gospel*," but Forde denies that there is anything gained by such language.[230] The history of the third use of the Law, rooted as it is in the doctrine of the *lex aeterna*, gives no hope for this kind of theological language to advance a Gospel-centered ethic. Such an approach would only "impose a new kind of legalism."[231]

The radical discontinuity between the old age and the new age makes even Paul Althaus's proposal of a third possibility beyond Law and Gospel untenable.[232] *Gebot* is a Trojan horse for the third use of the Law. Interestingly, Forde criticizes Althaus for the division of time into a threefold scheme—before the fall, after the fall, and after conversion.[233] "Althaus' scheme presupposes the believer's ability to place himself beyond the real threat of the Law simply by disposing of it in a neat *Urstand*, fall, and *Endzeit* scheme."[234] Forde thought that Althaus's scheme failed because it rendered the Law a harmless word from God. In other words, it entailed an implicit denial of the *semper accusat*.

In contrast to all attempts to rescue a "third use of the Law," there was no way to rescue the larger concept of the Law in the new age. "It seems quite evident, however, that once the eschatological character of revelation has been asserted, the Law which is now to be used in a 'third way' must be redefined so radically that it bears little or no relationship to the former uses whatsoever."[235] Forde is quite correct in warning against a Law that has been redefined in this way because the redefinition is usually in terms of attributing Law concepts to the Gospel, resulting in Gospel as admonition or ethical instruction. According to Forde, the greater problem is that either any third use is so unlike the "old uses" that it ceases to be Law altogether, or it becomes a *tertium quid*, as in Althaus's approach, "which is after all only the old way in disguise."[236]

The eschatological approach to the relationship between Law and Gospel precipitated a crisis for the doctrine of the Law. "The assertion of the eschatological character of revelation has created a crisis for the doctrine of the Law, a crisis so severe that one can perhaps speak even of a bankruptcy in the attitude of Protestantism toward the Law."[237] Law, of whatever kind, has no place in the time created by the eschatological discontinuity of the cross.

Forde proposes that the nature and function of the Law can be understood only in terms of the eschatological dialectic shaped by the intrusion of the cross. Forde gives the Law a purely functional definition.

> Law is a general term for the manner in which the will of God impinges upon man in the old age, both in nature and in the words of Scripture. It is the demand and the judgment which confront him as a sinner. Even the words about the cross will initially be heard as demand, as a threat to his being. It is important to note here the Law is defined almost exclusively in terms of its function. Nature and function are taken together. The nature of the Law is that it terrifies.[238]

In this view, the Law has no place in the age defined by the cross. The Law is relegated to the old age. Ultimately, Law is what terrifies and what terrifies is Law. "Nothing *material* is said about the *content* of Law as such; that, apparently, may depend upon concrete circumstances."[239] The Gospel's task is to quiet the existential terror of the human heart. Here the Law can have no place.[240] The eschatological dialectic governs the relationship between Law and Gospel.[241]

Because the Law is set in the old age with its unfaith, nothing certain can be said about its content. The Law is merely and entirely a threat to being. Thus, the person does not know what a correct course of action would be in any given situation. The person only feels the unease caused by the threat of the Law. Even the Decalogue is only a proximate guide in any given situation.

> The Decalogue is the best statement of natural law. If man does not know the Law, he must be taught. But on this level, within the old age, it remains, it would seem, only a question of the relative appropriateness of a course of action in a given situation.[242]

The Decalogue, then, is a general guide to action useful only in a situational context.[243] This approach to the Decalogue is characteristic of existential ethics.[244]

Forde provided a clear summary of the battle between orthodoxy and *Heilsgeschichte.* He is correct in seeing that the battle was ultimately being waged over the place of the Law in theology and its relationship to the Gospel. Existentialism gave him the framework to criticize these historical approaches and to make suggestions about the place of the Law in Christian theology. Forde provides much to consider.

Once again existentialism is as much an intellectual or systematic framework for thought as any framework provided by the orthodox or Hofmann. Forde distinguished his view of the death and resurrection of Christ from the point of view of Hofmann and the orthodox in such a way that he implied that his eschatological point of view was not fraught with the difficulties inherent in being a systematic theme. "There is no 'system' as such which can distinguish between the ages or can provide a continuous transition from this age to the next. Only the death and resurrection of Christ, the act of judgment and grace, is 'the way.' "[245] However, existentialism is as much a point of view as orthodoxy or *Heilsgeschichte.*[246] An existential approach to Christian theology is not value neutral. Existentialism values being-in-existence over being-in-substance. Hence the static view of Law as *lex aeterna* is immediately ruled out.

While this is to be expected given Forde's existential presuppositions, there is something too neat about his bifurcation of time into "before the cross" and "after the cross." Certainly the cross is the source of eschatological discontinuity.[247] The intrusion of the Gospel into the world has a radical effect upon the Law and its significance. In this sense the temporal order should be Law, then Gospel.[248] Yet Forde has allowed his eschatological viewpoint to define how Law and Gospel relate to each other and how they function within Christian theology. Forde seems to have carried out a misordering of traditional Lutheran priorities, where Law and Gospel is the overarching theme that gives shape to the Lutheran theological enterprise.[249] In Forde's approach, eschatology has become that overarching theme.[250] Therefore, he has presented a strictly temporal ordering of Law and Gospel.[251]

The temporally ordered eschatological approach is helpful. Yet if it excludes other legitimate emphases, it is pushed beyond its usefulness. Missing in Forde's eschatological perspective is the significance of the sinner's real, and even existential, situation as *simul justus et peccator.* Forde's contention that the eschatological approach is thinking theologically about Law and Gospel is susceptible to the criticism that it is just thinking temporally, and not theologically at all.[252] The temporal order of Law and then Gospel fails to take seriously the proleptic eschatological reality of the "now and not yet" character of the Christian life.[253] This is a clear theme in Scripture and gives us another dialectical tension with which to balance Forde's temporal "before and after."[254] Forde fails to account for the character of the Christian as *simul*—at the same time righteous and sinner. In this way he has ignored the significance of the subject of Christian theology, the person.[255] This is not to say that there are not times when in Christian theology the order is rightly Law then Gospel. Often in proclamation that is the order that must prevail.[256] However, Christian "being" remains being in the *simul*. Law and Gospel are both involved, but the question remains, How is the Law involved in this mode of being? The third use of the Law still emerges as the response to the dilemma, without denying the ever-present *semper*, as a judgment against human unfaith.

Forde uniquely avoids the confusion of Law and Gospel that seems characteristic of those who deny the third use of the Law. The sharp temporal distinction of his eschatological approach keeps him from heading down this road. In fact, he is critical of all attempts to reintroduce the Law after the cross or the Gospel.[257] Forde struggles to resolve the problem of the relationship of Christian theology and ethics. He suggests that the problem of the Christian life is one of ontological understanding. "In the church the believer comes to understand his existence in terms of *two* ontological determinations of his being, being 'in Adam' and being 'in Christ.'"[258] How the "ontological determinations" relate to the existential character of being in faith, Forde does not say.[259] In any case, given the existentialistic tenor of Forde's work, the introduction of an ontological category at this point is methodologically weak at best. The introduction of ontology here is even stranger since he has criticized the orthodox approach to the Law because of its static-ontological character. Because of this, it is quite uncertain what Forde means by "ontological" at this point. Ethics remains a groping enterprise, enlightened only by the existential situation.

The third use of the Law, in whatever form, does not escape the criticism of the existential approach to Lutheran theology. Forde categorically denies the third use of the Law any place in the Lutheran theology.

SUMMARY ANALYSIS AND EVALUATION

The influence of existentialistic Luther scholarship and European theology shows in the work of the ELCA theologians during the period of 1961 to 1976. ELCA theologians still generally accepted the existential theological framework already in evidence in the previous period. As they applied it to their theology, they even suggested that existentialism was a neutral method, not carrying its own presuppositional freight. As was shown in the previous period, this approach has devastating effects on the third use of the Law because it calls into question the use and validity of the Law in the entire Christian theological endeavor.

ELCA theologians of this period definitely suspected the third use of the Law of being a Calvinistic-legalistic disease in the body of later Melanchthonian Lutheranism—a disease to be eradicated from contemporary expressions of Lutheran doctrine. Calvinism has been and remains a convenient Lutheran whipping boy. However, ELCA theologians failed to see that the Formula of Concord's doctrine of the third use of the Law is significantly different from Calvin's approach to the third use of the Law.

Haikola advanced the discussion among American Lutherans by pointing out that, for Lutheran theology, the doctrine of the Law does make a significant impact on the doctrine of the Gospel. The Law remains a starting point for proclamation. To do otherwise in Lutheranism is to fail to have a reason for the Gospel. Lutheran theology has to keep in balance the doctrinal dichotomies typified by the Law-Gospel dialogue. There can be no understanding of the Gospel apart from an understanding of the content and place of the Law in Lutheran theology.

Hordern was typical of those suspicious of the third use of the Law in that he reinvented the third use of the Law as a component of the Gospel. Hordern was deeply indebted to both Althaus and Elert in that regard. He not only voiced his suspicion of the third use of the Law, but also inserted legal claims and purposes into the Gospel.

Forde's work built most adroitly on Haikola's thesis. Forde perceived the significance of understanding the place of the Law in Lutheran theology. His study of 19th-century German Lutheranism was a great service to American Lutheranism by raising the issue and by communicating the data. By leaving the place of ethics in Christian theology dangling, however, his conclusions raised more questions than they answered. Forde had eliminated the third use of the Law as a reintroduction of a legalistic element, but then had no way to deal with ethics in the Christian life. Forde also presupposed an existentialistic approach to Lutheran theology. Yet he failed to account for its impact upon Lutheran theology as an external organizing principle by supposing it to be value neutral. Finally, Forde turned to eschatology to order the use of the Law and Gospel principle in Lutheran theology. It is not at all clear that this is a genuinely Lutheran approach to Law and Gospel or to eschatology. Lutheran theology tends to use Law and Gospel as its ruling or organizing principle. Law and Gospel resists being ruled by other theological principles, such as eschatology. Instead, Law and Gospel would rule eschatology.[260]

Forde's dangling problem of ethics in the Christian life exists because he realizes that he ought not inject legalistic concepts into the Gospel, which alone remains after the eschatological division of the cross is applied to Christian theology. This is remarkable because in the present discussion Forde is unique among American Lutheran theologians in avoiding the temptation to plant the Law in the Gospel after denying the third use of the Law.

THE MISSOURIANS

During the period of 1960 to 1976 the Missourians fought to establish the continuing validity of the third use of the Law. The validity and character of the third use of the Law was a central issue in the theological and political wars that accompanied the conflict over control of Concordia Seminary, St. Louis, and the LCMS itself.[261]

BACKGROUND AND INFLUENCES

The figure who towered over the LCMS theological and political scene in this period was Jacob A. O. Preus.[262] Preus championed the traditional position of the Synod that Scripture was the ruling authority over all doctrine and practice in the church. Preus insisted on the priority of Scripture in the theological task of the church. David P. Scaer, a Preus apologist, has summarized Preus's position:

> Scriptures are the source of all teachings to be taught in the church. These teachings if used according to the principles laid down in the Bible itself will convict the sinner of his sin (the Law) and will lead him to a knowledge of Jesus Christ as his personal Savior from sin (the Gospel).[263]

Preus intimately connects the doctrine of Law and Gospel with the normative authority of the Bible. This authority is the authority to convict of sin, that is, the Law, and to give knowledge of the Savior, that is, the Gospel.[264]

Preus's famous (and much vilified)[265] "A Statement of Scriptural and Confessional Principles" takes up Law and Gospel as its second major point. Preus issued "A Statement" on March 3, 1972, to serve as a basis for the ongoing doctrinal investigation at Concordia Seminary, St. Louis.[266] Preus placed himself squarely in the tradition of orthodox Lutheranism on the eternality of the Law. "The Law, as the expression of God's immutable will, is to be used by the church to bring men to a knowledge of their sins as well as to provide Christians with instruction about good works (SD, V, 17–18)."[267] Preus was defending the third use of the Law by writing that the Law provides Christians with instruction about good works. He concluded the points in "A Statement" with teachings he rejected. Preus rejected the following (among others):

2. That the Gospel is a norm or standard for the Christian life, or that the Gospel, in effect, imposes new Law upon the Christian.

3. That what God's Law declares to be sinful (for example, adultery or theft) need not be regarded as sinful in all times and situations.

4. That the Christians, as men who have been freed from the curse of the Law, no longer need the instruction of the Law to know what God's will is for their life and conduct.[268]

Each of these points has immediate application to the third use of the Law. Preus was trying to guard against the confusion of Law and Gospel, the denial of the *lex aeterna*, and the denial of the Law's power to instruct Christians after conversion.

Preus insisted that theology was the *a posteriori* reflection of the church upon her faith. This meant that reflection on the faith might not conform to experiential descriptions of the faith. It also meant that the church would continue to confess her faith in the authority, not to mention the absolute veracity, of the Scripture. The Missourians were on the opposite side of the battlefield from the theologians of the Valparaiso school.[269]

SUMMARY OF VIEWS

Like Forde, the Missourians held that there was a major dichotomy of doctrine in the Law and Gospel dialectic, but they dealt with the tension between Law and Gospel by focusing on anthropology instead of eschatology. While Forde made the old age–new age dichotomy govern the balance of Law and Gospel, the Missourians made the old Adam–new Adam

dichotomy the ruling theological principle. The Missourians were trying
to take the *simul* seriously.

HENRY J. EGGOLD

Henry J. Eggold emphasized that Law and Gospel must be preached
to the whole person, as a unified *concretum*. In his 1963 article "The Third
Use of the Law," Eggold argued that the Formula of Concord presents a
case that the Law does not apply to Christians only "if believers and the
elect children of God were perfectly renewed in this life."[270] Since this
hypothetical case never obtains in reality, the whole person as *simul justus
et peccator* must be taken into account. Eggold summarized his position: "It
is the intention of this essay to attempt to demonstrate that a person is in
danger of denying the necessity of the third use of the Law for the
Christian when he ascribes what is applicable only to the new man to the
concretum of the Christian."[271] Clearly, Eggold has employed a unitive
anthropology in his approach.

Eggold wanted to show that Luther did not reject the Law's use in the
Christian's life and that Luther's theology, therefore, is not at odds with the
Lutheran Confessions, especially the Formula of Concord. He supports
this contention with several quotations from the Wittenberg Reformer
that show that Luther believed the Ten Commandments remain in force
even for believers,[272] the Law is a friend and companion for the
Christian,[273] and the Christian can never be *ex legibus*.[274] Eggold is responding to the contention of contemporary Luther scholarship that Luther did
not apply the Law to the Christian in the sense of the third use, a contention taken up and repeated by existentialistic Lutheran theologians.[275]

The meaning of the *semper* is important to Eggold's interpretation of
the use of the Law in the Christian life.

> It is significant to note that when the *Formula* declares that the Law
> always accuses, it is not intending to say that it *only* accuses, as though
> this were its sole function. Rather, implicit in the emphasis on the
> Law as accuser is the antithetical idea that it does not promise.[276]

The accusatory function of the Law shows that it is not *promissio*, which
was Melanchthon's favorite word for the Gospel; he used it more than 260
times in the Apology of the Augsburg Confession. Only the Gospel
promises and gives forgiveness of sins. The Law cannot give such gifts.

Eggold thought it self-evident that the Law should function in a third-
use pattern. "In its very nature it is given as instruction for one's conduct."[277] But this contention does not solve the problem of the third use of

the Law. The Law might be a rule or rules for conducting life, but the question is, Should it function as a rule in the life of a Christian? For Eggold, who is following quite strictly the Formula of Concord, the Law continues to function in the life of the Christian as a guide for conduct. So while the Gospel might free the Christian from the coercion of the Law, the Christian now delights in the Law of the Lord in his new Adam.[278] The Christian's relation to the Law changes because of the Gospel.

While the third use of the Law might remain as an ethical guide, Eggold warns against a strict application of the principles of the Law. The Law cannot give answers to every ethical dilemma the Christian faces. "Although it lays down norms for conduct, it does not provide a specific, clearly defined rule to cover every situation in the Christian life."[279] The Law cannot provide casuistic answers for every situation. Instead the Law highlights the ways in which love might function, so where the Law does not give a specific directive, the Christian will know how love would give direction to ethical action.

Ultimately, Eggold pleads for the continuing application of the Law to the Christian person. Eggold considered it illegitimate to divide the old Adam from the new so only the Gospel would be preached to Christians. This would be a denial of the reality of sin. Christians are both old Adam and new Adam and thus need both Law and Gospel in the concrete situation of a whole life, taken as a *concretum*.[280] "Any view of the Christian man which fails to retain this duality of the Christian is a false view."[281] The preaching of Law and Gospel remains a *theologia viatorum*, striving for completion in the age to come but still, in this age, needing to provide the instruction of the Law. The third use of the Law must remain, simply because there remains the duality of the old Adam and the new Adam in the Christian life. The theological nexus of Law and Gospel is the Christian person as described by the *simul*. Law and Gospel are for the whole person, the Christian as a *concretum*, as Eggold puts it.

DAVID P. SCAER

Among the Missourians of this period, David P. Scaer[282] was one of the most eloquent defenders of the third use of the Law. Scaer was sharply critical of the Gospel reductionism evinced by those he labeled as "Valparaiso theologians." He argued that epistemological concerns were at the root of the disagreement between the two theological camps. Does the theologian begin with the Gospel, which leads to Scripture, or does he begin with Scripture, which leads to the Gospel? Those from the Valparaiso school defended the former, the Missourians the latter.

Scaer cited the position of J. A. O. Preus as representative of the Missourian view and the position of Paul Bretscher as representative of the Valparaiso view. Scaer summarized the Preus position:

> Scriptures, written, spoken, preached or paraphrased, tell me about sin (Law) and lead me to faith in Christ (Gospel). Dr. Preus certainly would not deny but obviously believes that faith leads one back to Scripture in accord with the command of Christ as Dr. Bretscher also holds by pointing to Luke 24:36–45.[283]

In contrast to the Missourian position, which began with Scripture and worked toward theology, theologians of the Valparaiso school began with Gospel and worked back toward Scripture. These theologians began with the commitment to the Gospel and subjected Scripture to its scrutiny.

> The position of Dr. Preus is that the Scriptures are the cognitive principle in theology, i.e., they tell us about Christ. Therefore everything taught in the church must be derived from the Scriptures and ultimately serve Jesus Christ. The position of Drs. Bretscher, Schroeder, and Schultz is that the Gospel is the basis of theology and whatever is not contrary to the Gospel is permissible in the church. The first position has been labeled legalistic and Calvinistic and the second, Gospel reductionism.[284]

The Valparaiso theologians began with *solum evangelium*. The result was that the Gospel functioned as a limit for the *sola Scriptura* principle of Lutheran theology.

This approach deemed that whatever was outside the Gospel became an *adiaphoron*, that is, a matter of theological indifference. In the judgment of Scaer, everything becomes a matter of theological indifference to those of the Valparaiso school. "In practice, as experience shows, nothing is found contrary to the Gospel."[285] Thus, the first principle in the Valparaiso approach is the Gospel, so the focus is not what Scripture teaches, but what the Gospel allows.[286] Scaer argued that the choice between the Gospel and Scripture offered by this principle is a false either/or.

> This offer of a choice between Christ and the Bible is not only misleading—it is downright deceptive. It is certainly not suggested by the Scriptures themselves. . . . No real choice can ever be made between Christ and the Bible, simply because the Bible centers in Christ and he submits himself totally to it. Christ is the chief content of the Bible and also the only key to its interpretation.[287]

The Missourians took into account the distinction between a phenomeno-logical approach to theology and a systematic approach. Systematic theol-ogy remains second-order thinking or reflection on the faith. Thus, sys-tematic theology does not follow the pattern of personal conversion or of apologetic uses. "The theological task, not to be confused with the mis-sionary task of the church, is begun by everyone, orthodox or otherwise, with apriori [sic] opinion of what the Bible is or is not."[288] Law and Gospel was set in the framework provided by Scripture as a whole. Scripture had priority. Law and Gospel was derived from it, not vice versa.

In this context, Scaer was critical of F. E. Mayer's acceptance of the Law and Gospel doctrine of Werner Elert.[289] The Missourian tradition was indebted to Francis Pieper, who criticized the Erlangen approach to the-ology in his *Christian Dogmatics*.[290] Scaer continued that tradition by criti-cizing Elert's organizing of theology around the Law and Gospel theme without taking into account the position of the Bible. "The elevation of 'Law-Gospel' as the controlling theological theme was the very weakness in Elert's position."[291] For Scaer and the Missourians, Elert had divorced theology from history by failing to ground it in the history-bound revela-tion of Scripture. This divorce of theology from Scripture earned Elert the charge from Scaer that he was a "Lutheran Barthian." "His 'Law-Gospel' principle hung suspended in theological thin air, almost in the same fash-ion as the Erlangen theology a century before."[292] Historical questions are simply suspended as unfruitful. Such an approach assumes the existence of the Word of God without tying it to a specific historical form. For Scaer this approach does not differ at all from Barth's.[293]

Scaer speculated how the Elertian position was so easily absorbed in the Missouri Synod during the previous period of 1940 to 1960. He sug-gested that the brand of Lutheran orthodoxy practiced in the Missouri Synod had prepared a fertile field in which Elertian theology could root and grow. Scaer chided the Synod's tendency to refuse to face difficult his-torical questions because of the Synod's inerrancy doctrine. "It was a kind of 'The Bible has settled it. Don't ask any questions' approach. Just believe! Of course, this is what Barth and Lutheran Barthianism was also saying: 'Just believe.' "[294] So the approach of the orthodox Missouri Synod readied it for the influence of Elertian theology.[295]

Scaer and the Missourians were uniformly concerned about the ten-dency to place into the category of adiaphora all theology outside their narrow definition of the Gospel. For example, Scaer reproached Schroeder for championing the ordination of women; in Schroeder's opinion it was opposed to the Gospel not to ordain women to the office of the public ministry. Once again the Law simply disappears from consideration.

Scaer charged that the Law is dissolved by the Gospel in the Gospel reductionistic scheme.[296] For Scaer the nexus between Law and Gospel is the person and work of Christ, who fulfills the Law and pays the penalty for the sin of the world in his vicarious suffering and death. The Law is not merely set aside by the Gospel, but in Christ the Gospel confirms God's righteousness and holiness in the Law.[297]

When the third use of the Law is denied, Gospel is turned into Law. The Gospel becomes the ethical regulating principle in the life of the Christian. Robert C. Schultz argued that murder is sin not because it infringes on the fifth commandment, but because it contradicts the Gospel.[298] The Law no longer has any power to condemn, but the Gospel itself has taken over the condemnatory function of the Law. Ultimately this is a denial not only of the third use of the Law, but also of the second use. Schultz's position also leads Scaer to wonder if the Law is binding on non-Christians. If Christians are not under judgment for breaking the Law, what status can the Law have for non-Christians?[299]

Gospel as defined by the theologians of the Valparaiso school becomes "a *carte blanche* for moral and doctrinal freedom."[300] Doctrinal and moral anarchy were, according to the Missourians, the real results of the denial by these theologians of the third use of the Law.

Scaer also charged that when the Gospel is treated as the "regulating principle" in the Christian life it becomes "little more than spiritualized pragmatism."[301] The Gospel had become the basis for all manner of doctrinal deviation.[302] The third use of the Law could not be applied to doctrine. In other words there were no legally based doctrinal norms in the public teaching of the church.[303]

Scaer was critical of what he saw as a misappropriation of the Law and Gospel dialectic. He argued that Law and Gospel is not a "doctrine" in the same sense as the other articles of the faith, but it is a way of looking at the articles of the faith. Law and Gospel is a filter for the articles of the faith. In this way Law and Gospel does not function independently of the articles of the faith. For Scaer, Law and Gospel cannot function to change the meaning or the content of the church's kerygma. The acts of God may be perceived through the filter of Law and Gospel, but they are not in and of themselves Law or Gospel.[304] Any divine act might be Law or Gospel depending on how it is preached.[305]

Law and Gospel deal with *how* God's creative and redemptive acts are related to God's people in preaching. A bare act of God is not Law or Gospel of itself. God's preaching or explaining his acts is Law and Gospel. The Gospel is the report of the act. Of course Christians recognized the apostolic preaching as the divinely sanctioned explanation of divine actions against which no other explanation in the church is to be tolerated. (*Sola Scriptura!*)[306]

The acts of God in the scriptural revelation cannot be mitigated or changed by the Law-Gospel dialectic. The kerygmatic acts of God in the scriptural revelation stand on their own and only become Law or Gospel in their being preached, whether by the apostolic authorities in the scriptural record or by their successors *viva voce* in the church. For Scaer, acts of God in Christ *become* Gospel when the apostolic authorities inform the world that God has acted *pro me*.

Scaer also argues for the continuing validity of the Law as inherent in God's creation. Generally, Lutherans have been suspicious of the Barthian rejection of natural theology, once again because it sets the word of the Law outside the realm of reality. While Lutherans might struggle with the precise content of the natural law, they do argue that the creating God firmly grounds the Ten Commandments in the reality of creation.

> The Law, reflecting God's own essence, is the regulatory principle for all of creation and is present in the creation simply because of God's creating activity. Man's abrogation of the Law puts him under God's condemnation *ipso facto*. Natural law alerts man that he has stepped outside the boundaries and the Law given verbally by special revelation reflects this Law negatively to man's sinful nature.[307]

A denial of the enduring validity of the Law is tantamount to a denial of reality for Scaer. Law is not only a *lex aeterna* situated in God, but it is also *lex naturalis*.

The Missourians perceived the Valparaiso theologians' view of Law and Gospel as an attack on the objective content of the faith. "The *for us* in theology rests on the fact that God *did something*. If 'Lutheran Barthianism' gains the field, the *for us* will also be lost."[308] A rejection of an objective Law implied a rejection of the Gospel and its results. The third use of the Law must remain where the Gospel is to be properly defended.

John W. Montgomery

John W. Montgomery was critical of the method of using Law and Gospel as an overarching hermeneutical theme. Montgomery himself coined the term "Gospel reductionism." He argued that by denying eternally valid categories of thought, the whole substance of the faith was in jeopardy. He warned against the tendency to boil down all biblical interpretive issues to Law-Gospel.

> Law-Gospel comes to function as an independent philosophical principle (like those of nineteenth century [sic] German idealism) by which Scripture is judged; and the Bible takes on the role of a book of illustrations for the principle. Not so the Reformers' view of Law-Gospel; for them, it derived *from* Scripture, and, like all theological truths, it could only be affirmed on the ground of the total reliability of God's Word.[309]

Law and Gospel was an extrabiblical *norma normans* now applied not only to theology, but also to the text of Scripture.

Montgomery traced the influence and disastrous results of existentialism upon Christian theology. He argued that existentialistic ethics necessarily leads to ethical relativism.

> The Protestant existentialist can never appeal to absolute Law; he can only say, "You're free, choose to love." But what does this mean in concrete terms? Theoretically it can mean "anything goes"—an antinomianism indeed—for each existential decision is unique and without precedent.[310]

Once again the fear of ethical anarchy drove the discussion of the third use of the Law by the Missourians. Sanctification in the traditional sense is rendered impossible where there is no absolute ethical standard.

The third use of the Law is an essential doctrine for two reasons, according to Montgomery. First, love does not give content to ethical action. In other words, love provides motivation and power to ethical action, but it cannot provide the "what." Only the objective word of God in the Law can provide that content.[311]

Second, the third use of the Law preserves the doctrine of sanctification. Because of the new birth in Christ, the Christian's relation to the Law has changed. The Christian now delights in the Law of the Lord.[312] "Only by taking the Third Use of the Law—the 'Law of Christ' (Gal. 6:2)—seriously do we take regeneration seriously; and only when we come to love God's revealed Law has sanctification become a reality in our lives."[313] The nomological situation of the Christian changes because of the Gospel. Montgomery readily concedes that the Law still accuses the Christian.

However, the Christian will also see the biblical Law in another light—"as the manifestation of God's loving will."[314]

KURT E. MARQUART

Kurt E. Marquart chronicled the LCMS doctrinal war that was center stage during this period of American Lutheran history in a book entitled *Anatomy of an Explosion*.[315] He took up the issue of Law and Gospel and the third use of the Law in this work. Marquart was decidedly opposed to the use of historical critical interpretive tools in the exegesis of the Bible.[316] He was also highly critical of the attempt to claim that Law and Gospel could provide objective controls for the application of higher-critical tools of interpretation. As we have seen, the theologians of the Valparaiso school and the ELCA theologians treated Law and Gospel as a norming authority for biblical studies. This was unacceptable to Marquart on at least three grounds.

First, like Scaer, Marquart insists on the historical facticity of Bible texts.[317] Marquart considers invalid the method of theology that places the Law and Gospel dialectic over the text of the Bible as a ruling or controlling principle. The Elertian or the "Lutheran-Barthian" approach, which separates the Bible's own story from its grounding in history so Law-Gospel controls it, fails because it leaves the Bible at the mercy of historical critical canons of interpretation. Marquart identifies this with a Bultmannian theological approach, where the historical content of Scripture is judged by a Law-Gospel distinction without any reference to its facticity.[318] Thus, the theologians of the Valparaiso school champion the Gospel content of Scripture above its authoritative character as the Word of God. The rejection of the authority of Scripture is a defense of the Gospel. Marquart suggests that this is a false dichotomy; instead, the principle of Scripture authority is intended to defend the Gospel itself. He employs this homey illustration to make his point.

> The Scripture-principle, then, is the Gospel's own authority-principle and not something separate on the side! To put it very crudely, the "formal principle" or "Scripture-principle" (that is, Scripture as sole authority, *sola Scriptura*) is simply the door of the Gospel's hen-house. The door is not there for its own sake but precisely to protect the whole house. If it is gone, it would be foolish to say smugly, "O [*sic*] well, that was only the door—the rest of the hen-house is still safe!" Once the door is gone, the historical critical fox is free to take whatever he pleases. The hen-house will be quite empty eventually, even if not after the first two or three visits.[319]

The principle of Scripture-authority is essential to defend not only the Gospel, but all the teachings of the faith. According to the Missourians, when the henhouse is unguarded, anything goes, including a rejection of the third use of the Law. Doctrinal and moral anarchy is the natural outcome of such an approach. This line of reasoning demonstrates the close relationship between a traditional biblical inspiration doctrine and the third use of the Law in LCMS theology.

Second, Marquart maintains that there is a distinction between systematic theology and apologetics. Systematic theology for the Missourians remains an enterprise of faith; that is, it is begun and carried out only with the presupposition of belief.

> The fallacy is to assume that because books on doctrine usually begin, very sensibly, with biblical inspiration as the basis and authority for all doctrine and practice, therefore the intention is to "prove" inspiration in order then to "reason" oneself or others into faith in Christ. This is arrant nonsense. Detailed manuals on Christian doctrine are normally written to instruct future public teachers of the church in the church's biblical faith. The standpoint of faith and of theology, therefore, can and must be presupposed. The Lordship of Christ is already a certainty from the outset and determines the whole treatment of the Bible; faith in Christ is not something still to be established in the middle or towards the end of the volume or set![320]

For Marquart and the Missourians, systematic theology primarily is the faithful teaching the faith to the faithful. Thus, a systematic theologian could correctly begin with the faith-normed presuppositions about the Bible as the starting point of systematic theology.[321] The missionary or apologetic approach is quite different. In mission work the proclamation of Law and Gospel is the priority. In apologetics putative barriers to the faith are dealt with apart from the presupposition of faith.[322]

Third, Marquart is deeply suspicious of a sharp division between doctrine and the Gospel. He argues that in modern Lutheran usage the terms *Law* and *Gospel* have been assigned functional meanings alien to their original intent. " 'Law and Gospel' also have been turned into 'a lifeless speculation.' In *chic* Lutheran usage, 'evangelical' means tolerant, and the 'Gospel' is identified with a kind of secular permissiveness."[323] In Marquart's analysis the Law loses its content and the Gospel is turned into a kind of new Law that provides only permission based on secularized canons of propriety. In such thinking, being Law oriented is the opposite of being Gospel oriented. Law and Gospel are no longer seen in tension with each other; instead, one simply neutralizes the other. A Gospel orientation extinguishes any hope of a third-use of the Law. The third use of the Law is a doctrine hopelessly inured in legalism. Such a view receives a resounding reprimand from Marquart, who sees it as an accommodation to secular values.[324]

SUMMARY ANALYSIS AND EVALUATION

The Missourians believed that to reject the third use of the Law would be to risk antinomianism. Characteristically they warned that by denying the third use of the Law there was a risk of falling into a denial of the Law altogether. Antinomianism threatened both doctrine and life by risking a dissolution of order. As the 1960s advanced, the theme of the importance of moral and doctrinal order became increasingly significant for the Missourians, who saw themselves fighting a battle for the life of their church body, not to mention Lutheran doctrine itself.

The concept of doctrinal discipline was important to that battle and thus the defense of the third use of the Law loomed large. Any disregard for the third use of the Law smacked of secularism and ethical permissiveness. The issue of doctrinal discipline created fierce contention within the Missouri Synod throughout this period.

The Missourians accepted the third use of the Law on the basis of the authority of the Formula of Concord. They rejected the notion that the Formula of Concord was a wrong-headed legalistic deviation from the dynamic Gospel-centered guidance of Martin Luther. They denied that there was a breach between the theology of Luther and the Lutheran Confessions on this point. As will be shown in chapter 4, their view of Luther is being vindicated by more recent Luther research, which has begun to focus more on the later Luther. That Luther himself never specifically denominated a third use of the Law mattered little. According to the Missourians, he had used the Law in a third-use fashion, even if he had never specifically named it "third use."

The theologians of the Valparaiso school suggested that there was an inherent weakness in the Missourian acceptance of the principle of Scripture authority. They thought it an attempt to coordinate two different principles of authority in Lutheran theology—Law and Gospel on the one hand, and Scripture authority on the other. Thus, the Missourians defended the importance of the principle of Scripture-authority by clarifying the distinction between systematic theology and mission endeavors. The approach to proclamation needed to be different from the approach to systematic theology. They refused to let the Gospel dissolve the tight doctrinal relationship among the articles of faith, as they thought others had. For the Missourians every doctrine was intimately related to the Gospel. This or that doctrine could not simply be relegated to the position of adiaphora.

SUMMARY AND CONCLUSIONS

American Lutheran theologians' approach to the third use of the Law in this period shows the clear division within American Lutheranism. Theologians of the Valparaiso school and the ELCA theologians traveled parallel paths, despite being concerned with different church institutional situations. The Valparaiso theologians were completely occupied with the battle at Concordia Seminary, St. Louis, over the LCMS. The ELCA theologians were not constrained by narrow confessional concerns and more openly espoused and supported European theological influences. The Missourians were attempting to preserve Lutheran orthodoxy and Old Lutheranism in America and were fighting to stop what they perceived to be the intrusion of historical-critical tools into the classrooms of the Synod's schools.

To a greater or lesser extent both the theologians of the Valparaiso school and the ELCA theologians used an existentialistic approach to theology. This approach ruled out the third use of the Law as a sub-Christian intrusion or a Calvinistic intrusion into Lutheran theology, which entered through Melanchthon's influence and the Formula of Concord and was observed by Melanchthon's students and their successors in the period of orthodoxy. Just a hint of Calvinism was enough to taint the third use of the Law as unLutheran and unevangelical.

The Missourians were much more accepting of the authority of the Formula of Concord and more critical of European theological influences. They argued that Luther's doctrine was represented accurately by the Formula of Concord, albeit in the language characteristic of Melanchthon. Given the volume of research on this subject and the textual ambiguity of some of that research, this issue will remain in dispute among Luther scholars and Lutheran theologians for some time to come.

Gospel reductionism had a devastating effect on the Christian use of the Law. Some theologians not only rejected the third use of the Law, but in more radical cases rejected any use of the Law in the church. The more radical treatments of the Law by the theologians of the Valparaiso school might well have been a theological overreaction calculated to shock and irritate the stodgy orthodoxy of the Missourians. As the two groups faced off over momentous issues, the political situation required swift responses, often fraught with too much passion and too little deliberation. The Missourians rejected the hermeneutical implications of the Valparaiso position for methodological reasons, but they could also see the impact Gospel reductionism would have on any number of Christian doctrines, including the third use of the Law. The ELCA theologians were not as deeply affected by the internecine fights wracking the LCMS and thus were more balanced in their consideration of the third use of the Law, though they clearly denied it a place in their theology. Forde's use of Haikola's thesis about the significance of the Law in Lutheran theology presents significant evidence of this balance.

The approach to the third use of the Law in this period shows once again that a denial of the third use of the Law inevitably entails an inclusion of the Law's content in the Gospel. This legal intrusion in the Gospel gets a variety of labels: Gospel imperatives, *paraklesis*, parenesis, encouragement, *Gebot*, and so forth. Whatever it is called, it remains a confusion of Law and Gospel. Forde saw this clearly in his work and steered clear of it by suspending judgment on the relationship between Christian ethics and the Law, an issue that cries out for a response.

Forde's eschatological approach to the place of the Law in Christian theology was also unique, but flawed by its one-sidedness. He failed to account for the way in which theological dichotomies actually cut in different directions across the *corpus* of Lutheran theology. An eschatological approach is but one perspective, cutting across Lutheran theology with the old age–new age dichotomy. The anthropological dimension of the Christian's life as *simul justus et peccator* can never be left out of the doctrinal equation. The *justus et peccator* dichotomy also cuts across Lutheran theology. The Missourians kept the *simul* as a constant part of the debate, attempting to emphasize the unitive nature of Christian anthropology. Ironically, in this period the defenders of orthodoxy in American Lutheranism approached the question of the place of the Law with anthropological concerns at the forefront.

NOTES

[1] For more on the connection of these theologians to Valparaiso University and Concordia Seminary, see p. 46 and p. 78, n. 38.
[2] Martin Heinecken, "Erlangen Theology," in *Twentieth Century Encyclopedia of Religious Knowledge*, vol. 1. (ed. Lefferts A. Loetscher; Grand Rapids: Baker, 1955).

[3] The theologians who gave the major impetus to this school were Johann Wilhelm Friedrich Hoefling, Gottlieb Christoph Adolph von Harless, Johann Christian Konrad von Hofmann, and Franz Reinhold Hermann von Frank. Gottfried Thomasius, Heinrich Schmid, Theodosius Harnack, Theodor Zahn, Christoph Ernst Luthardt, and Ludwig Ihmels were of the Erlangen school and generally provided a conservative trajectory to the development of the school, as in the case especially of Harnack. See Heinecken, "Erlangen Theology" in Loetscher, ed., *Encyclopedia of Religious Knowledge*.

[4] The major characteristics of the Erlangen school can be summarized in the following five points. First, the Erlangen school attempted to remain faithful to the Lutheran Confessions. However, the Erlangen theologians eschewed what was at the time called "*Zeitentheologie*." Instead, they pursued a course of developing theology. They began with the Lutheran Confessions but moved beyond them along the trajectory they thought was suggested by those Confessions. They believed that Lutheran theology could be positively developed by a "dynamic moving forward in the direction indicated by the Confessions." Second, while often criticizing Schleiermacher and his method, they accepted as central the "subjective starting point." Third, J. C. K. von Hofmann, a leading Erlangen theologian, championed the *Heilsgeschichte* method that attempted to overcome the orthodox tendency to treat the Bible as a source of proof texts to be mined for golden nuggets of divine wisdom. Fourth, the theologians of the Erlangen school treated faith and the Bible as a unified whole, centered in the doctrine of justification by grace alone. The goal of this unification of the human subject and the Bible is the reestablishment of communion between God and man. Schleiermacher's influence is clear at this point. Fifth, Erlangen theologians saw ethics as an integral component of dogmatics. See Heinecken, "Erlangen Theology," in Loetscher, ed., *Encyclopedia of Religious Knowledge*.

[5] Elert (1885–1954) was a parish pastor from 1912 until 1919, when he became the head of the *altlutherisch* seminary in Breslau before moving to Erlangen. He was professor of church history at the University of Erlangen from 1923 until his death. After the death of Philip Bachmann in 1931, Elert was also appointed professor of systematic theology.

[6] Breslau is now part of modern Poland. Breslau was a Prussian possession until the Versailles treaty at the end of the First World War. The Breslau Synod came into existence in 1830 as a protest against the Prussian Union. The pastors and congregations were subjected to government persecution until 1845 when the Prussian government granted toleration in the "*generalkonzession*." Persecution caused emigration to America (the Buffalo Synod is one example) and also a church wary of persecution and strongly polemical along "Old Lutheran" doctrinal lines. The Breslau Synod has been most closely allied with the independent Evangelical Lutheran Free Church (SELK). The Breslau seminary, which Elert ran until moving to Erlangen and which was abandoned in 1945, was replaced by the SELK seminary in Oberursel. See Erwin L. Lueker, ed., *Lutheran Cyclopedia* (rev. ed.; St. Louis: Concordia, 1975), s.v. "Germany, Lutheran Churches in."

[7] Lowell C. Green, "The Relationship of Werner Elert and America," *Concordia Historical Institute Quarterly* 70 (Summer 1997): 76–77.

[8] Green, "Relationship of Werner Elert and America," 90.

[9] Elert readily and rightly admits that for Melanchthon and Luther the authority of Scripture was not questioned and, therefore, was not in need of defense against the Roman Catholic party. See Werner Elert, *The Christian Faith* (5th ed.; trans. Martin

H. Bertram and Walter R. Bouman; master's thesis, Luther Seminary Library, St. Paul, 1974), 69.

[10] Elert, *Christian Faith*, 70.

[11] Elert, *Christian Faith*, 70.

[12] Wilfried Joest argues that though Luther does not use *expressis verbis*, he does use the concept. Wilfried Joest, *Gesetz und Freiheit: Das Problem des tertius usus legis bei Luther und die neutestamentliche Parainese* (Göttingen: Vandenhoeck & Ruprecht, 1951), 71–82. Armin W. Schuetze takes a similar approach, attempting to show that the basic ideas of the Formula of Concord were Luther's. See Armin W. Schuetze, "On the Third Use of the Law: Luther's Position in the Antinomian Debate," in *No Other Gospel* (ed. Arnold J. Koelpin; Milwaukee: Northwestern, 1980), 207–27.

[13] SC; *BS* 507–510; *Trig* 539–43. James M. Childs Jr., at the time an LCMS ethicist and theologian, suggested that the third use of the Law directs Christian ethics to accept some kind of rules. He sees the explanations to the Ten Commandments in Luther's catechism as the "prime example here." See Childs, "The Third Use of the Law and Constructive Ethics," *CurTM* 2 (February 1975): 36.

[14] Werner Elert, *Law and Gospel* (trans. Edward H. Schroeder; Philadelphia: Fortress, 1967), 46.

[15] The Formula of Concord was written by committee and has a convoluted literary history (see pp. 19–21), which makes it nearly impossible to attribute any particular section to a particular author or authors. An economy of language dictates the use of personification in this case.

[16] Elert, *Law and Gospel*, 40.

[17] Helmut Thielicke pointed out that the starting point of the Lutheran doctrine of Law and Gospel is the reality of the sinfulness of Christians. "In the state of justification the Law has to bear witness to our existence as de facto sinners [*peccatores in re*]. By keeping this fact before us the Law rescues us from the illusions that we are 'perfect Christians' who no longer live at the point where we must continually begin again [*incipere*], needing the forgiveness of Jesus Christ each day afresh" (Helmut Thielicke, *Theological Ethics*, vol. 1 [ed. William H. Lazareth; Philadelphia: Fortress, 1966], 94).

[18] For a similar argument, see Henry J. Eggold Jr., "The Third Use of the Law," *Springfielder* 27 (Spring 1963): 16.

[19] See SD VI, 18; *BS* 967; *Trig* 967–69.

[20] SD VI, 24; *Trig* 969–71. "*Bis das Fleisch der Sünden ganz und gar ausgezogen und der Mensch vollkommlich in der Auferstehung erneuert, do er weder der Predig des Gesetzes noch seiner Trauung und Strafen, wie auch des Evangelii nicht mehr bedürfen wird, die in dies unvollkommen Leben gehören*" (*BS* 969).

[21] Elert, *Law and Gospel*, 42.

[22] Elert's criticism of the third use of the Law is what logicians call the fallacy of an ambiguous term. He has not pinned down the meaning of the term "third use of the Law." Is he talking about Melanchthon's use of the term, the Formula of Concord's use of the term, Calvin's use of the term, or a modern use of the term? This is not clear. See Elert, *Law and Gospel*, 42–43.

[23] "*Tertius usus, qui et praecipuus est, et in proprium Legis finem proprius spectat, erga fideles locum habet, quorum in cordibus iam viget ac regnat Dei Spiritus*" (John Calvin, "*Institutio Christianae Religionis*," in *Opera Selecta*, vol. 3 [eds. Peter Barth and William

Niesel; Munich: Christian Kaiser, 1928], 337; [2, 7, 12]).

[24] See Calvin, "*Institutio Christianae Religionis*," 337–39. For more on Calvin's view of the Law, see, for example, John H. Leith, "Creation and Redemption: Law and Gospel in the Theology of John Calvin," in *Marburg Revisited* (eds. Paul C. Empie and James I. McCord; Minneapolis: Augsburg, 1966), 150.

[25] Both Paul M. Hoyer of the LCMS and Scott Ickert of the ELCA argued that Calvin actually confused Law and Gospel because he taught that the Law motivates for righteous living. See Paul M. Hoyer, "Law and Gospel: With Particular Attention to the Third Use of the Law," *CJ* 6 (September 1980): 193, 197; and Scott Ickert, "The Uses of the Law," *Lutheran Forum* 25 (February 1991): 20.

[26] Edward H. Schroeder, "Law-Gospel Reductionism in the History of The Lutheran Church—Missouri Synod," *CTM* 43 (April 1972): 233.

[27] Stephen A. Schmidt, "Law-Gospel: Toward a Model of Moral Education," *RelEd* 65 (November–December 1970): 476.

[28] See John W. Montgomery, *Crisis in Lutheran Theology*, vol. 1 (Grand Rapids: Baker, 1967; 2d rev. ed., Minneapolis: Bethany Fellowship, 1973), 94, n. 30.

[29] See Schmidt, "Toward a Model of Moral Education," 477.

[30] See Lueker, ed., *Lutheran Cyclopedia*, s.v. "Althaus, Paul August Wilhelm Hermann."

[31] See Paul Althaus, *The Divine Command* (trans. Franklin Sherman; Philadelphia: Fortress, 1966), 27–29.

[32] For a sympathetic summary, see William H. Lazareth, introduction to *Divine Command*, by Paul Althaus, iii–x.

[33] See Althaus, *Divine Command*, 2.

[34] Althaus, *Divine Command*, 2.

[35] See Raymond W. Albright, "Althaus, A. W. H. Paul," in Loetscher, ed., *Encyclopedia of Religious Knowledge*, vol. 1.

[36] See Althaus, *Divine Command*, 3.

[37] Althaus, *Divine Command*, 6.

[38] "*Welches ist der ewige, unverrückliche, unwandelbarer wille Gottes*" (WA 45:149, 20–21).

[39] Ep VI, 7; *Trig* 807. "*Ein einiges Gesetz, nämlich der unwandelbar Wille Gottes*" (*BS* 795).

[40] Althaus is not thinking of a literal Adamic encounter with God, but a state that precedes all history, including all biblical history. The concept of a primal state applies to every person. The fall is recapitulated in every person. "We have fallen, and continually fall, out of God's original relationship to us, out of the primal state" (Althaus, *Divine Command*, 12).

[41] Althaus, *Divine Command*, 8–9.

[42] See Althaus, *Divine Command*, 10.

[43] Althaus, *Divine Command*, 10. The terminology "*verbum proprium*" and "*verbum alienum*" is language derived from Isa 28:21. Note that Althaus changes the terminology slightly in his usage. Luther wrote of *opus proprium* and *opus alienum*. See SD V, 11–13; *BS* 955–56; *Trig* 955–57.

[44] Althaus, *Divine Command*, 9.

[45] See WA 40/1:558.

[46] See Althaus, *Divine Command*, 27.

[47] Althaus, *Divine Command*, 13. Helmut Thielicke shared this insight of the unity of the Law but did not accede to the addition of the term "command." He argued that the human relation to the Law changes after conversion but that it must remain "Law." For Thielicke, in distinction to Althaus, the Law has many aspects but remains Law. "Thus the Law itself is always the same; its authority too is unchanged throughout. Only my relation to it is different; I am no longer a servant but a son. I am no longer an opponent of a Law which confronts me as the Law of the 'Lord.' I am rather one who in free love actually wills what his Father wills" (Thielicke, *Theological Ethics*, 1:137).

[48] Althaus, *Divine Command*, 27.

[49] For example, John 6:63.

[50] Walter J. Bartling, in speaking of Pauline parenesis, wrote, "A surprising number of the imperatives are not negative prohibitions at all but positive exhortations that function as enticement and as reinforcement for the motive powers that are already functioning in the reality of the Spirit's fellowship" (Bartling, "Hermeneutics and Pauline Parenesis," in *A Project in Biblical Hermeneutics* [ed. Richard Jungkuntz; St. Louis: The Commission on Theology and Church Relations of The Lutheran Church—Missouri Synod, 1969], 61).

[51] Perhaps the imperative "Open your presents," uttered to children on Christmas Eve, would come close to illustrating this use of the imperative in everyday language.

[52] Althaus himself recognized the problem of the relationship between the imperative and command in the Bible when he made the same distinction in another context. Althaus criticized the use of Law as pointing purely to the imperative elements in the Bible. However, command is more indicative of imperative elements than Law, which is a broader term. See Althaus, *Divine Command*, 9.

[53] See Robert D. Preus, "The Significance of Luther's Term *Pure Passive* as Quoted in Article II of the Formula of Concord," *CTM* 29 (August 1958): 561–70.

[54] Althaus, *Divine Command*, 30.

[55] See SD IV, 10; *BS* 941; *Trig* 941.

[56] Althaus, *Divine Command*, 30.

[57] See Althaus, *Divine Command*, 30.

[58] Althaus, *Divine Command*, 45.

[59] Althaus, *Divine Command*, 45.

[60] Althaus, *Divine Command*, 46.

[61] For more on the process by which these mergers took place, see John H. Tietjen, *Which Way to Lutheran Unity?* (St. Louis: Concordia, 1966), 123–39; and E. Clifford Nelson, "The New Shape of Lutheranism 1930–" in *The Lutherans in North America* (ed. E. Clifford Nelson; Philadelphia: Fortress, 1975), 498–508.

[62] John W. Montgomery, an erstwhile outsider who joined the Missouri Synod on the basis of conviction, wrote in 1969 about the way in which Missouri was cut off from American denominational and cultural life. "The reason for Missouri's current theological crisis is to a large extent sociological. Here one observes the 'ghetto' phenomenon so characteristic of immigrant groups. During the first century of its existence, the Missouri Synod remained largely walled off from theological erosion because of

its commitment to the orthodox theological position (and even language) of its Saxon founders, who had left Germany expressly to avoid politically enforced ecumenical union" (Montgomery, *Crisis in Lutheran Theology*, 1:133).

[63] Nelson, *Lutherans in North America*, 515.

[64] Conrad John Immanuel Bergendoff (1895–1997) of the Augustana Synod, which merged into the LCA, was a respected American Lutheran theologian and church historian. See Loetscher, ed., *Encyclopedia of Religious Knowledge*, s.v. "Bergendoff, Conrad John Immanuel," 1:127.

[65] See Nelson, *Lutherans in North America*, 516.

[66] LCMS, *The Proceedings of the 46th Regular Convention of the LCMS* (St. Louis: The Lutheran Church—Missouri Synod, 1965), 80. Lutheranism as a "confessional movement" was the view taught to a generation of pastors trained under Arthur Carl Piepkorn, professor of systematic theology and the Lutheran Confessions at Concordia Seminary, St. Louis, from 1951 until his death in 1973. This view has been championed by some of Dr. Piepkorn's most influential students, including Richard John Neuhaus, editor of *First Things*.

[67] Nelson, *Lutherans in North America*, 517.

[68] Paul G. Bretscher said about the conflict in the Missouri Synod that "the first focus of that conflict was, after all, an educational institution, Concordia Seminary in St. Louis" (Bretscher, *After the Purifying* [River Forest: Lutheran Education Association, 1975], xi).

[69] Montgomery, *Crisis in Lutheran Theology*, 1:110.

[70] See pp. 45–53.

[71] Nelson, *Lutherans in North America*, 528.

[72] Bretscher, *After the Purifying*, 8.

[73] See The Board of Control of Concordia Seminary, St. Louis, Mo., *Exodus from Concordia* (St. Louis: Concordia College, 1977), 129.

[74] Nelson, *Lutherans in North America*, 533.

[75] Hermann Sasse, review of E. Clifford Nelson ed., *The Lutherans in North America*, *Lutheran Theological Journal* 10 (August 1976): 60.

[76] Edward H. Schroeder specifically called the term a "neologism." See Schroeder, "Law-Gospel Reductionism," 233.

[77] Bohlmann and Preus were both members of the faculty minority at Concordia Seminary, St. Louis.

[78] Schroeder, "Law-Gospel Reductionism," 232. The essays presented at this time were collected into Montgomery, *Crisis in Lutheran Theology*.

[79] In 1975 Paul G. Bretscher wrote, "Theologians who claimed to derive the authority of the Scriptures from the authority of the Gospel were suspected of 'Gospel reductionism,' and of trying to change the doctrinal basis on which the Synod had stood for 125 years" (Bretscher, *After the Purifying*, 7).

[80] See pp. 25–30.

[81] Schroeder astutely pointed out that the distinction between Law and Gospel was ignored in the Reformation studies of both Holl and Troeltsch and that Elert set out to remedy that lack of attention. See Schroeder, "Law-Gospel Reductionism," 233.

[82] For more on this metatheological import of Law and Gospel, see Scott R. Murray,

"Law and Gospel: The Lutheran Ethic," *Logia* 4 (July 1995): 15–24.

[83] Schroeder, "Law-Gospel Reductionism," 235; emphasis in the original.

[84] Schroeder said precisely the same of the hermeneutic of Luther. Schroeder commended Luther for what Lindsay Dewar called Luther's "one-sided" interpretation of the Scriptures. Dewar excoriated Luther for interpreting the Bible from the standpoint of justification by faith. See Lindsay Dewar, *The Holy Spirit and Modern Thought* (New York: Harper, 1959), 125. Schroeder suggested that this was the correct standpoint for interpreting the Bible. Edward H. Schroeder, "Is There a Lutheran Hermeneutics?" in *The Lively Function of the Gospel* (ed. Robert W. Bertram; St. Louis: Concordia, 1966), 81.

[85] The *quia* subscription simply means that Lutherans pledge themselves to the content of the Lutheran Confessions because they are true and correct expositions of the Word of God. The opposite position is that the Confessions could be subscribed to in a *quatenus* fashion, that is, insofar as they reflect the Bible's own teaching. This is ultimately no subscription at all. For more on the historical meaning of *quia* confessional subscription, see C. F. W. Walther, "Why Should Our Pastors, Teachers and Professors Subscribe Unconditionally to the Symbolical Writings of Our Church," *CTM* 18 (April 1947): 241–53; and Robert D. Preus, "Confessional Subscription," in *Evangelical Directions for the Lutheran Church* (eds. Erich H. Kiehl and Waldo J. Werning; Chicago: Lutheran Congress, 1970), 43–52.

[86] Schroeder, "Law-Gospel Reductionism," 235.

[87] Schroeder, "Law-Gospel Reductionism," 235; emphasis in the original.

[88] Robert C. Schultz, at the outset of a 1961 journal article, pointed out that Law and Gospel are systematic signposts intended to defend the doctrine of justification. "The distinction between Law and Gospel is one of the clearest systematic expressions of the doctrine of justification through faith without works formulated by the Lutheran Reformation" (Schultz, "The Distinction between Law and Gospel," *CTM* 32 [October 1961]: 591).

[89] See Ralph A. Bohlmann, "Principles of Biblical Interpretation in the Lutheran Confessions," in *Crisis in Lutheran Theology*, vol. 2 (ed. John W. Montgomery; Grand Rapids: Baker, 1967; 2d rev. ed., Minneapolis: Bethany Fellowship, 1973), 145–58, 161. See also Ralph A. Bohlmann, *Principles of Biblical Interpretation in the Lutheran Confessions* (rev. ed.; St. Louis: Concordia, 1983). Holsten Fagerberg pointed out that "the Confessions actually proceed to the interpretation of Scripture, but without telling us which principle is being employed in the process" (Fagerberg, *A New Look at the Lutheran Confessions* [trans. Gene J. Lund; St. Louis: Concordia, 1972], 35).

[90] Robert C. Schultz, one of the Valparaiso theologians, considered Law and Gospel to be a hermeneutical principle of the Lutheran Reformers. However, he did not argue that this was their only hermeneutic. See Schultz, "Distinction between Law and Gospel," 596.

[91] Here "hermeneutical principle" is used to refer to a rule applied by an interpreter to the text to discover its meaning. See Bohlmann, "Principles of Biblical Interpretation," 160.

[92] The position defended by Schroeder had support in the work of a number of European Lutherans, the best example of which was Edmund Schlink. However, even Schlink did not give the one-sided interpretation to the Law and Gospel hermeneutic that Schroeder did. "This intense concern with the Gospel suggests that the Gospel is the norm in Scripture and Scripture is the norm for the sake of the Gospel"

(Edmund Schlink, *Theology of the Lutheran Confessions* [trans. Paul F. Koehneke and Herbert J. A. Bouman; Philadelphia: Fortress, 1961], 6). Note that Schlink does not say that the Gospel is the norm *of* Scripture, but *in* Scripture. He also balances this idea with "Scripture is the norm for the sake of the Gospel."

[93] AC XV, 3–4; *Trig* 49. "*Admonentur etiam, quod traditiones humanae institutae ad placandum Deum, ad promerendam gratiam et satisfaciendum pro peccatis adversentur evangelio et doctrinae fidei; quare vota et traditiones de cibis et diebus etc. institutae ad promerendam gratiam et satisfaciendum pro peccatis inutiles sint et contra evangelium*" (*BS* 69–70).

[94] Kurt Marquart noted that LCMS moderates defend a false either/or in that, like Schroeder, they pit the Gospel against Scripture. "The 'formal principle' (or Scripture-principle), then, is not something additional, above, and beyond the Gospel and forced onto it from without. It is rather the Gospel's own authority-dimension, the criterion by which the Gospel distinguishes itself from false Gospels (Gal. 1:8, 9; Eph. 2:20)" (Kurt Marquart, *Anatomy of an Explosion* [Concordia Seminary Monograph Series 3; Fort Wayne: Concordia Theological Seminary Press, 1977], 130).

[95] Fagerberg, *New Look*, 36.

[96] Cf. Robert C. Schultz, "An Alternative to the Formula of Concord?" review of Holsten Fagerberg, *A New Look at the Lutheran Confessions*, *The Cresset* 36 (March 1973): 13.

[97] For more detail on this debate, see Fagerberg, *New Look*, 36, n. 7.

[98] Fagerberg, *New Look*, 63.

[99] Marquart, *Anatomy of an Explosion*, 131; emphasis in the original.

[100] "The Law and the Gospel cannot be looked upon as providing the hermeneutical key to every pericope in the Bible" (David P. Scaer, "Law and Gospel in Lutheran Theology," *Grace Theological Journal* 12 [Fall 1991]: 176). Robert Preus pointed out that Law and Gospel functions as a theological hermeneutic to rule out legalism. See Robert D. Preus, "The Hermeneutics of the Formula of Concord," in *No Other Gospel* (ed. Arnold J. Koelpin; Milwaukee: Northwestern, 1980).

[101] Robert J. Hoyer, "On Law and Gospel," *The Cresset* 29 (February 1966): 8.

[102] Schroeder, "Law-Gospel Reductionism," 235.

[103] Schroeder, "Law-Gospel Reductionism," 235.

[104] See George Stöckhardt, *Law and Gospel According to Their Several Effects* (trans. Walter H. Bouman; Valparaiso Pamphlet Series 9; Valparaiso: Valparaiso University Association, 1946), 5, 6, 27. Stöckhardt (1842–1913) was trained at Erlangen, Leipzig, and Berlin and emigrated to the United States in 1878. He taught at Concordia Seminary, St. Louis, from 1887 until his death. He is the only German-trained exegete to teach at Concordia Seminary in the early history of the LCMS. His influence was extensive, and his memory was revered in the LCMS long after his death. His studies are still used in translation by LCMS clergy. See William E. Goerss, "Stöckhardt, Karl George," in Lueker, ed., *Lutheran Cyclopedia*.

[105] No matter what else Stöckhardt is attempting to show in this article, he is not supporting Law and Gospel as a biblical hermeneutic.

[106] A great deal of significance was given to the opinions of the "fathers" in the practice of theology in the LCMS during this period. The fathers were the venerated theological professors of the LCMS of previous generations. The primary fathers were Walther, Francis Pieper, and Stöckhardt. Even today it is difficult to criticize the

work of these men in LCMS circles.

[107] Hoyer, "On Law and Gospel," 8.

[108] Hoyer, "On Law and Gospel," 8; emphasis in the original.

[109] See Hoyer, "On Law and Gospel," 8.

[110] Hoyer was by no means unique in his views. John S. Damm denied that the Law can be a guide for the Christian ethic. "Thirdly, the Law cannot be a guide for this ethic. If the Law is God's it can only expose our lack of love. And if the love is God's then the Law is too minimal to serve as any sort of guide. It becomes superfluous for the exercise of love. This is by no means a full discussion of the subject. It is not even an outline. The point here is simply that a third use of the Law as a guide for Christian life is impossible" (Damm, "Criteria for Evaluating Educational Materials," in *The Teaching of Religion* [ed. John S. Damm; River Forest: Lutheran Education Association, 1965], 42).

[111] Robert J. Hoyer, "On Second Thought," *The Cresset* 32 (November 1968): 17.

[112] The Commission on Theology and Church Relations of the LCMS defined Gospel reductionism as "use of the Gospel as the norm of theology in such a way as to suggest that considerable freedom should be allowed within the church in matters that are not an explicit part of the Gospel" (Commission on Theology and Church Relations, *Gospel and Scripture* [St. Louis: The Lutheran Church—Missouri Synod, 1972], 4).

[113] See pp. 96–100.

[114] Bartling, "Hermeneutics and Pauline Parenesis," 73.

[115] See Edward H. Schroeder, "The Relationship between Dogmatics and Ethics: An Investigation into the Theologies of Elert, Barth *und* [sic] Troeltsch" (Th.D. diss, The University of Hamburg, 1963), 62.

[116] Schmidt, "Toward a Model of Moral Education," 478.

[117] Schmidt, "Toward a Model of Moral Education," 478–79.

[118] This was precisely the problem that Karl Barth criticized in his *Gospel and Law*. See p. 26–27.

[119] *Die Haustafel*; BS 523–27; *Trig* 561–63.

[120] Schmidt, "Toward a Model of Moral Education," 478. Martin E. Marty also described the Law's work with the adverb "only" in his 1962 book on Lutheran ethics, *The Hidden Discipline*. "There is only accusation" (Marty, *The Hidden Discipline* [St. Louis: Concordia, 1962], 19).

[121] Hoyer, "On Law and Gospel," 8.

[122] See Hoyer, "On Law and Gospel," 9. Edward H. Schroeder held that the Law was not immutable only in a functional sense. The Law continues to demand and threaten as an expression of God's judging power. See Edward H. Schroeder and Stephen Hitchcock, *"A Statement" A Misstatement* (St. Louis: Evangelical Lutherans in Mission, n.d.), 2.

[123] Marty, *Hidden Discipline*, 32.

[124] Gwen Sayler, "Werner Elert and the Law/Gospel Dialectic," *CurTM* 2 (February 1975): 42.

[125] Sayler, "Elert and the Law/Gospel Dialectic," 42. See also Schultz, "Alternative to the Formula of Concord?" 13.

[126] Bartling, "Hermeneutics and Pauline Parenesis," 77.

[127] Bartling, "Hermeneutics and Pauline Parenesis," 60.

[128] See Albert Schweitzer, *The Mysticism of Paul the Apostle* (trans. William Montgomery; New York: Macmillan, 1931), 293–333.

[129] Bartling, "Hermeneutics and Pauline Parenesis," 61.

[130] Bartling, "Hermeneutics and Pauline Parenesis," 63.

[131] Bartling, "Hermeneutics and Pauline Parenesis," 75.

[132] Among the responses of the members of the Commission on Theology and Church Relations of the LCMS, this comment was made: "It isn't that the Gospel doesn't create a new ethos of its own, over and above what we might be demanded by the Law. It does indeed. And the shortest summary of that new ethos is, as Bartling says, agape. The negative converse of this agape in Romans—especially if you read the end of the epistle (chs. 14 and 15) as the paracletic reply to its beginning (ch. 2)—is the new power which the justified have: no longer to pass judgment (14:13). But is that new power available to them merely as a 'norm,' especially if that suggests one more criterion by which their lives are again criticized (κρινειν), evaluated? That the Gospel is not, and the Law is" (Bartling, "Hermeneutics and Pauline Parenesis," 79–80).

[133] Bartling, "Hermeneutics and Pauline Parenesis," 74.

[134] Bartling, "Hermeneutics and Pauline Parenesis," 75.

[135] Bartling, like Schmidt, adds an exhortative element to the Gospel. See pp. 107–08.

[136] For another example of this tendency in the LCMS, see Adalbert R. A. Kretzmann, *Law and Gospel* (St. Louis: Faith Forward Executive Committee, The Lutheran Church—Missouri Synod, n.d.), 17–19.

[137] Schroeder, "Law-Gospel Reductionism," 235.

[138] For example, Richard E. Koenig scorned the LCMS tradition of strict doctrinal discipline as rigid and unfeeling. See Richard E. Koenig, "What's behind the Showdown in the LCMS? Church and Tradition in Collision," *Lutheran Forum* (November 1972): 19.

[139] Schroeder, "Is There a Lutheran Hermeneutics?" 95; emphasis in the original.

[140] Schroeder, "Is There a Lutheran Hermeneutics?" 96.

[141] Martin Buber, *I and Thou* (trans. Ronald Gregor Smith; New York: Scribner, 1957).

[142] Schroeder, "Is There a Lutheran Hermeneutics?" 92.

[143] Holsten Fagerberg identified at least two different ways in which the word *Gospel* was used in the Lutheran Confessions. It is untenable that the Gospel is only promise in Lutheran theology. One of these usages directly contradicts Schroeder's contention. Fagerberg pointed out that for the Lutheran Confessions the Gospel can be New Testament Scripture and its content. See Fagerberg, *New Look*, 87–96. As one example, the Formula of Concord speaks of the Gospel as a doctrine that teaches and, therefore, has objective content. See SD V, 20; *BS* 958; *Trig* 957–59. See also LC IV, 29; *BS* 696; *Trig* 739.

[144] Paul G. Bretscher, "The Log in Your Own Eye," *CTM* 43 (November 1972): 645.

[145] See Bretscher, "The Log in Your Own Eye," 680.

[146] Schroeder, "Is There a Lutheran Hermeneutics?" 97.

[147] Kurt Marquart aptly pointed out the ultimate end of this process is to banish Law and Gospel from the theological process by putting it at the mercy of the so-called assured results of higher-critical interpretive tools. "The first and foremost point to be made is that any 'Law and Gospel' separated from strict biblical authority hang in the air and, far from 'controlling' higher criticism, are in fact totally at its mercy" (Marquart, *Anatomy of an Explosion*, 124).

[148] LCMS, "Constitution of The Lutheran Church—Missouri Synod," in *Handbook of The Lutheran Church—Missouri Synod* (St. Louis: The Lutheran Church—Missouri Synod, 1995), 9.

[149] Bretscher, *After the Purifying*, 17.

[150] Bretscher, though a writer of extraordinary beauty, was not always consistent in his presentation. While he at one point advocated a "Gospel-only" method of determining what was the word of God and what was not, farther along in the presentation he described the word of God as being a Law-Gospel "Word of God," rather than a Gospel-only word of God. To further complicate this, he adds that this Law-Gospel word of God must be normed by the Gospel. See Bretscher, *After the Purifying*, 19.

[151] See, for example, Robert C. Schultz, "Reflections on the Current Controversy in The Lutheran Church—Missouri Synod: An Attempt to Express Pastoral Concern," *The Cresset* 35 (October 1972): 10 et passim; Edward H. Schroeder, "Current Implications of the 'We Condemn' Statements in the Lutheran Confessions," *CurTM* 2 (February 1975): 5–9; and H. Armin Moellering, "A Rejoinder with Repristinating Notes," *CurTM* 2 (February 1975): 10–18.

[152] Paul G. Bretscher accounted for the past acceptance of the both/and of Scripture and Gospel. "Everybody still agreed that the 'true treasure' of Lutheranism was both the holy inspired Scriptures and 'the most holy Gospel of the glory and grace of God.' No one thought of himself as having to 'choose' between these two. . . . It was a matter of 'both . . . and,' not of 'either . . . or' " (Bretscher, *After the Purifying*, 99).

[153] Bretscher, *After the Purifying*, 5.

[154] For the purposes of this discussion, ALC and LCA theologians will be taken as a group and denominated ELCA. The ALC church historian E. Clifford Nelson is correct in his statement: "American Lutheranism was institutionally tripartite, but theologically it was bipartite" (Nelson, *Lutherans in North America*, 507).

[155] See the discussion of those influences on pp. 91–114.

[156] Carl Braaten, *The Future of God* (New York: Harper & Row, 1969).

[157] Haikola was professor of systematic theology at the University of Helsinki.

[158] Lauri Haikola, "A Comparison of Melanchthon's and Luther's Doctrine of Justification," *Di* 2 (Winter 1963): 32–39.

[159] Lauri Haikola, "*Melanchthons und Luthers Lehre von der Rechtfertigung*," in *Luther and Melanchthon in the History and Theology of the Reformation* (ed. Vilmos Vajta; Philadelphia: Muhlenberg, 1961), 89–103.

[160] See Haikola, "A Comparison," 33.

[161] Haikola, "A Comparison," 32.

[162] Haikola, "A Comparison," 32.

[163] See Haikola, "A Comparison," 33.

[164] See Ap IV, 32–35; *BS* 166; *Trig* 129–31.

[165] *"Decalogus autem requirit non solum externa opera civilia, quae ratio utcunque efficere potest, sed etiam requirit alia longe supra rationem posita, scilicet vere timere Deum, vere deligere Deum, vere invocare Deum, vere statuere, quod Deus exaudiat, et exspectare auxilium Dei in morte, in omnibus afflictionibus; denique requirit obedientiam erga Deum in morte et omnibus afflictionibus, ne has fugiamus aut averseremur, cum Deus imponit"* (Ap IV, 8; *BS* 160; *Trig* 121).

[166] Haikola, "A Comparison," 33.

[167] *Justitia propria, justitia aliena.*

[168] Haikola, "A Comparison," 33–34.

[169] Haikola, "A Comparison," 35.

[170] Haikola, "A Comparison," 35.

[171] Luther, too, used such conceptions to refer to the passivity of faith. However, he tends to use vivid parabolic language such as the beggar receiving riches from a prince or a householder. See, for example, WA 4:130–31. Melanchthon, however, used the drier language of philosophy to give his theology voice.

[172] This has been a matter of bitter debate among Lutherans since the 16th century. See John M. Drickamer, "Did Melanchthon Become a Synergist?" *Springfielder* 40 (September 1976): 95–101.

[173] See Haikola, "A Comparison," 36.

[174] See Haikola, "A Comparison," 39.

[175] Melanchthon's students faithfully upheld this distinction in the Formula of Concord. See, for example, SD III, 18; *BS* 920; *Trig* 921.

[176] See Tr 45; *BS* 486; *Trig* 517.

[177] Haikola, "A Comparison," 39.

[178] See Ap IV, 167–71; *BS* 194–95; *Trig* 169.

[179] Haikola, "A Comparison," 39.

[180] William Hordern is a well-known author and editor of theological works. He was president of Lutheran Theological Seminary, Saskatoon, Canada.

[181] William Hordern, *Living by Grace* (Philadelphia: Westminster, 1975), 198.

[182] Hordern, *Living by Grace*, 15.

[183] Hordern had a damning evaluation of Protestant preaching. "As one listens to the sermons from Protestant pulpits, it becomes clear that the Law has replaced the Gospel as the central theme" (Hordern, *Living by Grace*, 103).

[184] Hordern, *Living by Grace*, 108.

[185] The Lutheran Confessions use the term *fiducia* no less than 68 times, whereas they never use the term *credentia*. Interestingly, the Lutheran Confessions never contrast *credentia* with *fiducia*. However, the terms that are contrasted are *fiducia* and *notitia*. See AC XX, 26; *BS* 80; *Trig* 57. Melanchthon also contrasts *ignorantia* with *fiducia*, indicating that *fiducia* has a specific object of faith. See Ap II, 14; *BS* 150; *Trig* 109.

[186] See Hordern, *Living by Grace*, 110.

[187] See Hordern, *Living by Grace*, 28–29.

[188] Hordern, *Living by Grace*, 110.

[189] Hordern, *Living by Grace*, 111.

[190] See SD III, 18; *BS* 920; *Trig* 921. For more on the Osiandrian Controversy, see *Trig* 155.

[191] The foremost of those was Albrecht Ritschl, *The Christian Doctrine of Justification and Reconciliation* (trans. Hugh Ross Mackintosh and A. B. Macaulay; Clifton: Reference Book Publishers, 1966).

[192] Karl Holl, *Die Rechtfertigungslehre im Licht der Geschichte des Protestantismus* (Sammlung gemeinverständlicher Vorträge und Schriften aus dem Gebiet der Theologie und Religionsgeschichte 45; Tübingen: J. C. B. Mohr, 1922). Cf. Braaten, *Future of God*, 99. For a short and pithy criticism of Holl's view, see Adolf Köberle, *The Quest for Holiness* (trans. John C. Mattes; Minneapolis: Augsburg, 1936; repr., St. Louis: Concordia, 1982), 92, n. 12.

[193] For example, Melanchthon constantly denied that humans are capable of loving God sufficiently. "*Quis enim satis diligit, aut satis timet Deum?*" (Ap IV, 167; *BS* 194; *Trig* 169). The Formula of Concord distinguishes sharply between love and justifying faith. "*Es ist auch weder Reu oder Liebe oder andere Tugend, sonder allein der Glaub das einige Mittel und Werkzeug, damit und dardurch wir Gottes Gnade, das Vordienst Christi und Vergebung der Sünden, so uns in der Verheissung des Evangelii fürgetragen werden, empfangen und annehmen können*" (SD III, 31; *BS* 924; *Trig* 925).

[194] Hordern, *Living by Grace*, 112.

[195] See pp. 93–95.

[196] Luther does not denominate the uses of the Law in the Smalcald Articles. He describes two "offices" (*Ampt*) of the Law. He calls the second one the Law's "*fürnehmeste Ampt oder Kraft.*" This by no means rules out another use of the Law. Logically, a second use does not preclude a third use. To rule out a third use is an *argumentum ex silentio*. See SA III, 2–3; *BS* 435–38. Hordern does not engage in the question of whether or not Luther actually had a concept of a third use of the Law, nor does he deal with the material from the antinomian disputations. Once again Hordern's approach tends to be practical, and, therefore, he assumes a number of things because they are outside the scope of his work.

[197] See Ep VI, 4; *BS* 794; *Trig* 805–7.

[198] See Hordern, *Living by Grace*, 115. The doctrine of the third use of the Law has led some North American Lutherans to deny the Formula normative doctrinal status. The LCA did not accept the Formula from its inception, and its successor body the ELCA likewise does not accept the Formula as a confessional statement but merely as an interpretation of the church's faith. "2.05 This church accepts the Unaltered Augsburg Confession as a true witness to the Gospel, acknowledging as one with it in faith and doctrine all churches that likewise accept the teachings of the Unaltered Augsburg Confession.

2.06 This church accepts the other confessional writings in the Book of Concord, namely, the Apology of the Augsburg Confession, the Smalcald Articles and the Treatise, the Small Catechism, the Large Catechism, and the Formula of Concord, as further valid interpretations of the faith of the Church" (Evangelical Lutheran Church of America, *Constitutions, ByLaws, and Continuing Resolutions* [rev. ed. (1999)], 2.05–2.06). This position is not entirely because of the doctrine of the third use of the Law, but in large measure because of it. See ALC/LCMS Commission on Fellowship, *The American Lutheran Church and The Lutheran Church—Missouri Synod: A Statement on Doctrinal Differences* (St. Louis: The Lutheran Church—Missouri Synod, 1980), 10–12.

[199] Hordern, *Living by Grace*, 115–16.

[200] Hordern, *Living by Grace*, 116.

[201] William Lazareth stated that the third use of the Law in the sense of "guiding rule for life for the regenerate" is a Calvinistic-Melanchthonian doctrine. He, too, denies that Luther accepted a guiding use for the Law. "Moreover, the Formula of Concord (VI) should not be misinterpreted on this issue to sanction an unevangelical and pietistic conception of regeneration. Its so-called 'third use of the Law' is merely the specific application of the universal first use (usus theologicus) to the Christian insofar as he remains sinful, in keeping with Luther's teaching that the Christian is at once both sinful and righteous" (Lazareth, *Luther on the Christian Home* [Philadelphia: Muhlenberg, 1960], 125). ELCA theologians are quite consistent on the position advocated by Werner Elert. George W. Forell says of Article VI of the Formula of Concord, "However, if one keeps in mind the description of the human situation as *simul justus et peccator* it appears that this third use could easily be subsumed under the two uses as proposed by Luther. Luther's position has been the object of a number of significant studies since W. Elert rejected this 'third use' as attributable to Luther" (Forell, "Law and Gospel," in *Marburg Revisited* [eds. Paul C. Empie and James I. McCord; Minneapolis: Augsburg, 1966], 134). See also Eric W. Gritsch and Robert W. Jenson, *Lutheranism* (Philadelphia: Fortress, 1976), 63.

[202] See Braaten, *Future of God*, 99.

[203] Hordern, *Living by Grace*, 119.

[204] "*Es ist alles des Gesetzes Predigt, was da von unsern Sünden Zorn prediget, es geschehe wie oder wenn es wolle. Wiederumb ist das Evangelium eine solche Predigt, die nicht ander denn Gnade und Vergebung in Christo zeiget und gibt*" (WA 15:228).

[205] See, for example, SD VI, 10–15; *BS* 965–6; *Trig* 965–7.

[206] See Hordern, *Living by Grace*, 109.

[207] Hordern, *Living by Grace*, 119. Robert Jenson rules out both intellectual content and actions from the Gospel. "We have come to the root of a set of perfectly horrid confusions which set in when faith is conceived of as the act of the intellect or as the act of intellect properly seasoned with certain emotional attitudes, as any kind of act that performs" (Jenson, "Faith, Dogma and Theology," in *Theological Perspectives* [Decorah: Luther College Press, 1967], 2).

[208] Henry P. Hamann offers a perceptive evaluation of the denial of the place of the Law in Lutheran theology. "Any confusion of Law and Gospel means a loss of the Gospel. The Law never seems to be the loser, as the situation with Agricola illustrates. When the Law is thrown out of one window it comes back through another— by a wrong definition of the Gospel. The Law is not eliminated; finally, the Gospel is" (Hamann, "Article V: Law and Gospel," in *A Contemporary Look at the Formula of Concord* [eds. Robert D. Preus and Wilbert Rosin; St. Louis: Concordia, 1978], 186).

[209] Gerhard Forde, *The Law-Gospel Debate* (Minneapolis: Augsburg, 1969).

[210] See Forde, *Law-Gospel Debate*, 218–19.

[211] E. W. Hengstenberg (1828–69) was professor at Berlin.

[212] See Forde, *Law-Gospel Debate*, 10. Forde failed to cite a single orthodox theologian in his presentation of their position, and he admitted that the brief sketch of the orthodox position ran "the risk of caricature" (Forde, *Law-Gospel Debate*, 9). This is a common problem of the critics of orthodoxy. In his monumental work on the Lutherans in the period of orthodoxy, Robert D. Preus points out that most critics of

orthodoxy have never actually studied the literature. See Preus, *The Theology of Post-Reformation Lutheranism*, vol. 1 (St. Louis: Concordia, 1970), 20–21.

[213] J. C. K. von Hofmann (1810–77) was professor at Erlangen and is noted for being the father of the *Heilsgeschichte* method of theology.

[214] Forde, *Law-Gospel Debate*, 57; emphasis in the original.

[215] Forde, *Law-Gospel Debate*, 34.

[216] For a summary of Hegel's work, see H. B. Acton, "Hegel, G. W. F.," in *The Encyclopedia of Philosophy*, vol. 3 (ed. Paul Edwards; New York: Macmillan, 1972), 435–51.

[217] Harnack (1817–89) was professor at Dorpat and Erlangen and was the father of Karl G. A. von Harnack.

[218] Forde, *Law-Gospel Debate*, 54.

[219] Forde, *Law-Gospel Debate*, 74. Forde recognized the influence of Lauri Haikola on his views. See Forde, *Law-Gospel Debate*, 175–78. Forde also criticizes the Formula of Concord for perpetrating a compromise between the ontological and the eschatological point of view. "There seems almost a curious resistance among Lutherans to allow the work which Luther began really to do its work, an insistence, perhaps, that we can go no further than some of the confessional compromises take us, at best an uneasy wedding between ontology and eschatology" (Forde, "The Formula of Concord Article V: End or New Beginning?" *Di* 15 [Summer 1975]: 189). First, perhaps this compromise is the true genius of the Formula of Concord. Second, as I have suggested earlier, the Luther uncovered by the eschatological interpretive filter might not produce an adequate doctrinal portrait of the Wittenberg reformer.

[220] Forde, *Law-Gospel Debate*, 74.

[221] See Forde, *Law-Gospel Debate*, 12.

[222] Forde, *Law-Gospel Debate*, 12.

[223] See Forde, *Law-Gospel Debate*, 74–76.

[224] Forde, *Law-Gospel Debate*, 78.

[225] The Gospel-Law pattern championed by Karl Barth gets significant attention from Forde. See Forde, *Law-Gospel Debate*, 137–49; see also Thomas Coates, "The Barthian Inversion: Gospel and Law," *CTM* 26 (July 1955): 481–91.

[226] Forde, *Law-Gospel Debate*, 225–26; emphasis in the original.

[227] Forde, *Law-Gospel Debate*, 226.

[228] Forde, *Law-Gospel Debate*, 203.

[229] Forde, *Law-Gospel Debate*, 203; emphasis in the original.

[230] Forde, *Law-Gospel Debate*, 203; emphasis in the original.

[231] Forde, *Law-Gospel Debate*, 226–27.

[232] See also Forde, "End or New Beginning?" 190.

[233] See pp. 96–100.

[234] Forde, *Law-Gospel Debate*, 227.

[235] Forde, *Law-Gospel Debate*, 227.

[236] Forde, *Law-Gospel Debate*, 228.

[237] Forde, *Law-Gospel Debate*, 228.

[238] Forde, *Law-Gospel Debate*, 192–93. In a 1975 article, Forde indicates that the defi-nition of the Law must not be both functional and terminological. See Forde, "End or New Beginning?" 187.

[239] Forde, *Law-Gospel Debate*, 194. Law and Gospel are terms primarily denoting a kind of existence and only secondarily the content of the proclamation. "Law, or liv-ing under the Law, means a kind of existence in which everything turns on you and you are threatened and can only ask yourself, 'What shall I do?' " (Gerhard O. Forde, "Law and Gospel as the Methodological Principle of Theology," in *Theological Perspectives* [Decorah: Luther College Press, 1967], 62).

[240] While Forde is critical of Althaus's threefold scheme of orienting the Law before the fall, after the fall, and after conversion, Forde simply ignores the supralapsarian meaning of the Law. If Law is defined as threat, then what would the Law be before the fall? The functional definition of the Law falls into difficulty when faced with the meaning of the supralapsarian Law.

[241] "Thus Lutheranism has attempted to foster a theology which preserves the escha-tological dialectic between the two ages. This, in sum, is what the distinction between Law and Gospel is really all about" (Forde, *Law-Gospel Debate*, 213).

[242] Forde, *Law-Gospel Debate*, 193.

[243] Anders Nygren, Bishop of Lund, provides a salutary counterbalancing perspective to the situational approach of American Lutherans through his reflection on the European experience of totalitarianism, the positivistic approach to Law, and the Law is the Law movement of Europe after World War I. When the Law has no specific content, Nygren contended that the vacuum would be filled. "What is Law? With a certain stylizing one could express the interpretation which sets the tone for the posi-tivistic outlook in the following way: Law is not some eternal principle; Law is the order which the state, with the aid of its power and its devices of constraint and com-pulsion, maintains. The state and its power are therefore primary; they are that which constitutes Law" (Anders Nygren, "Christianity and Law," *Di* 1 [Autumn 1962]: 39).

[244] A great deal of what Forde writes about the Law is indicative of existentialistic or situationalistic ethics. "Existentialist ethics has sometimes concentrated on the agent's free choice and defended antinomianism because principles and rules lead to an inau-thentic existence" (James F. Childress, "Situation Ethics," in *The Westminster Dictionary of Christian Ethics* [rev. ed.; eds. James F. Childress and John Macquarrie; Philadelphia: Westminster, 1986], 586). For another example of an existentialistic approach to the Law, see George Forell, who writes, "Within the context of the Christian proclamation the Law is not a propositional code (doctrine) but a personal (existential) demand" (Forell, "Law and Gospel," 131). Because the Law is existential demand, it cannot be doctrine; therefore, it cannot provide objective doctrinal boundaries.

[245] Forde, *Law-Gospel Debate*, 223.

[246] An existential approach is more congenial to Reformed theology than to Lutheran theology. Existentialistic theology denies that words in and of themselves can carry the living content of the "Christ event." So Forde denies to theological assertions the power "to save." "No theology as such, no set of assertions—however cleverly con-structed—can 'save' man. Only Christ can do that. Only when the Gospel is heard as God's final word in Christ in a concrete existential sense can this come about" (Forde, *Law-Gospel Debate*, 211). Forde is saying that the finite, earthly means of human words cannot bear the weight of assertions about God. He is accepting a

philosophical principle of Reformed theology invoked by Huldreich Zwingli and used against the real presence in the Lord's Supper, the personal union of the two natures in Christ, and others, namely, *finitum non capax infiniti esse*. The Lutheran doctrine of the Word and the power of words to carry divine content are ruled by a strict denial of the Zwinglian anti-incarnational principle. For more on the *non capax*, see Hermann Sasse, *This Is My Body* (Minneapolis: Augsburg, 1959; rev. ed., Adelaide: Lutheran Publishing House, 1977), 122; and Franz Pieper, *Christliche Dogmatik*, vol. 3 (St. Louis: Concordia, 1920): 169–70.

[247] For example, Rom 10:4.

[248] Forde might well have been setting his sights on Karl Barth's Gospel-Law approach more than anything else in *The Law-Gospel Debate*.

[249] See, for example, SD V, 1; *BS* 951; *Trig* 951.

[250] The concern for the place of eschatology is especially important to 20th-century theology. Beginning with Albert Schweitzer, theologians have been trying to relate eschatology and ethics. See E. Clinton Gardner, "Eschatological Ethics," in Childress and Macquarrie, eds., *Dictionary of Christian Ethics*, 201–5.

[251] Werner Elert also places temporal concerns in the forefront of his approach to the use of the Law. However, he places temporal sequence in the Christian life, rather than in eschatology. "This God-bestowed freedom can best be actualized in the temporal sequence of the free man's life" (Elert, *The Christian Ethos* [trans. Carl J. Schindler; Philadelphia: Muhlenberg, 1957], 233).

[252] See Forde, *Law-Gospel Debate*, 223.

[253] With his characteristic precision, Adolf Köberle said, "Whoever tries to speak without paradoxes and would consider each one of these realms [justification and sanctification] alone, who tries to find a solution of the paradox now, betrays either Good Friday or Easter and fails to understand our present status between Pentecost and the Parousia, in which it is equally sin and disobedience against God if we do not 'grow in grace' or if we seek to anticipate the glory of the final perfection" (Köberle, *Quest for Holiness*, 263).

[254] "For the most part (the major exceptions being the Fourth Gospel, Colossians, and Ephesians), the 'already' and the 'not yet' of the promised salvation exists in dialectical tension" (Gardner, "Eschatological Ethics," in Childress and Macquarrie, eds., *Dictionary of Christian Ethics*, 204).

[255] Forde is far more Hegelian than he would admit. He is attempting to produce a synthesis drawn from the thesis of orthodoxy and the antithesis of *Heilsgeschichte*. The synthesis is produced through the strainer of eschatology. However, there are certainly more elements of Christian theology that must be added to the mix to produce this synthesis, to borrow the Hegelian term. While it might be admitted that for methodological clarity theologians must narrow their focus, they must not lose sight of the multiplicity of factors that lead to doctrinal conclusions. Forde warns: "When the term 'dialectic' is used here it must be understood that this is a dialectic determined entirely by eschatology, and not by other concerns" (Forde, *Law-Gospel Debate*, 222). Forde has been too narrow in his approach. Indeed Forde is even more pointed in his insistence that eschatology is the Occam's razor of Law and Gospel in a later article. "If one is not prepared to make a clean eschatological distinction, one is forced to make distinctions elsewhere of a dubious sort" (Forde, "End or New Beginning?" 190). Despite Forde's judgment against "distinctions . . . of a dubious sort," theology is usually a great deal more complicated than can be worked by "clean distinctions."

Maintaining the mystery of the Gospel might require a theological balancing act among several competing concerns.

[256] See C. F. W. Walther, *The Proper Distinction between Law and Gospel* (trans. W. H. T. Dau; St. Louis: Concordia, 1986), 89–99.

[257] "The attempt to maintain that the Gospel properly speaking produces repentance obscures the proper work of Christ and turns the Gospel into new Law. It is an attempt on the part of the preacher to force the issue, to avoid the Law, to avoid legalistic repentance which only succeeds in producing more of the same under a different guise" (Forde, "End or New Beginning?" 188).

[258] Forde, *Law-Gospel Debate*, 225.

[259] In a 1975 article, Forde doesn't give any more insight about what he means when he writes about a battle between ontology and eschatology in the Formula of Concord. In this article ontology and eschatology are opposite ideas. Christian life is lived in the eschatologically shaped tension between the accusing Law and the saving Gospel. Ontology implies static doctrinal concepts and formal definitions that are neither salvific nor condemning. See Forde, "End or New Beginning?" 189.

[260] "*Nachdem der Unterschied des Gesetzes und Evangelii ein besonder herrlich Licht ist, welches darzu dienet, das Gottes Wort recht geteilt und der heiligen Propheten und Apostel Schriften eigentlich erkläret und verstanden*" (SD V, 1; *BS* 951; *Trig* 951).

[261] For two representative but opposing views on the ecclesiastical battle in the LCMS, see Frederick W. Danker, *No Room in the Brotherhood* (St. Louis: Clayton Publishing House, 1977); and Marquart, *Anatomy of an Explosion*.

[262] Preus was president of the LCMS from 1969 until 1981 and before that was president of Concordia Theological Seminary, Springfield, Illinois.

[263] David P. Scaer, "The Law Gospel Debate in the Missouri Synod," *Springfielder* 36 (December 1972): 159. See also J. A. O. Preus, "A Statement of Scriptural and Confessional Principles," quoted in Danker, *No Room in the Brotherhood*, 76–86.

[264] Preus, "A Statement," quoted in Danker, *No Room in the Brotherhood*, 76.

[265] For example, Walter E. Keller, "A Scrutiny of 'A Statement on Scripture,' " *The Cresset* 35 (June 1972): 6–9; Walter E. Keller, et al., review of J. A. O. Preus, "A Statement of Scriptural and Confessional Principles," *The Cresset* 36 (May 1973): 6–19; Edward H. Schroeder, "Critique of President Preus' [*sic*] Statement" (TMs [Mimeograph]; Archive Stacks; Ludwig Fuerbringer Library, Concordia Seminary, St. Louis, n. d.); Schroeder and Hitchcock, "*A Statement*" *A Misstatement*; and Danker, *No Room in the Brotherhood*.

[266] The Board of Control, *Exodus from Concordia*, 30.

[267] Preus, "A Statement," quoted in Danker, *No Room in the Brotherhood*, 76.

[268] Preus, "A Statement," quoted in Danker, *No Room in the Brotherhood*, 76–77.

[269] Scaer, "Law Gospel Debate," 156–59.

[270] SD VI, 6; *BS* 964; *Trig* 963–65.

[271] Eggold, "Third Use of the Law," 16.

[272] See WA 46:569.

[273] See WA 10/1:467.

[274] See WA 40/3:631.

[275] For another similar response, see Eugene F. Klug, "Confessional Emphasis on

Law and Gospel for Our Day," *CTQ* 42 (July 1978): 241–57.

[276] Eggold, "Third Use of the Law," 20; emphasis in the original. Eggold misstates his case. The Formula of Concord never explicitly mentions the *semper*. Instead, it is Melanchthon's teaching in the Apology of the Augsburg Confession: Ap IV, 128; *BS* 185. Ap IV, 167; *BS* 194. Ap IV, 204; *BS* 199.

[277] Eggold, "Third Use of the Law," 20.

[278] Eggold, "Third Use of the Law," 21; Ps 1:2; Rom 7:22.

[279] Eggold, "Third Use of the Law," 21.

[280] Eggold is following Pieper, *Christliche Dogmatik*, 3:280. The Formula of Concord uses the term only once. See SD I, 52; *BS* 860. It never is used in SD VI. The use of this term in the Lutheran dogmatic tradition warrants further investigation.

[281] Eggold, "Third Use of the Law," 19.

[282] David P. Scaer has been professor of systematic theology at Concordia Theological Seminary, Fort Wayne, Indiana, since 1966.

[283] Scaer, "Law Gospel Debate," 159.

[284] Scaer, "Law Gospel Debate," 159. For an example, Paul E. Schuessler charged that the LCMS had two competing influences in her theology—one Lutheran, the other Reformed. "Like two birch trees growing along side one another, evangelical Lutheranism and evangelical Reformed theology have competed with one another in the Missouri Synod. Since 1969 the evangelical Reformed has gained the ascendancy" (Paul E. Schuessler, "Using the Law," *Lutheran Forum* [May 1978]: 23).

[285] Scaer cites an essay by Horace Hummel, then a member of the LCA, illustrating this point. "The LCA is a perfect example of what happens when one abandons all possible thought of discipline, refuses to state what is being rejected as well, and appeals to the 'adequacy of the historic Confessions' or simply to 'Gospel': these become code words for anything goes; in practice anything contrary to the Gospel simply will never be found" (Horace Hummel, "Law and Gospel in the Old Testament" [Mimeographed Conference Essay 4]; quoted in Scaer, "Law Gospel Debate," 159; emphasis in the original).

[286] See Scaer, "Law Gospel Debate," 159.

[287] David P. Scaer, "Christ or the Bible?" *Christianity Today* 12 (10 November 1967), 113.

[288] Scaer, "Law Gospel Debate," 161.

[289] See pp. 69–73.

[290] See pp. 62–64.

[291] Scaer, "Law Gospel Debate," 162.

[292] Scaer, "Law Gospel Debate," 163.

[293] See Scaer, "Law Gospel Debate," 163.

[294] Scaer, "Law Gospel Debate," 165.

[295] Of the Missourians, Scaer was most likely to be critical of traditional approaches to theology.

[296] See Scaer, "Law Gospel Debate," 166.

[297] See Scaer, "Law Gospel Debate," 166.

[298] See Robert C. Schultz, "Missouri Synod History and Doctrine: Variant Readings,"

The Cresset 35 (October 1972): 32.

[299] See Scaer, "Law Gospel Debate," 166. Richard Klann summarized this issue: "The Christian no longer lives under the Law (legalism), nor above the Law (antinomianism), but in the Law. 'To live in the Law' is the equivalent of asserting the congruence of the will of the Christian with the will of God in sanctification. The Christian never asserts any kind of moral or ethical autonomy. Christian discipleship is obedience to God's will" (Klann, "Reflections on Disputes Regarding the Proper Distinction between Law and Gospel," *CJ* 1 [January 1975]: 35).

[300] Scaer, "Law Gospel Debate," 167.

[301] Scaer, "Law Gospel Debate," 166.

[302] See also Moellering, "Rejoinder with Repristinating Notes," 12–13. Moellering defends the importance and validity of doctrinal discipline as not incompatible with love. The theologians of the Valparaiso school commonly contended that doctrinal discipline was unloving and thus incompatible with the Gospel. For example, see Schroeder, "Current Implications," 5–9; and Waldemar W. Wehmeier, "Missouri and Public Doctrine," *CurTM* 2 (February 1975): 23–34. Cf. Hermann Diem, "Is Doctrinal Discipline Possible?" *Lutheran Forum* (February 1971): 11–15; and Walter Künneth, "Responsibility for Doctrine Today," *Lutheran Forum* (February 1971): 8–10.

[303] Horace Hummel, who at the time was professor of Old Testament at the Lutheran School of Theology, Chicago, Illinois, pleaded for the importance of doctrinal discipline in American Lutheranism in a seminal and much-read article in *Lutheran Forum* in 1969: "The problem of how to take a firm stand against breakdown of discipline and dogmatic aberrations without stifling theological creativity and genuine ecumenical engagement is anything but new. It is, however, especially acute today, especially among those whose concepts of 'freedom' are apparently more informed by certain modern ideologies than by the Gospel, and for whom, as a result, the very notion of doctrinal discipline is offensive and to whom virtually any authority represents 'authoritarianism.' The possibilities of miscarriages of church discipline are great (how liberalism loves to highlight them!) and, obviously, everything should be done to prevent them. But I submit that most recent Protestant history better illustrates the sad results of its absence than its excesses. Any organization maintains some sort of discipline consonant with its *raison d'etre*, and if doctrine ceases to be a significant part of the Church's discipline, then obviously only factors really extrinsic to the essence of the Church are externally holding it together" (Hummel, "No Other Gospel!" *Lutheran Forum* [October 1969]: 4). Hummel later joined the LCMS and taught at Concordia Seminary, St. Louis.

[304] The Formula of Concord quotes Luther, who pointed out that the cross may be a preaching of Law or Gospel. See SD V, 12–13; *BS* 955–56.

[305] The practical emphasis on preaching is central to C. F. W. Walther's doctrine of Law and Gospel.

[306] Scaer, "Law Gospel Debate," 167–68.

[307] Scaer, "Law Gospel Debate," 168.

[308] Scaer, "Law Gospel Debate," 170; emphasis in the original.

[309] Montgomery, *Crisis in Lutheran Theology*, 1:121.

[310] Montgomery, *Crisis in Lutheran Theology*, 1:125.

[311] See Montgomery, *Crisis in Lutheran Theology*, 1:126.

[312] Psalm 119; Psalm 1.

[313] Montgomery, *Crisis in Lutheran Theology*, 1:127.

[314] Montgomery, *Crisis in Lutheran Theology*, 1:127.

[315] Marquart was a 1959 graduate of Concordia Seminary, St. Louis, who after serving a long pastorate in Queensland, Australia, returned to the United States in 1975 to take a post as professor of systematic theology at Concordia Theological Seminary, Fort Wayne, a position he continues to hold.

[316] See Marquart, *Anatomy of an Explosion*, 124 et passim.

[317] See Marquart, *Anatomy of an Explosion*, 124.

[318] See Marquart, *Anatomy of an Explosion*, 124.

[319] Marquart, *Anatomy of an Explosion*, 125.

[320] Marquart, *Anatomy of an Explosion*, 129.

[321] Francis Pieper, often the whipping boy of those of the Valparaiso school, pointedly rejects that an unbeliever must be convinced of the inspiration of Scripture before he can be brought to faith in the salvation won by Jesus Christ. See Pieper, *Christliche Dogmatik*, 1:157–58. Faith is *a priori* to systematic theology; systematic expression of doctrine is *a posteriori* to faith.

[322] See Marquart, *Anatomy of an Explosion*, 128.

[323] Marquart, *Anatomy of an Explosion*, 137–38.

[324] See Marquart, *Anatomy of an Explosion*, 138.

4

AMERICAN LUTHERANISM 1977–98

A PERIOD OF CONCERN FOR BALANCE

A clarification of the status of doctrine and the relationship among the major Lutheran church bodies characterized American Lutheranism between 1977 and 1998. The LCMS officially severed its pulpit and altar fellowship with the ALC in 1981, citing irreconcilable differences over the status of the Bible and other points of doctrine.[1] This move left the trinity of the ALC, the LCA, and the AELC[2] free to negotiate toward an organic denominational union, the nuptials of which were January 1, 1988. This denominational unification created the ELCA. Now there was only left and right and nothing in the middle. The clarity of the division caused the uneasy peace of a doctrinal cease-fire in American Lutheranism (a peace now showing signs of being broken). E. Clifford Nelson's judgment that there were only two theological parties in American Lutheranism now had become a denominational reality as well.[3] This generalization, true though it is, is also significant for its exceptions. In the discussion of the third use of the Law there has been a rapprochement between younger theologians of the ELCA and their LCMS counterparts.

The theological signpost marking the beginning of this period was the 400th anniversary of the Formula of Concord. A flurry of conferences, books, and articles accompanied this celebration. Predictably, given the recently concluded ecclesiastical battles and the renewed focus on the Formula itself, the issue of the third use of the Law surfaced again. As the period progressed, the third use of the Law was given more eloquent defenses, in part because of new insights into the theology of Luther, which were by now percolating down to American Lutheran theologians from both European and American Luther scholars.

167

ELCA Theologians

Background and Influences

The influence of the doctrinal battles that raged within the LCMS continued to have an impact upon the theology of the ELCA well into this period. The Valparaiso University conference to celebrate the 400th anniversary of the Formula of Concord occurred with those battles fresh on everyone's mind. The walkout from Concordia Seminary in 1974 occurred in part as a response to the imposition of church discipline from the national church organization.[4] Thus, the issue of doctrinal discipline in the church was a burning issue at the time of the anniversary celebrations, causing several questions to surface: Could church discipline be enforced as a function of the Law? What role did the Gospel have in church discipline? Did the church have the right to enforce discipline? Is the enforcement of discipline the third use of the Law? The third use of the Law remained a topic of much debate.

As the period progressed and the church political situation settled down, the merger of the LCA, ALC, and AELC to create the ELCA became a turning point for ELCA theologians. The merger set in motion a series of events that ensconced "quota goals" for ethnic, gender, and sexual diversity within the ELCA. The issue of diversity, driven by liberal, egalitarian ideals quite apart from the Christian Gospel, had dire consequences for theology in the ELCA. Those consequences bloomed in the battle over sexual ethics that erupted in the early 1990s. The discussion within the ELCA pitted those who denied the third use of the Law against those who were now beginning to see the need for Law as a norm for Christian ethics. Concern about sexual ethics generated concern about the third use of the Law.[5]

Summary of Views

William H. Lazareth

In late 1977 William H. Lazareth presented a paper titled "Foundation for Christian Ethics: The Question of the 'Third Use' of the Law" at the Conference for Parish Leaders at Valparaiso University commemorating the 400th anniversary of the Formula of Concord.[6] The paper had two major characteristics. First, Lazareth continued to interpret the Formula of Concord's doctrine of the third use of the Law using the results of the Luther renaissance and the work of Werner Elert and Paul Althaus.[7]

Second, Lazareth rejected the either/or of a Law that either instructs or accuses, which was inherent in his earlier work, *Luther on the Christian Home*.[8]

Law-Free Gospel and the Luther Renaissance. Lazareth began with the assumptions of the Luther renaissance. He recounted again how scholars of the Luther renaissance had denied that Luther had held a third use of the Law, at least in the sense of an informatory use of the Law for Christians. "They have concluded from Luther's whole conception of the Law that he could not possibly have taught a third use in this didactic sense."[9] This presupposition had not changed for Lazareth since 1960. He also repeated the Elertian position that there is no "purely" informatory function for the Law in Luther's thought.[10] Lazareth's *Lutheran Identity and Mission*, published in 1994, repeats the same views.[11] There was no advance here.

Lazareth was arguing that since Luther himself did not teach a third or informatory use of the Law, the Formula of Concord could not be teaching an informatory use of the Law. In other words, the result of the Luther renaissance was the determining factor in the interpretation of the Formula of Concord. This anachronism was heartily criticized by Theodore R. Jungkuntz, who responded to Lazareth's conference paper.[12]

> The historical context of the Formula of Concord has been reduced to certain discoveries stemming from the "Luther renaissance," discoveries which supposedly have established that Luther could not possibly have taught a third use of the Law in a didactic sense.[13]

ELCA theologians stressed the importance of interpreting the Lutheran Confessions within their historical context.[14] However, Lazareth did not take the Confessions within their own context, but within the context of the existentialistic Luther renaissance. Because the Luther renaissance declared Luther incapable of having a third use of the Law, the Formula could not be taken at face value, at least not if the Formula was an accurate reflection of Luther's own teaching—an assumption doubted by many theologians.

Luther, Mosaic Law, and Natural Law. Luther rejected the old threefold division of the Mosaic law into moral law, civil law, and ceremonial law. In fact, Luther denied that the Mosaic law was at all binding upon the Christian. However, he did believe that the natural law was binding upon the Christian. The natural law was comprehended in, but not circumscribed by, the Ten Commandments. For example, the commandment

enjoining Sabbath observance was part of the Mosaic law, not part of natural law, and thus was not binding upon the Christian.

> Luther concludes that insofar as the Ten Commandments provide us
> with a concise statement of the natural law governing all of sinful
> mankind, they are carefully to be obeyed. But insofar as they include
> special matters above and beyond the natural law which are peculiar
> to the Jewish theocracy, they may be regarded as time-bound statutes
> of the Jewish Law code which are not binding upon Christians.[15]

What was universal was universally binding. What was unique to the
Jewish theocracy was binding only upon it. The Decalogue was binding on
Christians only insofar as it reflected the natural law.[16]

However, the question as to how and to what extent the natural law
applies to the Christian remains to be answered. Lazareth does not represent accurately the language of the Formula of Concord regarding the
relationship between the Christian *in concreto* and the Christian *quatenus
renati sunt*. The Formula of Concord always speaks of the Christian insofar as he or she is reborn, not insofar as he or she is a Christian.

> In this way Christians are not under the Law, but under grace,
> because by faith in Christ the persons are freed from the curse and
> condemnation of the Law; and because their good works, although
> they are still imperfect and impure, are acceptable to God through
> Christ; moreover, because insofar as they have been born anew
> according to the inner man, they do what is pleasing to God, not by
> coercion of the Law, but by the renewing of the Holy Ghost, volun-
> tarily and spontaneously from their hearts; however, they maintain
> nevertheless a constant struggle against the old Adam.[17]

The Formula describes the Christian as a *concretum* made up of the new
and old Adam. The Law applies to a Christian *soviel, quatenus* he or she is
a sinner. The person is free from coercion from the Law *soviel, quatenus* the
person is reborn. Lazareth puts the *quatenus* too soon in his description of
the Christian's relationship to the Law and the Gospel. In this way he does
not adequately take into account the *simul*. "Insofar as the Christian
remains sinful, he is bound only to that part of the Decalogue which coin-
cides with natural law."[18] The unifying character of the Christian person is
that God has placed the person under grace and the person lives in the
simul, never just as sinner or just as righteous. Properly speaking then, the
Christian person *in concreto* is never the subject of the *quatenus*. The
Christian person is *simul*. The *quatenus* must remain a description of the

ambiguity of the Christian's situation in Law and Gospel as *den alten Adam* and *neugeboren Mensch*.

Lazareth continued the rigid Law, then Gospel pattern exhibited by Forde in the previous chapter.[19] He contended that Luther's placement of the Ten Commandments before the creed in his catechisms is proof that Luther believed that the Ten Commandments were not applicable as third-use Law. "Luther treats the Decalogue before, rather than after, the Creed. Why?—because the Law's function is to accuse us before our confession of Christ, not to guide us after our confession of Christ."[20]

Lazareth commits a variation of the *post hoc ergo propter hoc* fallacy.[21] Lazareth's argument goes something like this: Because the creed comes after the Ten Commandments in Luther's catechisms, the Ten Commandments prepare for the faith of the creed by accusing human unbelief. This error is unaccountable because Luther specifically addresses the content of the explanations of the commandments to Christians.[22] For example, in the Small Catechism Luther explains the first commandment with these simple words: "*Wir sollen Gott über alle Ding fürchten, lieben und vertrauen.*"[23] The terms to fear, love, and trust in God above everything are characteristics that both Luther and Melanchthon attribute to believers alone. Unbelievers do not truly do these things.[24] Luther writes the explanations to the Ten Commandments for Christians, and they are not only preparatory to the Gospel.[25] If the order of the parts of the Small Catechism is significant, then it is significant that the catechism is drawn to a close with the *Die Haustafel*,[26] which includes ethical instruction for various human callings.[27] Not only does Luther begin the Small Catechism with the Law for Christians in the Ten Commandments, but he also ends it with ethical instruction.[28] Later in his article even Lazareth is forced to admit that Luther reworked the Ten Commandments to be an illustration of the "solely-binding *Gebot* of the first commandment."[29] In other words, Luther's explanations of the Ten Commandments are not merely the accusatory use of the Law. Lazareth seems caught between the opinions of the weighty European scholars of the Luther renaissance on the third use of the Law and the clarity of the text of the Formula of Concord and Luther's catechisms.

In an attempt to extricate himself from this dilemma, Lazareth follows a *via media* in the form of the *Gesetz und Gebot* approach of Althaus. This is purely an imposition on the Formula of Concord, which knows nothing of the term "*Gebot*" in the sense used by Althaus. The word is used only once in the Formula of Concord and in a context that indicates it is being used in a second-use fashion. The *praeceptum* is a threatening word from God.[30] "*Gesetz*" is used 47 times in the sixth article of the Formula of Concord alone. The Formula of Concord does not contain the distinction between *Gesetz und Gebot*.

Lazareth claims that "the Law (as *Gebot*) never accuses and is joyfully obeyed as the loving will of God in which the Christian—as righteous— 'delights and meditates on it day and night.' "[31] This claim might be coherent with Lutheran theology taken as a statement about a narrow concern for the reborn person's relationship to the Law. However, this statement is not adequate taken as a description of the teaching of the Formula of Concord, and it might be misleading on its own terms. The idea would be better expressed that the Gospel enables the Christian insofar as he or she is reborn to delight in the Law.

Finally, Lazareth makes the claim that the third use of the Law is really the " 'second' use of the Gospel: i.e., justifying faith active in sanctifying love" and that the "so-called 'third' use does not essentially differ from the first and second uses."[32] This view presents a critical difficulty. It is a confusion of Law and Gospel. Lazareth has called "*Gebot*" both Law and Gospel. But it cannot be both. If it is Law it must still threaten and accuse. If it is Gospel, it must be radically different from the first and second uses of the Law and, therefore, in no sense whatsoever Law.

Lazareth's view ultimately raises the question of the rationality of the formulators of the Formula of Concord. If the third use is either the second use of the Gospel or the second use of the Law for Christians, then the formulators were either ignorant or dishonest in using a term (third use of the Law) that Lazareth thinks is completely tainted by Calvinistic overtones.[33] First, we may wonder why they denominated a third use of the Law at all. Lazareth's evaluation leads to the conclusion that the third use of the Law is a distinction without a difference. If there is literally no third use of the Law, why denominate something as a third use of the Law?

Second, the formulators were extremely sensitive to any intrusion of Calvinism into Lutheran theology. A main issue that catalyzed the writing of the Formula of Concord was the uncovering of "crypto-Calvinism" in the faculty of the University of Wittenberg. It was called crypto-Calvinism because its proponents claimed to be Lutherans though all the while they worked for the adoption of the Calvinistic doctrine, especially of the Lord's Supper, in Saxony. Elector August of Saxony decided that a clear exposition of the Lutheran doctrine of the Lord's Supper was needed, lest Lutheranism be repudiated in favor of Calvinism right at the heart of the

Lutheran Reformation, the University of Wittenberg. Elector August was apprised of the calumny of the crypto-Calvinists when in 1574, through a mix-up of private correspondence, it became apparent that the crypto-Calvinists had intentionally deceived the Elector and were actively, though quietly, campaigning for Calvinism among the Saxons. Predictably, Elector August was furious about this deception. August jailed the leaders of the crypto-Calvinistic conspiracy. Some conspirators languished in jail for more than ten years.[34] Suffice it to say that when the formulators began to write a Lutheran confessional statement not long after the unmasking of the crypto-Calvinistic conspiracy, they did everything they could to avoid making statements that in any way could be interpreted as inspired by the Genevan Reformation.[35] If the term "third use of the Law" necessarily brings with it an entanglement with Calvin, they would have avoided it like the plague. Yet they did not.

Lazareth claimed that the modern employment of the term "third use of the Law" is pastorally misleading because of its supposed connection to (or even dependence upon!) Calvin's use.[36] The term would have been even far more misleading, not to mention dangerous, in the 16th century than it is today. Yet the Lutheran confessors used the term and titled an article using it.

Passion for a "Law-free Gospel,"[37] as Lazareth put it, need not deteriorate into a Law-free proclamation. Unfortunately, his laudable passion for a Law-free Gospel gave birth to a Law-tainted Gospel. Theodore R. Jungkuntz warned that Lazareth's sloganeering approach to the subject was dangerous. "Slogans like 'Law-free Gospel' may become Satan's occasion for sowing confusion."[38] Lazareth is closer to the theologians of the Valparaiso school than is Forde, who was much more cautious about confusing Law and Gospel. In the end, Lazareth is attempting to vindicate the opinions of the scholars of the Luther renaissance at the risk of his own theology's internal coherence and methodological consistency.[39] The third use survives neither Lazareth's incoherence nor his misinterpretation of the Formula of Concord. For him the third use of the Law remains at best a question.

GERHARD O. FORDE

Gerhard O. Forde's locus "Christian Life" in *Christian Dogmatics,*[40] published in 1984 by Fortress, repeated the arguments advanced in his earlier *The Law-Gospel Debate.*[41] Forde continued to shape the doctrine of justification by an eschatological outlook, even to the exclusion of other emphases. In Forde's thinking the third use of the Law is a return to the life before Christ. To return to the Law is to make Christ useless. However, according to Forde, this return to the Law would be rendered impossible if the proper eschatological perspective could be maintained. "The confusion (caused by a reintroduction of the Law as third use) results, once again, from failure to argue consistently from an eschatological perspective."[42] The eschatological perspective exclusive of any other concerns remained the ruling principle in Forde's views on the third use of the Law. Forde covered no new ground here.

Forde assumed that the third use necessarily entails a manipulation of the Law, by which the preacher or the believer treats the Law as first, second, or third use according to his or her need or whim. This theological and ethical presumption does appear in some literature of the LCMS in the period of 1940 to 1960.[43] However, this view is hardly characteristic of Lutheran theology and is not required by the acceptance of a third use of the Law. Forde is correct when he denies that we can manipulate the Law because it remains entirely God's Law. "We cannot preside over the Law's use in order to speak of a third use which neither restrains evil nor convicts of sin."[44] In truth, there is only one Law, which God uses however it pleases him. The Law does not become third use because the believer deems it to be so. Instead, the impact of the Law varies according to the personal situation of the hearer. In this sense it may be correct to say that the Law's uses are really functions.

Without any evidence, Forde claims that Luther agrees with him and "is thus generally regarded as opposing a 'third use' of the Law."[45] However, the most that could be said about the position of Luther is that he simply did not use the appellation "third use" of the Law. As for the idea of the Law's applicability to the Christian, evidence abounds that Luther held that the Law still applies to the Christian after conversion as direction for good works and this precisely because the Christian stands in the two realms created by eschatological ambiguity and the Christian's own dilemma in the world, as summarized by the *simul*.

Forde remained critical of the *Gebot* doctrine of Althaus. Even more clearly he rejected the idea of a third concept suspended between Law and Gospel.

> There are only two possibilities vis-à-vis Law as the expression of the will of God. It is either an enemy or a friend, but never a neutral guide. It impinges on us either as the letter which kills or as the Spirit which gives life, but never as something in between.[46]

The word of God remains either Law or Gospel, never an amalgam of the two. Forde has overstated his case when he says that the Law is "never a neutral guide." If he means that there is no time when the Law does not threaten, or that there is never a time when the Law offers only neutral direction, then Forde is correct. He is incorrect if he means that the Law never functions as a guide at all. The Law still functions as a guide, and in that sense there is a third use.

If nothing else, Forde is decisive. He directly rejected the third use of the Law because it entails "covert antinomianism."[47] This charge requires a transvaluation of definitions because normally antinomianism would lead to a rejection of the third use of the Law. The latter was the view of LCMS interpreters. Forde argued, however, that a third use of the Law was created to tame or limit the Law's impact—to make it manageable or able to be fulfilled by the inchoate righteousness inhering in the Christian.

> What are we to say of a Law that has become a more or less harmless guide? What is actually proposed is an alteration in the view of the Law to fit the view of the Christian life as immanent moral progress. Because one does not want to die, one disarms the Law and makes it relatively harmless. Law is changed to accommodate sin.[48]

Once again the weakness of this view is that Forde has caricatured the view of those who hold a third use of the Law. No supporter of the Lutheran doctrine as taught in the Formula of Concord has contended that the Law becomes in any way "harmless" in the third use. The Formula holds together the ambiguity of the situation because it teaches that the Law threatens, instructs, and is delighted in by the individual. The same Law functions in different ways depending on the situation into which the Law is preached. These different functions may also occur simultaneously because of the spiritual complexity of humans and the situations into which God places them. Humans do not determine how the Law will function; God only commands that humans preach it. This word of Law will accomplish the purposes for which God sends it.[49]

While Forde alerted the reader to ways in which the third use of the Law may be abused in taming the accusatory nature of the Law, he does not advance at all beyond his 1969 work founded in the presuppositions of the Luther renaissance.

WALTER H. WAGNER

Walter H. Wagner, a church historian and an LCA official, established the groundwork for the acceptance of the third use of the Law among

ELCA theologians in an article in the *Journal of Religious History* entitled "Luther and the Positive Use of the Law." Wagner avoided the term "third use of the Law" throughout his article because he realized it would elicit an immediate rejection from his LCA and ALC colleagues. Wagner maintained that Luther scholarship had not surveyed a sufficiently broad sample of the Luther literature in studying Luther's attitude about the uses of the Law. He surveyed Luther's writings in three different periods in the life of Luther: 1515–19, 1520–29, and 1530–35. Wagner stated that Luther's views did not change significantly after 1535. In contrast to the method of the Luther renaissance, Wagner's approach was more broadly based and also accounted for the changes in Luther's views over time.

According to Wagner, Luther emphasized the second use of the Law between 1515 and 1519. This was because of the polemical situation in which the Wittenberg Reformer found himself. He had become convinced that the church was hopelessly Pelagianized and needed a strong dose of the second use of the Law to disabuse her children of the notion that righteousness before God could be claimed by the Law. Along with this clear emphasis, Wagner perceived that Luther's dependence in this period upon Augustine's *De Spiritu et Littera* also led him to hold that the Law had a positive role in the life of the Christian. Luther spoke of the Law in a positive fashion when he spoke of the work of the Spirit as the finger of God writing on the human heart.[50]

The period of 1520 to 1529 witnessed a change in Luther's situation. After the issuance of the papal bull of excommunication (1520) and the Diet of Worms (1521), Luther became increasingly convinced that the breach with Rome was irreparable. The problem of maintaining congregations apart from papal jurisdiction arose. Luther started to solidify the gains of the Lutheran Reformation in sociopolitical structures demanded by the vacuum left by separation from Rome and by the political chaos fomented by the radical reformers and the Peasant Revolt of 1525. Like James Kittelson, who showed Luther to be a church bureaucrat as the Reformation progressed,[51] Wagner pointed out that the changing situation "challenged the professor to act increasingly like a bishop."[52] Luther reached for the Law in its various uses in this situation.

Luther's catechisms, issued at the end of this penultimate period, were a clear indication to Wagner that Luther held a positive, or third, use of the Law.[53] Luther's treatments of the Decalogue indicate that he considered the Ten Commandments to have a positive and normative role in the life of the Christian.[54] Luther still held that the Law remained a threat, but the Law also could be a guide for the Christian life. "A Spirit-inspired life in Christ, held Luther, would affirm and use the commandments as a guide for evangelical ethics."[55] This presupposition was the guiding force in the Saxon Visitation Articles of 1528 as well.[56]

The final period of 1530 to 1535 saw the outbreak of the conflict with John Agricola.[57] Luther again emphasized the Spirit as the one who leads the believer into a positive delight in the Law. Wagner argued that with differing emphases throughout the periods, Luther in every case still saw a positive use for the Law in the life of the Christian, in other words, a third use of the Law. Because the Christian has been freed from the curse of the Law, the Law no longer accuses the Christian, *qua justum*. Thus, the Law can provide "abundant instruction."[58]

VIEWS OF MORE RECENT ELCA THEOLOGIANS

ELCA theologians, such as Scott Ickert and David S. Yeago, who did not cut their teeth on the bitter controversies of the 1960s and 1970s, have taken a more sanguine view of the place and function of the third use of the Law in Lutheran theology. These theologians sounded the alarm about the antinomian tendencies in the ELCA and its "rights"-driven bureaucracy, based at its national headquarters in Chicago.

SCOTT ICKERT

In 1991 Scott Ickert charged that the ELCA had capitulated already in 1972 to what David P. Scaer had called "Lutheran Barthianism."[59] The desire of the ELCA to provide social justice in the world resulted in an unbridled antinomianism, which attempted to satisfy all the culturally normed social concerns.[60] Ickert identified two significant results. First, Ickert identified the liturgical anarchy and moral license that threaten his church body.

> The result (of the attempt to provide social justice in the world) has been an antinomianism to rival that of the 16th Century, if not surpassing it in scope. This is played out today in many areas, ranging from mindless liturgical license, to wholesale capitulation to liberal agendas regarding abortion and homosexuality, as well as to persistent pressures from society's most ardent ideologues.[61]

Ickert recommended a rediscovery of the Formula of Concord's doctrine of the third use of the Law so the Gospel itself might not be lost by being turned into new Law. In other words, Ickert thought the doctrine of the

third use of the Law is a theological defense of the Law-free character of
the Gospel.

Second, Ickert identified the corrosive effects of the ELCA's quota system in hiring staff for the national headquarters in Chicago. Ickert argued
that a new doctrine of the church was arising from the practice. "Raw and
unabashed legalism is forging a new conception of the church; and the
ELCA's quota system is a prominent example."[62] The ELCA was attempting to bridge the gap between the promised fulfillment of justice in the
eschaton and the present struggle toward that end by legalistic means
through the imposition of quotas. Scorn for such an attempt was Ickert's
response.

> All fanatical and vain exertions to achieve what only God can estab-
> lish are but faithless efforts to construct this or that utopia. Thus by
> *heightening* our differences through the quota system on the one hand,
> and *furthering* self-righteousness on the other through a crude revival
> of Social Gospel, we supplant the righteousness of faith with civil
> righteousness, revealing only the extent of our sin and pride.
> Legalism always has this result, to turn Christian freedom into
> bondage by transforming the object of faith into a new and different
> Gospel (cf. Gal. 1:6), i.e. into a curse.[63]

Ickert is troubled by the progress of the ELCA as an Americanized
denomination. He suggested a revival of the third use and attention to the
distinction between Law and Gospel to rescue the third use from its
plight.[64] Ickert remains ambivalent about what he perceives as the quasi-
Calvinistic character of the third use of the Law. Yet reviving the third use
is the only way he can see to return the ELCA to its Lutheran roots. Like
Jungkuntz, Ickert is concerned about moral license and sees in the third
use a defense against such moral deterioration in his church body.
Pragmatically he turns to a doctrine that according to him may not have a
clear Lutheran pedigree.[65] This is ironic indeed. However, Ickert's
approach indicates an openness to reviving the third use of the Law among
theologians of the ELCA.

DAVID S. YEAGO

David S. Yeago, professor of systematic theology at Lutheran
Theological Southern Seminary, Columbia, North Carolina, has been an
eloquent defender of the third use of the Law among ELCA theologians.
Yeago criticized the one-dimensional Law-Gospel approach of Werner
Elert in a provocative and hard-hitting 1993 article published by *Pro*

Ecclesia. In the article Yeago argued that Law-Gospel is not the "ultimate horizon" for the coherence of Lutheran doctrine.[66] Law and Gospel's centrality had become the ultimate, and even only, functioning hermeneutic in much of American and European Lutheran theology. Yeago argued that the narrow view of the Law as only accusatory was gnostic. With this narrow view, Law and Gospel are treated as disconnected opposites in constant conflict and, despite all protests to the contrary, are treated as an antinomy. This antinomy leaves Lutheran theology mired in a dualistic organizing principle.[67]

Yeago suggested that modern Luther scholarship, which shaped 20th-century theology, contributed to this false understanding of the place of Law and Gospel in Lutheran theology.

> In this essay, I want to suggest that the standard modern account of Luther's contribution to a doctrine of revelation has in one central way involved a disastrous *misconstrual* of the coherence of the Christian faith, and that this misconstrual has contributed significantly to the gnostic and antinomian devolution of contemporary Protestantism.[68]

While Yeago denied that Law and Gospel was "the ultimate structuring horizon of Christian belief," he did not intend to say that Law and Gospel was dispensable or unimportant.[69] "I am suggesting that the Law/Gospel distinction is *not* the principle in terms of which Christian belief hangs together, and that to assume that it is such a principle has disastrous consequences which we can see all around us."[70] The consequences about which Yeago was concerned were the results of the prevailing antinomianism, which affected morals and doctrine in American Protestant churches.

Yeago argued that the theoretical antinomianism inherent in the Law-Gospel principle had grave practical consequences, which authors such as Elert, Tillich, Bultmann, and others might not have foreseen.

> Much twentieth century Protestant theology has been antinomian all along; the practical antinomianism now regnant in many churches is simply a long-standing theoretical antinomianism achieving the courage of its convictions. If the Law/Gospel distinction is a final antithesis, then *any* commandment, *any* call for one ordering of life rather than another, will by definition be the Law from which the Gospel frees us.[71]

Yeago charged that Elert set ethics outside the church's realm of concern because for Elert the Law only accused.[72]

Yeago rejected the idea that the Law was oppressive because of its own character as Law.

> If the grounds for the oppressiveness of the Law lay outside the Law, say in our disobedience, then the Law would have to be placed in some wider context. Its oppressiveness and its antithesis to the Gospel would then not be a primitive datum, and the Law/Gospel distinction would not be the last horizon. So it becomes necessary to say that the Law oppresses *because it is Law*, that is, because it is an ordered demand, a requirement, a command.[73]

The Law's accusatory power results not merely from its character as command but from a combination of its character as command *and* human disobedience. The Law would not have been accusatory before the fall. The prohibition in Eden would have been purely informatory. The Law's threat is attributable to human depravity, not simply to its character as demand. Yeago does not deal with the *semper accusat* here, but his point about the oppression of the Law suggests that the *semper* results from the fallen nature of humans, not purely from the internal character of the Law. Therefore, the Law may not only threaten but also inform. The Law informed first; it always accused only later.

Yeago's debate with Walter R. Bouman on the place of Law in Lutheran theology clarifies this point. Bouman argued that if the Decalogue always accuses, then "how can it also be the will of God to guide the lives and actions of Christians?"[74] If the Law accused, it could not also guide and direct. For Bouman the Law could function only one way. He, too, was modifying the *semper accusat* into *solum accusat*. "If the primary purpose of the Decalogue/parenesis is to instruct, to exhort, to guide, then what accuses? Is there a *lex*, a Law of God, which 'always accuses?' "[75] First, no Lutheran has argued that the third use of the Law is the primary use. That is strictly the doctrine of Calvin.[76] Second, there is no reason that the Law cannot function to both threaten and guide.[77]

If the Law as accusation is not the foundational datum of the Christian faith, then it would be incorrect to construe the Gospel merely as a response to or a resolution of the guilt and unfaith pointed out by the Law. The Law would not shape the content of the Gospel, as critics claimed Lutheran orthodoxy had done.

Yeago pointed out that the Law-Gospel dialectic must share the wider context of Christian theology. He criticized the approach of 20th-century Protestant theologians. "Because there is no larger interpretive context for the Law/Gospel distinction, and because the Law is prior to our experience of the Gospel, the only point of reference for our understanding of the 'goodness' of the good news is the Law itself: the Gospel is 'good news' because it is not-Law, because it terminates the Law."[78] The Law-Gospel dialectic becomes gnostic when it rules without regard to the "larger interpretive context" of Christian theology.

The larger interpretive context of Christian theology is dogma. Yeago claimed that the common 20th-century view of Law and Gospel as sharp antinomy leads to a rejection of dogma. One of the components of the Law-Gospel dialectic according to Yeago is the dialectic between form and freedom—form having its source in the Law and freedom having its source in the Gospel.[79]

> But the principled antithesis of form and freedom involved in this construal cannot logically be restrained within the realm of the ethical. It is also corrosive of the very idea of dogma. A dogma is, after all, a rule; it is precisely a call for a particular ordering of thought and language, for a determinative reflective response to the love of God.[80]

If the Gospel truly terminates Law, and freedom overcomes form, then by implication a Gospel-centered church will be form-free, rejecting formation by dogma. Here Yeago has hit upon the antidogmatic bias of modern Christianity. This bias impoverishes the theology of the church by making the confession of the canons and decrees of the church's councils unthinkable.

Yeago argues that this kind of rejection of dogmatic formulations leads to a rejection of the specific and historically bound self-revelation of God in Christ.

> The church *formulates* dogma, one might say, in order to acknowledge the concrete *form* of God's self-giving in Christ. The dogmatism characteristic of catholic Christianity arises directly from the conviction that God has definitely and unreservedly given himself to human beings in a particular history, in the person, life and destiny of a particular first century Palestinian Jew.[81]

If the Gospel liberates from form and order, then it liberates from the form and order of dogma. "The logic is simple: if form is enslavement, then a God who took form in history would be an enslaving God."[82] Thus, modern theology has created a god who can be imagined under a multitude of images, but who must not under any circumstances take on a specific form and whom Christians must not confess.[83] Nothing less than the incarnation of God is at stake here. Where there is no incarnation, there can be no holiness.

Law and Gospel must not be divorced from the catholic truth, lest Law and Gospel actually attack that truth. Yeago indicated that the primal horizon of the Christian faith is the confession of the centurion, "Truly this man was the Son of God."[84] Christ is the primal datum of the faith, and only in that context does the Law have meaning. "The negativity of the Law is not located in its formal character as commandment, as proposal of form and order; its ground is rather in our *disorder*, our sin, our non-conformity to Christ."[85] With this proposal Yeago has cleared the ground for a positive, or third, use of the Law, without using the term. He has also shown that where the third use is taken seriously, there is a greater chance that the formation of doctrine will also be taken seriously. Where there is order, there will be both doctrinal and moral order.

The differences between the previous generation of ELCA theologians, who rejected the third use and were weaned on the theology of Elert and Althaus, and the younger generation, who were concerned about the ethical laxity in the ELCA, were typified by an exchange between Walter R. Bouman, professor of systematic theology at Trinity Seminary, Columbus, Ohio, and Yeago in the pages of *Lutheran Forum*. Bouman was one of three members of the "Human Sexuality II" task force of the ELCA that was charged with giving the church body guidance in matters of human sexuality and Christian morals. In 1994 this task force published a draft statement, "The Church and Human Sexuality," which was permissive to say the least and generated much opposition, not the least of which was from the editor of *Lutheran Forum*.[86] In response to *Lutheran Forum*'s editor, Bouman had much to say about the Bible's own sexual "endorsements," but most important for this discussion he expounded a particular way of using Law and Gospel.[87]

Bouman returned to the themes of the 1960s and 1970s to defend the work of the task force, evincing Gospel reductionism in precise terms. "It seems to me that by making a distinction between Law and Gospel primary in its approach to the Bible (Apology, Article IV), the Lutheran tradition demonstrates that what I have called 'slogan biblicism' does not represent the authentic Lutheran tradition, nor the authentic Christian tradition."[88] Bouman is correct in pointing out that the Bible may not provide a handbook-like program for the Christian life. However, Law and Gospel functions to shape Lutheran theology, not Lutheranism's approach to the Bible. The Bible norms Law and Gospel, not the opposite. In Gospel reductionism, every theological issue is reduced to the Gospel or not-the-Gospel.[89] In the Gospel reductionist view of the 1960s, the Law provides no norming authority to the church's moral or doctrinal teaching. Bouman suggested that biblical precepts and the Law are unrelated. "The *theological* experience of the 'Law' does not have to do, in the first instance, either with violating or with honoring biblical precepts."[90] While Lutheran theology does avoid treating the Bible as a legal guidebook, full of nuggets of wisdom for life, the Law of God still must in some sense be derived from, or based on, Scripture. The third use of the Law is much more than "slogan biblicism." Certainly there are ambiguities and struggles with the Law as a scriptural word of God; nonetheless, it remains a word from God.

While Bouman chides the practitioners of "slogan biblicism," implying that those who reject Gospel reductionism are more than a trifle simplistic, he himself fails to be carefully nuanced in his understanding of New Testament prohibitions.

> At best Christians derive "torah" (the so-called third use of the Law) from the parenesis of the New Testament. But in its "just war" or "justifiable violence" teaching (Augsburg Confession, Article XVI), the Lutheran tradition is not obedient to the clear and consistent teaching of the New Testament that Christians do no violence to an enemy.[91]

Lutheran theology holds a doctrine of two kingdoms as well as the ethical necessity to love an enemy. Lutheran just war theory is not a bald rejection of the scriptural ethic of nonviolence. Just war theory is an attempt to hold in tension spiritual life and life in the world.[92] Even if one disagrees with the point of view of the Lutheran approach, Bouman cannot argue that the position is merely "slogan biblicism." The two kingdoms doctrine fails to shape Bouman's approach to understanding and putting into context the New Testament's prohibitions against violence. A Gospel reductionistic approach at this point leaves the theologian without the tools to set spiritual and ethical concerns in the larger theological universe of meaning. Gospel reductionism results in its own naive simplicities.[93] In any case, for Bouman the third use of the Law remained a derivation of New Testament parenesis still relegated to the numinous intellectual category of the "so-called."[94] The Law just does not apply.[95]

Yeago responded[96] to Bouman's views by hearkening back to the actual text of Luther's catechisms. "The problem, it seems to me, is that Professor Bouman has brought to bear a particular systematic construal of Luther's theology of the Law in a way that leaves no conceptual space for the Catechisms and so for the church whose *Gestalt* the Catechisms expound."[97] Yeago perceived that Bouman's views did not account for the actual content of Luther's catechisms and the theological universe from which they arose.

Bouman's view of Law in Luther was derived from Werner Elert. Yeago thought this point of view was profoundly mistaken.[98] But even that was not the most significant issue for Yeago. Most significant was that Bouman had elevated a peculiar interpretation of Luther to be the ruling consideration in his theology, at the expense of the texts of the binding confessional documents of the Lutheran church.

> The Lutheran Church is not bound to Luther's theology of the Law, and certainly not to Elert's or Bouman's or Yeago's or anyone else's systematic reconstruction of it. The Lutheran Church is bound to the Scriptures and, because they are a correct exposition of Scripture, to the Confessions. Some of the latter were, to be sure, written by Martin Luther, though more, in fact, were written by Philip Melanchthon and his students. But even those confessional documents written by Luther himself are not being read doctrinally if we simply take them as case studies for our reconstructed image of his larger theological system. It's the texts, not the system, that make doctrine.[99]

If the texts of the Confessions are to be doctrinally binding, then they must not be subjected to the kind of reconstruction that guts them of their doctrinal content. The Lutheran Confessions must not be reinterpreted according to anyone's particular portrayal of Luther's views. This is precisely what theologians such as Elert and Althaus did. American theologians such as Bouman clearly pushed their peculiar Law-Gospel construct into Gospel reductionism. What Yeago called Bouman's "misconstrual" of the Lutheran doctrine of the Law "has simply replaced the relevant confessional texts as the locus of authority."[100] The modern systematic reconstruction of Luther has permitted Lutheran theologians to make an end run around the texts of the catechisms, which give clear direction, indeed "authoritative public doctrine," on human sexuality in the exposition of the sixth commandment.[101] Yeago pointed out that Luther treated the Ten Commandments in the very way that Bouman described as inadequate, even "biblicistic."

> The Ten Commandments are clearly expounded as "biblical precepts": Luther makes appeal neither to an autonomous existential realm nor to an autonomous political realm but explicates them intra-

biblically, from within the scriptural canon. The commandments make up the content of the natural law on all our hearts, but this doesn't seem to mean that the church discovers that content by exegeting the human heart rather than the Bible! Nor does the purpose of the commandments, as the Large Catechism represents it, fit tidily into an Elertian *duplex usus*.[102]

Finally, the Ten Commandments are and remain "divine doctrine." They are a reflection of what is pleasing to God and must be followed by everyone.[103]

Yeago also rejected the contention that the Law is entirely ambiguous. He pointed out that in some sense the catechisms take the Law to be the *telos* of the Gospel.[104] Yeago believes that the Law must be honored and upheld so there are explicit commandments in the church. The church may not be left with an existentialistic revision of the Ten Commandments. "Professor Bouman condemns us, very much against his own intentions, to a therapeutic reduction of the Gospel: the Law is what makes us feel bad, so the Gospel must be what makes us feel better."[105]

Yeago recognized the generational gap between himself and Bouman.[106] Bouman was of the generation of theologians that fought for the right to treat the Bible critically, Yeago of the generation "that learned biblical criticism from official Sunday School curricula."[107] Consequently, Yeago wondered if the changing of the guard might not signal a return to simplicity. "I wonder if, the battle for sophistication having been won, the new battle that faces my generation of theologians is not a fight for the right to *simplicitas*, which the whole Christian tradition, including the Reformers, regarded as a virtue closely related to faith."[108] The *simplicitas* that is being sought here is the simplicity of being faithful to the text, instead of to an esoteric and unbending construct.

SUMMARY ANALYSIS AND EVALUATION

During this period, among the ELCA theologians the Law-Gospel construct of American Lutheran existentialists was collapsing for at least five reasons. First, the weighty complexity of the Law-Gospel construct invented by the Gospel reductionists was now contributing to its collapse. Second, the construct was seen to be contradicting the clear texts of the Lutheran Confessions. Third, the existentialistic and church historical presuppositions that supported this view were now increasingly discredited. Fourth, especially the younger ELCA theologians were alarmed at the moral excesses that were being excused on the basis of the freedom of the

Gospel. They were concerned that a Law-free Gospel had given way to antinomianism. Fifth, the methodological weakness of a ruthlessly applied Law-Gospel dichotomy, which ignored other central points of Christian doctrine, was becoming apparent.

THE MISSOURIANS

BACKGROUND AND INFLUENCES

In the late 1970s Luther scholarship took a decisive turn away from the existentialistic approach characteristic of the previous periods. Luther had been understood as an existentialist. Melanchthon had been seen as the villain who succumbed to the reinstatement of Aristotelianism and its attendant intellectual evils. Bengt Hägglund pointed out the weakness of this point of view in a 1980 article entitled "Melanchthon versus Luther: the Contemporary Struggle."[109] Hägglund judged that "the difference between the two reformers is often over-estimated and overplayed."[110] In fact, he argued that Melanchthon could not be shown to have misunderstood Luther's theology, as the scholars of the Luther renaissance had argued.

> The learned and skillful way in which Melanchthon interpreted evangelical theology was gratefully accepted and highly esteemed by Luther. In much modern research, however, it has often been evaluated in a negative way: Melanchthon supposedly did not really understand the deepest intentions of the Reformation, and with him began the decline of Lutheran theology. The blame is laid partly on the influence of contemporary sixteenth-century philosophy and the combination of theology with philosophical education which was introduced by Melanchthon. Clearly this evaluation is untenable.[111]

Increasingly, LCMS theologians took up this view that Melanchthon had articulated Luther's views clearly and that Luther had not been an existentialist. For example, Wilbert H. Rosin denied that Luther had taken up an existentialistic approach to theology. Contrary to the opinion set forth in the Luther renaissance, he argued that Luther was an ontologist. .

> He was philosophically not an existentialist but held the concept of essence prior to existence and experience. He believed that reason tells us that there is a God; Luther did not rule out *all* use of reason, and to that extent Luther could also make room for an Aristotelian approach to the question of realism.[112]

The mature Luther had a mature program for the Lutheran Reformation.[113] Lewis W. Spitz, professor of history at Stanford University, also supported the view that the existentialistic interpretation of Luther left theology with a flawed view of Luther. Spitz lauded more balanced historical appraisals of Luther, which began with the work of Heinrich Bornkamm, who alerted Luther scholars to the validity of the so-called late Luther.[114] "There has in recent years been a movement in theology beyond the reductionism of existential theology."[115] This movement has had a significant impact upon the doctrine of the third use of the Law.

SUMMARY OF VIEWS

THEODORE R. JUNGKUNTZ

Theodore R. Jungkuntz was a professor of theology at Valparaiso University in this period. However, he was not a theologian of the Valparaiso school in the way the term is being employed in this volume. Instead, on the topic of the third use of the Law, he was a Missourian. Jungkuntz was a careful and informed interpreter of the Formula of Concord, having written a book in 1977 on the authors of the Formula.[116] He responded to the ELCA and Valparaiso theologians' views on the third use of the Law in a number of sources. At the Valparaiso Conference for Parish Leaders, he responded to William Lazareth. The debate at that conference generated so much discussion that they continued it in the pages of *Lutheran Forum* in 1977 and 1978.[117] Jungkuntz listed seven areas of concern on the third use of the Law addressed by the Formula of Concord.

First, Jungkuntz contended that the Formula of Concord sided with those who insisted that the Law needed to be preached to Christians for their instruction in Christian morality but that the formulators also attempted to take into account the concerns of those who took the other side.[118] One of the aspects of the controversies leading up to the Formula of Concord was whether good works are extorted from Christians or are produced by Christians spontaneously. The Formula opted for both. Because the Christian remains a sinner, he needs the coercion of the Law. Because the Christian is reborn of God, he does the works of the Spirit spontaneously, even "without any instruction."[119] Jungkuntz pointed out the analogy that the Formula of Concord draws between the uncoerced motion of heavenly bodies in nature and the spontaneous obedience of the Christian. However, the spontaneous motion of the heavenly bodies has an impersonal character about it. The Formula also taught that the angels render a spontaneous obedience, yet it remains a personal obedience.[120]

Nonetheless, the Formula is quite clear that even spontaneous obedience is an obedience to the immutable will of God.[121] "Even spontaneity does not function independently of 'the will of God.' "[122]

Second, Jungkuntz argued that in Article VI the Formula focuses on the proper relationship of Law and Gospel rather than the distinction between them, as in Article V.[123]

> The Law insists on the fact "that" we should walk in the new life and it gives instruction as to "what" the content of the new life is. But it is completely helpless when it comes to actually producing the new life in us. That remains purely and entirely the function of the Gospel.[124]

The Gospel functions as motivator and the Law functions as pattern for the Christian life. Jungkuntz was careful to reiterate that in this context the Law that instructs also always accuses.[125] Once again the false either/or was avoided.

Third, Jungkuntz denied that the immutable will of God can be reduced to the love of God or the loving will of God to save all people. Both the Law and the Gospel are God's will for humans. The Formula of Concord explicitly rejects the idea that there can be two wills in God.[126] Edmund Schlink justified the Formula's position by saying, "The unity of the divine will is beyond the sphere of rational solution as much as the unity of Law and Gospel."[127] What troubles Lutherans at this point is the apparent contradiction between the eternalness and immutability of the Law, on the one hand, and the acknowledgment that Christ is the end of the Law, on the other.[128]

The inability of humans to rationalize the ways of God is an eschatological fact. The Formula itself hints at this eschatological reality when it declares that at the resurrection people will need the word of neither the Law nor the Gospel.[129] Although the Word is God's immutable will, there is a limit to its applicability as Law and Gospel. This unity in God is beyond our knowing, until we know as we are known.[130] Until then humans are bound to the Word.

Jungkuntz believed that the rejection of an immutable Law is inextricably joined to the contemporary challenges to the traditional moral order. The rejection of an immutable Law opens the door to the devil and all manner of immorality. Jungkuntz argued that the Lutheran Reformation had closed the door on moral relativism by rejecting that the Law's demands could be reduced or "relativized," which insight in turn made unconditional grace central. Where the Law could not be relativized or tamed down into manageable tasks, the necessity of grace was paramount and unconditional. Unconditional Law made unconditional grace necessary.[131] However, the task of the Reformation was incomplete. Antinomianism as well as moralism could relativize the Law.[132] "If only Satan could convince the Christian that precisely as justified Christian he no longer needed the Law at all but only the Gospel, God's glory in Law and Gospel would quickly again be relativized."[133] Jungkuntz felt that modern ethical relativism was a greater threat to the church's life and teaching than was moralism. Sexual ethics and gender issues were of special concern.[134] These problems are not unique to the late 20th or early 21st centuries.

The temptation is to face these problems with an absolutizing of the Mosaic laws. Thus, the Ten Commandments become of one level, so the observance of the Sabbath and the forbidding of images, for example, become important functions of the Law, as they were for Andreas Karlstadt. Luther avoided this pitfall. "In order to escape such absolutizations of that which was merely historically conditioned, Luther appealed to 'natural law.' "[135] The absolutized character of the natural law was its immutability. Jungkuntz argued that the content of the natural law needs to be protected from modern relativization.

> And it is to this same Law [natural law] that I should like to appeal at a time in our own history when we are experiencing not only a false absolutization of certain norms but also a false relativization of other norms. Whichever of the two our problem might be, the Lutheran confessions and the theology of Luther behind them would appear to direct us not only to the "absolute" of God's love as revealed in his will to save through the "Gospel," but also to that same love as it is revealed in his will to govern his creation through the "Law" running through that very creation.[136]

Natural law is discerned by a study of Scripture, which reveals God's will to humans.

Fourth, Jungkuntz pointed out that because the Law was revealed by God in Scripture, the Lutheran Reformation rejected the self-appointed righteousness of the radical reformers. Spirit guidance could always and only be guidance by Scripture and could never be guidance by the autonomous self cut off from God's immutable will. Lutherans roundly condemned the 16th-century "*Schwärmer*" because of the *Schwärmer's* rejection of the "external" word as unnecessary. The enthusiasts thought that the "internal" word was sufficient for both doctrine and life. The

Formula of Concord taught that the Law was to keep Christians from making up their own service to God.[137] Self-generated service could not be God-pleasing and would detract from the glory of God.

Jungkuntz perceived the applicability of this principle to his contemporary context.[138] The position of the Formula of Concord meant that the claim to guidance by the Spirit could not justify the transgression of any of the Ten Commandments (presumably defined as natural law). Situationism could not liberate the Christian, or anyone for that matter, from obedience to the Law, a Law with a specific content.[139] "Rebellion, murder, sexual unchastity, robbery and lusting of any kind are forbidden in any and every 'situation' and because of them God's Law 'always accuses' us, particularly should we think we could thereby be pleasing to God."[140] Jungkuntz still considered situation ethics to be a threat to Christian moral teaching in 1978. It is the opinion of this author that Jungkuntz believed ELCA theologians at the time to be at least tainted by, if not wholehearted supporters of, situation ethics.

Fifth, Jungkuntz affirmed that the Formula of Concord does not lose sight of the principle that *lex semper accusat* and in that way wards off legalism. "If by 'legalism' is meant a relationship to God based on 'good behavior,' the Formula in Article Six will have none of it."[141] Yet this accusing character of the Law does not preclude its being an instruction to Christians about the nature and necessity of good works. The both/and of Lutheranism is confirmed once again in the Formula. "It is certainly in keeping with the dialectical nature of Lutheran theology to say: the Law simultaneously accuses and delights the believer. That in no way smacks of legalism."[142] The *semper* guards against self-righteousness; the Law as instruction defends the importance of good works and offers content for the Christian life.

Sixth, Jungkuntz stated that when troubled by the immutability of the Law there remains the eschatological limit set upon both the Law and the Gospel by the Formula of Concord. However, little is said about this eschatological limit.[143] That limit has no significance until the faithful stand before God's judgment throne. Until then, God limits the church to his Word. Further speculation beyond the Word is both impossible and blasphemous.

Seventh, Jungkuntz recognized that the battle over the third use of the Law among American theologians may be mere logomachy. He also suggested that some of the wrangling may be caused by the desire to defend the professional reputation of theologians,[144] in which case the *semper* also applies to theologians. Nevertheless, he proposed a revision of the language employed in Article VI of the Formula of Concord along the lines suggested by Article V.

Article V resolved the conflict over the question of whether the Gospel, properly speaking, could be a preaching of repentance.[145] The resolution was a recognition that the word *Gospel* was not used in one simple sense in Scripture, but had several meanings. Gospel in the broad sense could include the preaching of repentance, but Gospel in the narrow sense, Gospel in contrast to Law, could not.

On the basis of this pattern Jungkuntz proposed that the third use of the Law be denominated as the Law in the broad sense, that is, Law that both accuses the sinner and delights the reborn child of God. Law in the narrow sense would be the preaching of God's wrath against sin. How this distinction advances the argument remains unclear. Jungkuntz made the suggestion to show that the problem is more than a word game and that there is more at stake than finding the correct term to speak of the Law's use in the life of the Christian. By identifying the issue as more than an argument over words, Jungkuntz gets to the heart of the conflict.

> If the problem is in fact theological, it is one that goes to the very roots of Christian theology—the basis of the Gospel in the vicarious atonement wrought by our Lord Jesus on the cross. Are deniers of the Third Use of the Law still agreed that the Gospel gives precisely what the Law demands? Are they agreed that the "immutable will of God" is not merely some Marcionitic "Law-free Gospel" but the Law-fulfilled Gospel of the New Testament (Matt. 5:17–20; Rom. 8:3–4)?[146]

Jungkuntz recognized that the rejection of the third use of the Law had a number of serious theological entailments. Apparently, he suspected that Lazareth brought those entailments along with his dislike of the third use of the Law. In any case, it remains clear that in Lutheran theology one's views on the Law have an enormous impact on the meaning of the Gospel. Jungkuntz believed that the foundation of the Christian faith was at stake in the debate over the third use of the Law.[147] For that reason alone Lazareth is incorrect when he calls Jungkuntz a moralist. The third use functions as a defense of the purity of the Gospel.

It is instructive that Lazareth does not understand why there is such a fuss about the third use of the Law. He can see no reason that it should be considered "a storm signal on the theological scene" and does not know why anyone else would consider it so. Jungkuntz returns to the *simul* to answer Lazareth's disregard for the significance of the third use. "It appears to me to be a crisis in the consistent application of Luther's *simul justus et peccator*."[148] Jungkuntz regards it essential that the *simul* be consistently and continuously applied for the sake of the third use of the Law. The third use highlights central issues that demand a balanced application of hermeneutically significant theological principles, such as the *simul*. The Gospel is at stake in its correct application. A balanced theology cannot be too highly regarded.

EUGENE F. KLUG

In his work on the third use of the Law, Eugene F. Klug[149] defended the truly "Luther-an" character of the Formula of Concord.[150] As has been shown, many modern interpreters of the Formula take it to be an orthodox-Melanchthonian betrayal of Luther's Reformation. Given this presupposition it is no wonder that Klug pointed out modern Lutheranism's basic disinterest in and disregard for the Formula of Concord.[151] The existential Luther is far removed from the spirit of the Formula of Concord.

Klug was well aware that this presents a significant dilemma for orthodox Lutheranism in the LCMS. If the Formula of Concord does not truly reflect Luther's theology, he argued, then its doctrinal validity is questionable. The wedge between Luther and his successors cannot be permitted to endure. Thus, Klug aimed to show that Luther's view on the Law is really congruent with and gives shape to the Formula of Concord, Article VI.

The question to be answered about the Formula of Concord is, "Who had the mind of Luther and of the confessors at Augsburg, 1530?"[152] First, Klug presented material from Luther showing that though Luther did not use the term "third use of the Law," he taught a third use. Second, he recounted the errors of Elert, Althaus, and Ebeling in this regard. "The strategy in each case is to demonstrate that either Melanchthon or the architects of the Formula, or both represented a caricature somehow of the Reformer's true views."[153]

Klug charged Elert with having denied the third use of the Law though there was plenty of evidence that Luther had included the substance of that doctrine in his teaching. "But to dismiss out of hand the fact that Luther nonetheless used the *concept* of the third use of the Law, if not the exact term, is without substantiation."[154] Klug saw Elert as desiring to defend the *semper* at all costs. Klug considered Elert's argument a straw man, stating that no genuinely Lutheran theologian has ever denied the *semper*. "He apparently is unaware, or prefers to have it that way, that no Lutheran theologian worth his salt ever denied that *lex semper accusat* is a principle basic to Scriptural theology."[155] In fact, Klug concluded that Elert himself is an antinomian of the same sort as Otto, Poach, and Neander, who denied that the Christian needs a teacher of what is good or godly and that the Gospel teaches him or her. Klug thought no better of Althaus, with the exception that Klug admitted that the *Gebot und Gesetz* scheme was an attempt to blunt Althaus's own rejection of the third use.[156] Yet in Klug's opinion, this attempt puts Althaus in worse company because Althaus considers *Gebot* an element of the Gospel.

> By stating that command is an element in the Gospel, Althaus has surrendered to the Barthian (and Romanist!) position, that the Law is the necessary form of the Gospel whose content is grace! Precisely this is the conclusion to which antinomianism inevitably leads.[157]

While Althaus does admit that the Spirit wants to teach the Christian, he is uncertain of the vehicle for that instruction. Like Scaer, Klug wanted to ground the divine revelation in the means of grace, specifically in Scripture. Klug offered a response that he believed reflected Luther's own position:

> And the Reformer would immediately have bunched Althaus with the rest of the "new spirits" who want to pitch out the Law of God in favor of their own so-called "Gospel-prompted" pieties. In place of the third use of the Law Althaus makes a nebulous gesture towards "the voice of Scripture" and, of all things, to "Christendom" and "Christian tradition," as though these indeed could rescue him from a terrible dilemma.[158]

Klug thought that the European Lutherans had complicated a teaching that was quite simple. They were guilty of overtheologizing.[159]

Klug pointed out that the writers of the Formula of Concord were themselves "Luther scholars," intimately acquainted with the work of the Wittenberg Reformer. They quelled a raucous theological controversy within a divided Lutheranism. The key to their success had to be finding the mind of Luther. But they could accomplish that only by reflecting Luther's own understanding on the controverted points. They offered in the Formula of Concord a reflection of Luther's theology that motivated thousands of pastors and teachers to subscribe in token of their agreement. For Klug it was inconceivable that Martin Chemnitz, "himself one of the greatest Luther scholars that ever lived," could have failed to be genuinely Lutheran on the third use of the Law.[160]

DAVID P. SCAER

David P. Scaer advanced the discussion of the third use of the Law by probing the relationship between the doctrine of the Law and several other points of Christian theology in a series of articles on the third use of the Law and the Lutheran doctrine of sanctification. His approach can be summarized under the following topics: the Holy Spirit, Scripture, anthropology, the *simul*, and the Christological view of sanctification.

The Holy Spirit. Scaer considered the relationship of the Holy Spirit to the Law, a theme also hinted at by Theodore R. Jungkuntz,[161] by pointing out the unity of the persons within the Godhead. Theologians with antinomian tendencies had argued that with the arrival of the Holy Spirit in the new life, the Law becomes superfluous. Scaer rejected this idea by asserting a harmony between the Spirit and the Law. According to Scaer, God sends the Spirit to complete the work of the Son in the world.[162] Scaer also contended that the Spirit is sent to complete the work of creation.[163] The Spirit of God was the source of life for Adam in the Garden of Eden. Therefore, the Spirit is the link between humans and God. "The Spirit is responsible for the perfect harmony in creation, known as the natural law, and He is responsible for man's created understanding of the Law."[164] Scaer is arguing for a close relationship between the Spirit and God's creation-shaping word of Law.

That close relationship would render invalid any attempt to divide the work of the Spirit from the Law. "With this concept of creation, natural law, and the Holy Spirit, the Lutherans had to object to any claim about the presence of the Holy Spirit replacing the need for Law."[165] Only those whom the power of the Holy Spirit has converted have the power to perceive the Law as an expression of God's will for their lives. If God has embedded the natural law in creation and the Holy Spirit is a creative power in that Law-shaped nature, as Scaer contends, then the Holy Spirit's creative actions are within the Law. "The Spirit *cannot* work against the natural law as He would be condemning His own work. This would involve Him in an internal contradiction."[166] Scaer sees a high level of coherence between God's patterns of salvation and creation.

Continuing with Scaer's thought process, despite the fact that the Gospel is an entirely new word and work of God in the world, God the Holy Spirit seeks to use creaturely means or vehicles by which he saves humans. Law as reflected in the creation is a means of sanctification. Scaer is building an analogy with the Lutheran doctrine of the means of grace, in which Lutheranism maintains that God uses creaturely means—such as the incarnation, the sacraments, and the Word—to give, offer, and convey his grace to humans. Means of grace are significant for their human accessibility and tangibility.[167] Scaer pushes that analogy here to include the use of the natural law as the means through which God communicates his Law to the converted. Conversion does not invalidate the natural law.[168] The natural law will be done away with as an eschatological act of God to be awaited in faith and groaning. Thus, for Scaer a rejection of the Law after conversion in favor of pure Spirit illumination is tantamount to the arrival of the eschaton.

> Those who do not see the Law as valid in the life of the Christian must also assert that this world has passed away and that the new world has already been inaugurated. This proposition must be firmly rejected because only at Christ's coming will this world end and the new one be established.[169]

Here Scaer is clearly rejecting the thesis proposed by Gerhard Forde nearly ten years before in his *The Law-Gospel Debate* as well as in his later locus "Christian Life" in *Christian Dogmatics*.[170] Forde emphasized the decisive nature of the eschaton inaugurated by the cross of Christ. Scaer is emphasizing the yet-to-come feature of eschatology. In the Christian's now-imperfect relationship to the Law, what is yet to come must be awaited in faith; it must not be presumed. A Law-free existence is part of the age yet to come.

Scripture. Scaer saw a close connection between the third use of the Law and the doctrine of Scripture as divine revelation. For him the parallel was simple: "Just as Lutherans see the entire Scripture as inspired, so they see the entire Scriptural message, both Law and Gospel as applicable to the life of the Christian."[171] This was a clear rejection of Gospel reductionism, and especially of the position of Edward H. Schroeder.[172] Here Scaer based his approach on the Formula of Concord's own argumentation. The formulators had defended their position on the third use of the Law by citing Psalm 1 and 2 Tim 3:15–17,[173] though, according to Scaer, these passages refer to the entire Scripture, not just the Law. The Law is applicable to the Christian life because it remains a part of the unseamed garment of the revelation of Scripture. "Natural law, sin, and Scriptural inspiration are related to each other."[174]

For Scaer, Scripture provided a clarification of the Law already in nature, a clarification made necessary by human depravity. The fallen human heart could no longer read clearly God's word in creation. Thus,

Scripture provided Law as a condemnation of that depravity. The primary use of the Law for Scaer is the second use.[175] The Law is a part of God's whole plan of salvation for the world. The Gospel cannot make alive until the Law has killed.[176] Scaer inferred that the Law cannot be taken out of the working of God after conversion either. He denied that what is "not-the-Gospel" is not the word of God, as others had implied.[177] "Those who rejected the Law did not only have a faulty concept of the Law itself but of divine revelation and of the Scriptures themselves."[178] Here is the Missourian answer to Lazareth's question about why there is such a fuss about the third use of the Law.[179] The Missourians intimately related Law, revelation, and the nature of Scripture.

Anthropology. In a thoroughly Augustinian fashion Scaer looks at the Law's impact on humans in four different conditions: before the fall, after the fall, after conversion, and in the eschaton.[180] The differing impact of the Law in each condition is attributable not to a change in the Law itself, but to the changes in the human condition. In the state of innocence there was no distinction between the imperative and the indicative. Humans delighted in the Law, and there was nothing negative in its impact upon humans. "There was no tension between what man *did* and what man *could, must,* and *should* do."[181]

After the fall humans were instantly threatened by the Law. Now there was a gap between what humans did and what the Law demanded. There could be no more indicative, only the threat of the imperative. The change here was not in the Law itself, but in the character of the postlapsarian heart.[182] It could no longer hear the Law as indicative, but it heard the Law as the threatening wrath of God.[183]

After conversion the changed character of the human transforms the perspective on the Law so now the Law not only threatens, but also instructs and is delighted in. Insofar as he or she is *peccator*, the Law threatens the Christian; insofar as he or she is *justus*, the Christian is delighted and instructed by the Law. This all occurs simultaneously because the Christian lives under the Law and in the Gospel simultaneously. "Understanding the Law in this Third Use is predicated on understanding the Lutheran view of the regenerate Christian."[184]

Part of that understanding is the view of the struggle that goes on within the regenerate person. The regenerate person stands in two persuasions in relation to the Law. An internal conflict and struggle is triggered as each nature, the regenerate and the sinful, strives against the other.[185] "The Law of God remains one and immutable, but as it approaches the Christian, its positive directions apply to the converted part and its negative prohibitions with the threats of punishments are directed to the unregenerated condition."[186] Between cross and eschaton the Christian remains absorbed in the struggle between the two natures, certain of the ultimate outcome by grace for Christ's sake but struggling faithfully nonetheless.

Scaer's choice of terms at this point is not the best. To talk of "the converted part"[187] of the Christian is to risk a psychical bifurcation of the regenerated person. Such a bifurcation might imply that the Law can be applied as threat at one time and as instruction at another. Scaer did not intend this conclusion. The Law functions as threat or instruction not based on its character in communication, but on its reception by the Christian. Any word of Law could be both instruction and threat at the same time—a threat to the old Adam, instruction for the new Adam. The Law is not susceptible to human manipulation. Preachers do not make it first, second, or third use, but the Law functions as any of the uses according to circumstances.[188] It remains *God's* Law. Because of its untamed nature, the Law continues to demand the need for the Gospel. Thus, the pattern of the Christian life is a continuous circle from Law to Gospel and back to Law.

At the resurrection Christians will need neither Law nor Gospel. Until the consummation of the age, the third use of the Law hints at the perfect union of human acts and divine intentions for creation. Only then will the Law be unneeded. "Even in the final condition, it is not the nature of the Law that has changed but rather that man has become totally regenerated."[189]

***The* Simul.** Understanding the *simul* is essential to properly understanding the third use of the Law. The Law provides to the Christian both a description of the Christian life and the condemnation of his or her sin. Christians see themselves as totally justified but also see that they are sinners. "What is important in this understanding is the Latin word *simul*, at the same time, and not in a sequential sense as if one followed the other in point of time."[190] A purely temporal sequence of Law, then Gospel—or sinner, then regenerate—is a totally inadequate description of the relationship between the old and new Adam and of God's revelation of himself to the Christian. The historical case of this kind of superficial treatment of the *simul* is the Pietism that affected the Lutheran church and its theology in the 17th and 18th centuries. Scaer claimed that the *simul* was turned into a temporal progression, which resulted in a mild form of perfectionism.

> The matter is viewed in this way: After a person is justified by faith, the new life of obedience sets in and progresses. Justification is seen as a past event in the Christian life and sanctification as a temporal result, separate and distinct from justification as the cause. Wherever justification and sanctification are separated from each other with this kind of temporal understanding, Lutheran theology is brought to ruin.[191]

The temporal order of Pietism is justification or conversion and then sanctification, whereas in Lutheran theology justification and sanctification remain two sides of one coin, inseparable and simultaneous. "In the phrase *simul justus et peccator* the *simul* carries the weight."[192] The Christian is simultaneously justified and sanctified.

Christological View of Sanctification. In the 1980s Scaer emphasized the Christological nature of all theological truth. If Christ is the center of the Christian faith, then Christology must have an effect on all doctrine. Scaer argued that Luther's explanation of the Apostles' Creed situated sanctification in the second article, rather than the third.[193] Thus, sanctification includes overcoming sin, but more important it needs to be Christlike in its shape. Scaer contended that Luther's explanations to the Ten Commandments are not describing life lived under the Law, but the life of Christ himself. There is a reciprocity between the Law and the life of Christ.

> Luther is frequently cited as saying that every Christian is Christ to his neighbor. I am not so sure that those who speak in this way fully understand what this means. Frequently it may be an excuse for an existential Christianity to treat the historical Jesus without any real significance. It is, however, a valuable distinction if it means that the life flowing from faith is, in fact, practicing Christology in the world.[194]

The third use of the Law puts the life of Christ into practice. The device of Christocentricity functioned to emphasize the positive aspects of the third use of the Law, rather than prohibitions, which may lead to moralism or legalism. Scaer was concerned that an improperly nuanced approach to the third use of the Law has the potential to be moralistic. He was striving to use Christocentricity to avoid that pitfall.[195]

SUMMARY ANALYSIS AND EVALUATION

During this period the Missourians did not move from the position they had held in the previous period (1961–76). However, they were more thorough and more creative in their support of the third use of the Law. David Scaer advanced the discussion by presenting cogent arguments for the ways in which Law and Gospel overlapped and interrelated with other teachings of Lutheran doctrine. The Missourians held that the organic interrelationships of the points of Christian theology were relatively complex.[196] The interdependence of doctrine meant that Law and Gospel could not be ruthlessly or crudely applied to Lutheran theology. Law and Gospel shapes Lutheran theology but not at the exclusion of other hermeneutically significant and organically related doctrinal themes.

From the late 1950s there had been a significant shift in the views of Luther scholarship. The "late Luther" was no longer ignored. His contributions to catechesis and church organization were now interpreted as legitimate expressions of his theology, rather than as betrayals of an existentially defined Gospel. The gap between Melanchthon and Luther was narrowed after Luther scholarship divested itself of the shackles of an existentialistic interpretation of the Gospel. The adjustments in theologians' views of Luther began to significantly affect Lutheran theology in this period. A positive assessment of the later Luther ultimately contributed to a turn toward a positive assessment of the third use of the Law. The Missourians readily used these changes in perspective on Luther to defend the third use of the Law.

The Missourians also renewed their own research into Luther. They attempted to show that the Formula of Concord had indeed correctly portrayed the mind of the Wittenberg Reformer. A renewed interest in the catechisms and their organization was especially helpful. Research into Luther's approach to the Ten Commandments had a significant impact on the Law-Gospel debate. This research showed that Luther had interpreted the Ten Commandments for use by Christians. This was the third use of the Law in Luther's most enduring work.

The dire predictions of antinomianism made in the previous period and at the beginning of this presently discussed period seemed to be vindicated. This led the Missourians to reinforce the importance of having the third use of the Law. External discipline required reinforcement of a third use.

Finally, conceptual space was created for a Law that could both inform and accuse. The Missourians emphasized the *simul* over the eschatological construct of Forde. At the same time, however, they recognized how Law and Gospel cut across all topics of theology both to be shaped by them and to shape them in return. The interrelationships of the topics of theology were perceived to be intricately connected and carefully balanced. The Missourians also maintained that theological anthropology was not able to be accounted for by a simple division of the church's time into old age and new age. The Missourians wanted to maintain the tensions of balancing the "now and not yet" character of Christian life in the world.

SUMMARY AND CONCLUSIONS

The third use of the Law went through a dramatic revival among American Lutherans in this period (1977–98). Convergence of the Missourians and younger ELCA theologians on the third use of the Law began in this period. Older ELCA theologians tended to maintain their conceptual grounding in the results of the Luther renaissance and in the work of Elert and Althaus.

The conflict between two different generations of ELCA theologians over sexual ethics sparked renewed interest in the third use of the Law and demonstrated the generational divide in the ELCA. David Yeago showed the weaknesses of relying on Elert's views on Law and Gospel. This dispute also clarified the function of Law and Gospel in Lutheran theology.

Law and Gospel functions as a theological hermeneutic in Lutheran theology. Yeago pointed out that this hermeneutic has valid limits set upon it by other central points of Lutheran theology. The Elertian theologians' narrow application of Law and Gospel to the exclusion of other emphases increasingly looked imbalanced. That imbalance was in large measure exposed by the conflict over sexual ethics in the ELCA.

The existentialism of the Luther renaissance no longer held sway among Lutheran theologians who sought to interpret Luther's legacy to the church. Luther was now understood to be a solid churchman who saw the need for the Law in the nascent Lutheran church. His catechisms were now interpreted as containing a Law that was both accusing and positive.

The Lutheran Confessions were treated with a renewed sense of their positive norming authority for the life of the church. Such doctrinal norms were increasingly seen as useful and enriching rather than limiting and constraining. The possibility of doctrinal discipline became more significant as theologians fretted about moral and doctrinal decline among Lutherans. Doctrine was now seen as something more than mere formalism as long as it was a valid expression of the Lutheran confessional tradition.

NOTES

[1] See ALC/LCMS Commission on Fellowship, *The American Lutheran Church and The Lutheran Church—Missouri Synod: A Statement on Doctrinal Differences* (St. Louis: The Lutheran Church—Missouri Synod, 1980).

[2] The AELC was the denominational organization that grew out of the LCMS's ecclesiastical conflict. First known as Evangelical Lutherans in Mission, it was organized by those who left the LCMS in December 1976. See E. Clifford Nelson, "Supplement," in *The Lutherans in North America* (ed. E. Clifford Nelson; Philadelphia: Fortress, 1975), 560.

[3] See E. Clifford Nelson, "The New Shape of Lutheranism 1930–," in *The Lutherans in North America* (ed. E. Clifford Nelson; Philadelphia: Fortress, 1975), 507.

[4] See, for example, The Board of Control of Concordia Seminary, St. Louis, Mo., *Exodus from Concordia* (St. Louis: Concordia College, 1977), 61–62 et passim; Richard E. Koenig, "Post-mortem on the Showdown in the LCMS: The Issue Was Conscience," *Lutheran Forum* (September 1976): 6–11; Koenig, "What's after the Showdown in the LCMS? Epilogue to New Orleans," *Lutheran Forum* (November 1973): 10–12; and Koenig, "What's behind the Showdown in the LCMS? Church and Tradition in Collision," *Lutheran Forum* (November 1972): 17–20.

[5] See, for example, Marc Kolden, "Posing a Question," *Forum Letter* 23 (7 October 1994): 6–8.

[6] William H. Lazareth, "Foundation for Christian Ethics: The Question of the 'Third Use' of the Law," in *Confession and Congregation, The Cresset Occasional Paper, III* (ed. David G. Truemper; Valparaiso: Valparaiso University Press, 1978), 48–56.

[7] That Lazareth puts the term *third use* in quotation marks in the title of his paper is instructive.

[8] See pp. 57–58. William H. Lazareth, *Luther on the Christian Home* (Philadelphia: Muhlenberg, 1960).

[9] Lazareth, "Foundation for Christian Ethics," 48.

[10] See Lazareth, "Foundation for Christian Ethics," 49.

[11] William Lazareth and Péri Rasolondraibe, *Lutheran Identity and Mission* (Minneapolis: Augsburg Fortress, 1994), 44–46.

[12] Jungkuntz reported that Lazareth labeled his response "moralism" at the conference. Theodore R. Jungkuntz, "Gamesmanship or Dialogue?" *Lutheran Forum* (Lent 1978): 22.

[13] Theodore R. Jungkuntz, "Response to Dr. Lazareth," in *Confession and Congregation*, 57.

[14] Robert Preus considered the approach of some ELCA theologians to be a historical relativizing of the Lutheran Confessions. See Robert D. Preus, "Confessional Subscription," in *Evangelical Directions for the Lutheran Church* (eds. Erich H. Kiehl and Waldo J. Werning; Chicago: Lutheran Congress, 1970), 44. In other words, according to the ELCA theologians, since the Lutheran Confessions were historically conditioned documents they are valid witnesses to the truth of Jesus Christ only within their original historical context. For example, Theodore Tappert wrote, "When subscribing the confessions today, Lutherans assert that, in view of the issues which were then at stake and the alternatives which were then offered, the confessors were right" (Theodore G. Tappert, "The Significance of Confessional Subscription,"

in *Essays on the Lutheran Confessions Basic to Lutheran Cooperation* [New York: The Lutheran Church—Missouri Synod and National Lutheran Council, 1961], 29).

[15] Lazareth, "Foundation for Christian Ethics," 50–51.

[16] Melanchthon held precisely the same view of natural law. "*Porro ius naturale vere est ius divinum, quia est ordinatio divinitus impressa naturae*" (Ap XXIII, 12; BS 336).

[17] *Trig* 968. "*Solchergestalt sind die Christen nicht unter dem Gesetz, sondern unter der Gnaden, weil die Person von dem Fluch und Verdammnus des Gesetzes durch den Glauben an Christum gefreiet, und weil ihr gute Werk, ob sie gleich noch unvollkommen und unrein, durch Christum Gott angenehm sein, weil sie auch nicht aus Zwang des Gesetzes, sondern aus Verneuerung des Heiligen Geistes, von Herzen, willig und ungezwungen tuen, was Gott gefällig ist, soviel sie nach den innerlichen Menschen neugeboren sein; gleichwohl aber führen sie ein stetigen Kampf wider den alten Adam*" (FC SD VI, 23; BS 969).

[18] Lazareth, "Foundation for Christian Ethics," 51. Lazareth uses the same language elsewhere in his article (p. 53), indicating that this is not merely imprecise language.

[19] See pp. 123–31.

[20] Lazareth, "Foundation for Christian Ethics," 51.

[21] James E. Creighton, *An Introductory Logic* (4th ed.; New York: Macmillan, 1920), 189.

[22] See, for example, Richard Klann, "Reflections on Disputes Regarding the Proper Distinction between Law and Gospel," *CJ* 1 (January 1975): 34–45.

[23] SC I, 1; BS 507.

[24] "*Decalogus autem requirit non solum externa opera civilia, quae ratio ut cunque efficere potest, sed etiam requirit alia, longe supra rationem posita, scilicet vere; timere Deum, vere diligere Deum, vere invocare Deum, vere statuere, quod Deus exaudiat, et exspectare auxilium Dei in morte, in omnibus afflictionibus; denique requirit obedientiam erga Deum in morte et omnibus afflictionibus, ne has fugiamus aut aversemur, quum Deus imponit*" (Ap IV, 8, 27; BS 160, 165). The Formula of Concord uses the terms in precisely the same way. See SD II, 3; BS 871.

[25] In this regard, the comments of Michael Rogness about the Decalogue in the Small Catechism are instructive. "They [the Ten Commandments] come first, after all, and the pastor probably spends a lot of time on them. And since Luther's explanations (wonderful explanations, to be sure) are written for us in our Christian living, we get a full dose of the third use of the Law without having any idea of the first two uses at all, or even that there are three uses" (Rogness, "Dusting Off the Book of Concord," in *Confession and Congregation*, 95). See also David P. Scaer, "Formula of Concord Article VI: The Third Use of the Law," *CTQ* 42 (April 1978): 154; and Hans Schwarz, "The Dynamics of the Word," in *Christian Dogmatics*, vol. 2 (eds. Carl E. Braaten and Robert W. Jenson; Philadelphia: Fortress, 1984), 275.

[26] BS 523–27; *Trig* 561–63.

[27] Lazareth does not account for the *Haustafel* in *Lutheran Identity and Mission*, 43.

[28] Edmund Schlink provides a salutary summary of the catechism's approach to the Law. See Schlink, *Theology of the Lutheran Confessions* (trans. Paul F. Koehneke and Herbert J. A. Bouman; Philadelphia: Fortress, 1961), 121–22, n. 8.

[29] "Incidentally, and correspondingly, that is also why Luther, in his treatment of the Ten Commandments in his Small Catechism, took the Mosaic Decalogue and relativized its binding authority (as Gesetz) for baptized Christians. How?—by using the

last nine commandments simply as paradigmatic illustrations of the solely-binding *Gebot* of the First Commandment. 'We should so fear and love God that. . . .' We glorify and serve him in all of life—ecclesiastically, domestically, socially, economically, politically, etc" (Lazareth, "Foundation for Christian Ethics," 55).

[30] *"Früchte aber des Geistes seind die Werk, welche der Geist Gottes, so in den Gläubigen wohnet, wirket durch die Wiedergebornen, und von den Gläubigen geschehen, soviel sie wiedergeboren sind, als wann sie von keinem Gebot, Trauen oder Belohnung wußten; dergestalt dann die Kinder Gottes im Gesetz leben und nach dem Gesetz wandeln, wölchs S. Paulus in sein Episteln das Gesetz Christi und das Gesetz des Gemüts nennet, und gleichwohl nicht unter dem Gesetz, sondern unter der Gnaden sein, Röm. 7 und 8"* (Ep VI, 6; *BS* 794–95; *Trig* 806). The vast majority of Luther's uses of the term in the Lutheran Confessions are references to the Decalogue. See, for example, SC, preface, 17–18; *BS* 504–5; *Trig* 535–37.

[31] Lazareth, "Foundation for Christian Ethics," 55.

[32] Lazareth, "Foundation for Christian Ethics," 55.

[33] Scott Ickert perpetuates the presupposition that the Lutheran doctrine of the third use of the Law is basically taken from Calvin, who provides the classic case. "But it is in Calvin's Institutes (II. vii. 6–12) that we discover what may be considered the *locus classicus* for the definition of the third use of the Law" (Ickert, "The Uses of the Law," *Lutheran Forum* 25 [February 1991]: 20). A similar point of view was evinced by Hans Schwarz, who quoted Calvin's opinion on the third use of the Law, then claimed that "a similar line of thought was pursued by Philip Melanchthon" (Schwarz, "Dynamics of the Word," in *Christian Dogmatics*, 2:275). Schwarz more strongly connected Calvin's opinion with Melanchthon's in his own work, *Responsible Faith*: "This was also the line of thinking taken by Melanchthon, the Lutheran Book of Concord, and the theologians of Lutheran Orthodoxy" (Schwarz, *Responsible Faith* [Minneapolis: Augsburg, 1986]). The editors of *Christian Dogmatics* appear to have edited out the stronger statement, which Schwarz added to his later work.

[34] *Trig* 190.

[35] Even as early as 1559 and long before the uncovering of the crypto-Calvinistic conspiracy, Jacob Andreae, one of the primary authors of the Formula of Concord, saw that the gap between Lutheranism and Calvinism was irreparable. This was partially caused by the defection of the Palatinate to Calvinism in that year. Martin Chemnitz was also ardently anti-Calvinistic because of the opposition of the Wittenberg crypto-Calvinists to his work. See Theodore R. Jungkuntz, *Formulators of the Formula of Concord* (St. Louis: Concordia, 1977), 28, 62.

[36] See Lazareth, "Foundation for Christian Ethics," 55.

[37] Lazareth, "Foundation for Christian Ethics," 55.

[38] Jungkuntz, "Response to Dr. Lazareth," 58.

[39] Jungkuntz lauded Lazareth for committing himself to the principle that the Lutheran Confessions had to be interpreted within their historical context. However, Jungkuntz complained, "I am quite dissatisfied with the manner in which Dr. Lazareth has handled this principle" (Jungkuntz, "Response to Dr. Lazareth," 57).

[40] Gerhard O. Forde, "Christian Life," in *Christian Dogmatics*, 2:395–474.

[41] See pp. 123–31. Gerhard Forde, *The Law-Gospel Debate* (Minneapolis: Augsburg, 1969).

[42] Forde, "Christian Life," in *Christian Dogmatics*, 2:449.

[43] See p. 66.

[44] Forde, "Christian Life," in *Christian Dogmatics*, 2:450.

[45] Forde, "Christian Life," in *Christian Dogmatics*, 2:450.

[46] Forde, "Christian Life," in *Christian Dogmatics*, 2:451.

[47] Forde, "Christian Life," in *Christian Dogmatics*, 2:450. In an earlier chapter of the same work, Hans Schwarz takes a different tack to the third use of the Law. Schwarz adopted the *Gebot* teaching of Althaus. For Schwarz Lutheran theology needs to account for the place of ethics for the converted: "Christians certainly need moral directives and guidelines; they need to hear God's will to order their lives." He appears to be guilty of what Forde called "covert antinomianism." The Law still applies but only as an admixture of Law and Gospel, in the form of the *tertium quid* of *Gebot*. See Schwarz, "Dynamics of the Word," in *Christian Dogmatics*, 2:275.

[48] Forde, "Christian Life," in *Christian Dogmatics*, 2:450–51.

[49] Isa 55:10–11.

[50] See Walter H. Wagner, "Luther and the Positive Use of the Law," *JRH* 11 (January 1980): 52.

[51] See James M. Kittelson, "Luther, the Church Bureaucrat," *CJ* 13 (October 1987): 294–306.

[52] Wagner, "Luther and the Positive Use of the Law," 52.

[53] See also Timothy Wengert, " 'Fear and Love' in the Ten Commandments," *CJ* 21 (January 1995): 14–27; Lowell C. Green, " 'What Does This Mean?' Luther's Exposition of the Decalogue in Relation to Law and Gospel, with Special Reference to Johann Michael Reu," *Logia* 7 (Eastertide 1998): 3–10; and Charles P. Arand, "Luther on the God behind the First Commandment," *LQ* 8 (1994): 397–423.

[54] See Wagner, "Luther and the Positive Use of the Law," 54.

[55] Wagner, "Luther and the Positive Use of the Law," 56.

[56] See pp. 16–17.

[57] See pp. 16–19.

[58] Wagner, "Luther and the Positive Use of the Law," 60.

[59] "At least in America, the present antinomianism in Lutheranism reflects a post-Barthian Calvinism which was uncritically adopted by Lutherans eager to fit into the American religious culture" (Richard J. Niebanck, "Law and Gospel: Essential Proprium or Embarrassing Peculiarity?" *Lutheran Forum* 29 [November 1995]: 45).

[60] See, for example, Russell E. Saltzman, "A Discredited Debacle," *Forum Letter* 22 (28 December 1993): 1–3.

[61] Ickert, "Uses of the Law," 22.

[62] Ickert, "Uses of the Law," 23.

[63] Ickert, "Uses of the Law," 23; emphasis in the original.

[64] Marc Kolden of Luther Seminary, St. Paul, Minnesota, is another articulate opponent of the rejection of the third use of the Law. "The sorry history of separating Law and Gospel and holding that the Gospel alone is enough for everything is revealed in the frequent and typical examples of 'lazy Lutheranism' which are all too familiar: unchanged lives, pale cultural Christianity, ethical and political quietism and passivity, thoughtless universalism, and practical relativism. These alone ought to be

sufficient to discredit the separation of Law and Gospel" (Kolden, "The Scope of Forgiveness," *WW* 16 [Summer 1996]: 313).

[65] See Ickert, "Uses of the Law," 20.

[66] David S. Yeago, "Gnosticism, Antinomianism, and Reformation Theology," *ProEccl* 2 (Winter 1993): 38–39.

[67] See Yeago, "Gnosticism," 38–39.

[68] Yeago, "Gnosticism," 38; emphasis in the original.

[69] Yeago, "Gnosticism," 38.

[70] Yeago, "Gnosticism," 39; emphasis in the original.

[71] Yeago, "Gnosticism," 42; emphasis in the original.

[72] Yeago quoted Elert at length. "Only sinners belong to the Lutheran Church; not willful sinners, to be sure, but penitent sinners—yet always only sinners, who in this life can never be anything else. . . . What its members do or do not do, miss or do not neglect, in an ethical respect belongs in the domain of sociology and has nothing at all to do with the nature of the church. The evangelical human being is answerable for this, not the evangelical church, insofar as it owes the individual the Gospel, which engenders his faith and thus becomes indirectly perceptible in the ethical dynamic" (Yeago, "Gnosticism," 42; quoted from Werner Elert, *The Structure of Lutheranism* [trans. Walter A. Hansen; St. Louis: Concordia, 1962], 363). The ellipsis is in some sense misleading because it reads, "On principle the Lutheran Church has nothing to offer to the righteous people whose saintliness one can observe in the cut of their clothes, in their bill of fare, and in the 'language of Canaan.' " Elert means that social status and the external righteousness that is derived from it has no significance in the church. However, Yeago remains essentially correct in that the quote leads to antinomianism in the church, even if that was not the intention of Elert.

[73] Yeago, "Gnosticism," 40; emphasis in the original.

[74] Walter R. Bouman, "The Law of God: Response to Professor David Yeago," *Lutheran Forum* 29 (November 1995): 13.

[75] Bouman, "Response to Professor David Yeago," 13.

[76] Richard Klann pointed out that Calvin's doctrine of the Law was different than the Lutheran doctrine. "We face an entirely different conception of the third function of the Law in Calvin's *Institutes of the Christian Religion*, Bk II, Chapter VII, Section XII ff. . . . An analysis of the position of Melanchthon as of the teachings of Calvin will show that the positions of these two men cannot be reconciled without modification of their views" (Klann, "Reflections on Disputes," 41).

[77] "Even as the Law instructs us in the holy will and Law of God, it continually reminds us that we have failed to live up to its demands. It 'always accuses.' Yet Article VI of the Formula of Concord clearly distinguishes between the two [Law and Gospel]. A failure to distinguish involves a denial of the third use of the Law. A separation of the two easily leads to a 'code book' approach to the exhortations of the Law that must keep us from 'daily contrition and repentance' and from a continual return to the vivifying and motivating power of the Gospel" (Karl L. Barth, "Cardinal Principles of Lutheranism and 'Evangelical Theology,' " *CJ* 7 [March 1981]: 52).

[78] Yeago, "Gnosticism," 41.

[79] "While in Luther the simultaneity of freedom and obligation was maintained for

the whole person, in the enlightenment the freedom and obligation were related to the separation of the public and private use of reason so drastically expressed in Kant" (Vítor Westhelle, "Proclamation and Obligation: On the Demonstration of the Spirit and of Power," *WW* 16 [Summer 1996]: 332–33). Westhelle also criticized Elert for his "negative definition of power as coercion and accusation" (Westhelle, "Proclamation and Obligation," 335).

[80] Yeago, "Gnosticism," 43.

[81] Yeago, "Gnosticism," 43.

[82] Yeago, "Gnosticism," 44.

[83] See Yeago, "Gnosticism," 44.

[84] Mark 15:39.

[85] Yeago, "Gnosticism," 48.

[86] See Leonard Klein, "Disaster Averted, Disaster Invited," *Lutheran Forum* 29 (February 1995): 4.

[87] See Walter R. Bouman, "Walter Bouman on HSII," *Lutheran Forum* 29 (May 1995): 12–14.

[88] Bouman, "Bouman on HSII," 13.

[89] See pp. 103–11.

[90] Bouman, "Bouman on HSII," 13.

[91] Bouman, "Bouman on HSII," 13.

[92] For more on the impact of the two kingdoms on Lutheran ethical thinking, see Scott R. Murray, "Law and Gospel: The Lutheran Ethic," *Logia* 4 (July 1995): 15–24.

[93] It is instructive that Ronald F. Marshall, when offering "Four Lutheran Rules of False Teaching," lists as his first rule that Law and Gospel both must be used. "A *twosome*. Nothing is more closely joined together than . . . Law and Gospel (LW 26, p. 343). Both 'must be constantly and diligently in the church of God until the end of the world' (BC, p. 562). Keeping only the Law suffocates us with *legalism*. Keeping only the Gospel intoxicates us with *antinomianism*. Only the Law can break our pride in ourselves. Only the Gospel can waylay our fear of death. Both are needed all our days" (Marshall, "Four Lutheran Rules of False Teaching," *Lutheran Forum* 29 [May 1995]: 18; emphasis in the original).

[94] Bouman, "Bouman on HSII," 13.

[95] See Bouman, "Bouman on HSII," 14.

[96] The disagreement between Yeago and Bouman was not over the specific sexual issues in the "Human Sexuality" draft. "My remarks relate to Professor Bouman's comments on the doctrine of the Law, and shouldn't be read as taking a position one way or the other on the revised Human Sexuality draft" (David S. Yeago, "Bouman on the Law: *Amica Responsio*," *Lutheran Forum* 29 [August 1995]: 10). Bouman replied, "It is good that the topic is *lex*, not sex" (Bouman, "Response to Professor David Yeago," 12).

[97] Yeago, "Bouman on the Law," 10.

[98] See Yeago, "Bouman on the Law," 10.

[99] Yeago, "Bouman on the Law," 10.

[100] Yeago, "Bouman on the Law," 10.

[101] Yeago, "Bouman on the Law," 10.

[102] Yeago, "Bouman on the Law," 10.

[103] See Yeago, "Bouman on the Law," 10.

[104] *"Aus dem siehest du nu, daß der Glaube gar viel eine andere Lehre ist denn die zehen Gepot; denn jene lehrt wohl, was wir tuen sollen, diese aber sagt, was uns Gott tü und gebe. Die zehn Gepot sind auch sonst in aller Menschen Herzen geschrieben, den Glauben aber kann keine menschliche Klugheit begreifen, und muss allein vom heiligen Geist gelehret werden. Darümb macht jene Lehre noch keinen Christen, denn es bleibt noch immer Gottes Zorn und Ungnade über uns, weil wir's nicht halten können, was Gott von uns fordert. Aber diese bringet eitel Gnade, machet uns fromm und Gott angenehme. Denn durch diese Erkenntnis kriegen wir Lust und Liebe zu allen Gepoten Gottes, weil wir hier sehen, wie sich Gott ganz und gar mit allem, das er hat und vermag, uns gibt, zu Hülfe und Steuer, die zehen Gepot zu halten: der Vater alle Kreaturn, Christus alle seine Werke, der Heilige Geist alle seine Gaben"* (LC II 67–69; BS 661; *Trig* 697).

[105] Yeago, "Bouman on the Law," 12.

[106] "I cannot help but wonder if this is not the memory of old battles speaking rather than a clear perception of the one we are in now" (Yeago, "Bouman on the Law," 12).

[107] Yeago, "Bouman on the Law," 12.

[108] Yeago, "Bouman on the Law," 12.

[109] Bengt Hägglund, "Melanchthon Versus Luther: The Contemporary Struggle," *CTQ* 44 (July 1980): 123–33.

[110] Hägglund, "Melanchthon Versus Luther," 123.

[111] Hägglund, "Melanchthon Versus Luther," 124.

[112] Wilbert H. Rosin, "In Response to Bengt Hägglund: The Importance of Epistemology for Luther's and Melanchthon's Theology," *CTQ* 44 (July 1980): 136. This more recent view of Luther as an ontologist contradicts the earlier views of the Luther renaissance which were appropriated by American theologians such as Gerhard O. Forde. When discussing his opinion that American Lutheran theologians have failed to work a fully functional view of Law and Gospel, Forde pointed out that there is a battle between ontology and eschatology. Forde obviously resolved the battle in favor of eschatology. This leads to the rejection of the Law as an eternal order because the Law has no ontological existence. See Gerhard O. Forde, "The Formula of Concord Article V: End or New Beginning?" *Di* 15 (Summer 1975): 189. However, if Rosin is correct, then ontology must be accounted for in the Law's use. The Formula of Concord cannot merely be dismissed as less than Lutheran because it holds that the Law is an eternal order.

[113] See James M. Kittelson, *Luther the Reformer* (Minneapolis: Augsburg, 1986), 248.

[114] See Heinrich Bornkamm, *Luther in Mid-Career, 1521–1530* (ed. Karin Bornkamm; trans. E. Theodore Bachmann; Philadelphia: Fortress, 1983).

[115] Rosin, "Response to Bengt Hägglund," 138.

[116] Jungkuntz, *Formulators*.

[117] Theodore R. Jungkuntz, "The 'Third Use of the Law': Looking for Light on the Heat," *Lutheran Forum* (May 1978): 10; and Jungkuntz, "Gamesmanship or Dialogue?" 22.

[118] For more on the historical context of the debate, see *Trig* 169–72; and Robert Kolb, "Historical Background of the Formula of Concord," in *A Contemporary Look at*

the Formula of Concord (eds. Robert D. Preus and Wilbert Rosin; St. Louis: Concordia, 1978), 14–16, 26–29, 33–36.

[119] *Trig* 965. *"Ohne alle Lehre"* (SD VI, 6; *BS* 961).

[120] See *Trig* 965. *"Ohne alle Lehre"* (SD VI, 6; *BS* 961).

[121] *"Wenn aber der Mensch durch den Geist Gottes neugeboren und vom Gesetz freigemacht, das ist, von diesem Treiber ledig worden und von den Geist Christi getrieben wird, so lebet er nach den unwandelbaren Willen Gottes, im Gesetz begriffen und tut alles, soviel er neugeboren ist, aus freiem lustigem Geist; und solchs heißen nicht eigentlich Werk des Gesetzes, sondern Werke und Früchte des Geistes, oder wie es S. Paulus nennet, das Gesetz des Gemüts und Gesetz Christi; Dann solche Leute sind 'nicht mehr unter dem Gesetz, sondern unter der Gnaden,' wie S. Paulus sagt, Ro. 8"* (SD VI, 17; *BS* 967; *Trig* 967).

[122] Jungkuntz, "Looking for Light on the Heat," 10.

[123] See Jungkuntz, "Looking for Light on the Heat," 10.

[124] Jungkuntz, "Looking for Light on the Heat," 10.

[125] See Jungkuntz, "Looking for Light on the Heat," 10.

[126] See SD XI, 35; *BS* 1074; *Trig* 1075.

[127] Schlink, *Theology of the Lutheran Confessions*, 278.

[128] Rom 10:4.

[129] See SD VI, 24; *BS* 969; *Trig* 969–71.

[130] 1 Cor 13:12.

[131] See Theodore R. Jungkuntz, "Ethics in a Relativizing Society: Between the Relativisms of Moralism and Antinomianism," in *Confession and Congregation*, 12.

[132] A helpful definition of moralism was provided by David P. Scaer: "Moralism might be defined as living one's life according to certain directives, most of which seem to be negative prohibitions. Another definition might be making morality a goal in itself. Right or proper behavior becomes the end or goal of the philosophical or religious system" (Scaer, "Sanctification in the Lutheran Confessions," *CTQ* 53 [July 1989]: 165).

[133] Jungkuntz, "Ethics in a Relativizing Society," 12.

[134] See Jungkuntz, "Ethics in a Relativizing Society," 14; and Jungkuntz, "Looking for Light on the Heat," 11.

[135] Jungkuntz, "Looking for Light on the Heat," 11.

[136] Jungkuntz, "Looking for Light on the Heat," 11.

[137] *"So ist auch solche Lehre des Gesetzes den Gläubigen darum nötig, auf das sie nicht auf eigene Heiligkeit und Andacht fallen und unter dem Schein des Geistes Gottes eigen erwählten Gottesdienst, ohn Gottes Wort und Befehl, anrichten, wie geschrieben steht Deuter. 12: 'Ihr sollet deren keines tuen, ein jeder was ihm recht dünket, sondern höret die Gebot und Rechte, die ich euch gebiete,' und 'sollet auch nichts darzutuen noch darvontuen'"* (SD VI, 20; *BS* 968; *Trig* 969).

[138] David G. Truemper, a professor of theology at Valparaiso University, was critical of the Missouri Synod's insistence upon a significant and binding subscription to the Lutheran symbols. He asserted that the Confessions were used as a source of "orthodox utterances" designed to enforce doctrinal conformity. He called this the " 'electric fence' theory of confessional loyalty." Truemper advocated "theology without boxes." See Truemper, "Confession and Congregation: An Approach to the Study of

the Formula of Concord," in *Confession and Congregation*, 3. Jungkuntz responded to "theology without boxes," rejecting it as atheistic, at bottom. "Ethics in our contemporary, secularized society often means ethics without God, and its corollary, ethics without boxes. It means an ethics of relativism. And the Formula of Concord has taught us something about how to deal with that" (Jungkuntz, "Ethics in a Relativizing Society," 15).

[139] Roger D. Pittelko, then an LCMS parish pastor, concurred with Jungkuntz's concern. "If there is one thing that troubled us and continues to trouble us, it is the place of the Law. We live in a culture that was formed with a very different view of the Law from that of the Formula of Concord. How has that colored and affected our teaching? Legalism is not an unknown emphasis that many Lutherans have experienced. And it is one extreme. That emphasis is quite at home in a Calvinistic-Puritan setting. But what of the other extreme, that of no Law, of 'do your own thing' as the decade of the sixties taught us, or of 'situation ethics' of recent memory? Law and its place, or the lack of any place, is a question that faces every Christian. Have we bothered to use the resources of Articles V and VI of the Formula of Concord?" (Roger D. Pittelko, "Confession and Congregation: Resources for Parish Life and Work," in *Confession and Congregation*, 35).

[140] Jungkuntz, "Ethics in a Relativizing Society," 15.

[141] Jungkuntz, "Ethics in a Relativizing Society," 15.

[142] Jungkuntz, "Ethics in a Relativizing Society," 12.

[143] *"In der Auferstehung erneuert, do er weder der Predig des Gesetzes noch seiner Trauung und Strafen wie auch des Evangelii nicht mehr bedürfen wird, die in dies unvollkommen Leben gehören; sondern wie sie Gott von Angesicht zu Angesicht anschauen, also werden sie durch Kraft des einwohnenden Geistes Gottes freiwillig"* (SD VI, 24–25; BS 969; *Trig* 969–71).

[144] The famed *rabies theologorum*.

[145] See Ep V, 6–7; *BS* 791; *Trig* 803).

[146] Jungkuntz, "Looking for Light on the Heat," 12.

[147] Jungkuntz considered the debate on the third use of the Law to have significant implications for church fellowship. He responded to the wrangling at the Valparaiso University conference with a clear application of biblical church fellowship principles. "However, it was startling to me to have Dr. Lazareth publicly label me a 'moralist' in his presentation and shortly thereafter give to me 'the right hand of fellowship' (Gal. 2:9), only then to return to calling me a 'moralist.' I should prefer his 'anathema.' That, at least, seems consistent with the biblical and confessional implication given to the concept. Paul never treated the moralist with 'sloppy agape,' although he did speak the truth in love" (Jungkuntz, "Gamesmanship or Dialogue?" 22).

[148] Jungkuntz, "Response to Dr. Lazareth," 59.

[149] Klug is professor of systematic theology at Concordia Theological Seminary, Fort Wayne, Indiana.

[150] Jeffrey Silcock wrote two theses at Concordia Seminary that further detail Luther's views on Law and Gospel. These theses are useful gatherings of the data. See Silcock, "Law and Gospel in Luther's Antinomian Disputations, with Special Reference to Faith's Use of the Law" (Th.D. diss., Concordia Seminary, 1996); and Silcock, "Luther and the Third Use of the Law, with Special Reference to His Great *Galatians Commentary*" (S.T.M. thesis, Concordia Seminary, 1993).

[151] See Eugene F. Klug, "Confessional Emphasis on Law and Gospel for Our Day," *CTQ* 42 (July 1978): 241–42.

[152] Eugene F. Klug, "The Third Use of the Law," in *Contemporary Look*, 192.

[153] Klug, "Third Use of the Law," in *Contemporary Look*, 202.

[154] Klug, "Third Use of the Law," in *Contemporary Look*, 200.

[155] Klug, "Third Use of the Law," in *Contemporary Look*, 201.

[156] Robert Kolb suggested that a use of *Gebot* could be beneficial in his discussion of the "Instructive Use of the Law." "It has been suggested that the distinction between Law and command may be a useful way of describing two different functions of God's Law in daily Christian living. Law designates the oppressive functions of God's plan as it makes its condemning or curbing impact upon the believer's sinful will. Command designates the instructive function of that same plan, as God offers guidance for what the believer does—or will do, or should do, or ought to do" (Kolb, *The Christian Faith* [St. Louis: Concordia, 1993], 119–20). This is a significant deviation from the LCMS position and leaves unanswered the question of the relationship between the Law and *Gebot*. Kolb fails to give a compelling reason why *Gebot* is superior to the term "third use of the Law."

[157] Klug, "Third Use of the Law," in *Contemporary Look*, 202.

[158] Klug, "Third Use of the Law," in *Contemporary Look*, 202.

[159] See Klug, "Third Use of the Law," in *Contemporary Look*, 203.

[160] Klug, "Third Use of the Law," in *Contemporary Look*, 203.

[161] See Jungkuntz, "Looking for Light on the Heat," 11.

[162] Acts 1:1–2.

[163] See Scaer, "Formula of Concord Article VI," 147. Scaer probably has Gen 1:2 in mind, in which classic Lutheran exegesis takes אלהים רוח to be the Holy Spirit. See, for example, LW 1:9. Although Gen 1:2 may come to mind as a reference to the original work of creation, the closest the Bible gets to saying that the Spirit completes creation is Rom 8:22–23, where the redemptive work of God is also communicated to the groaning creation.

[164] Scaer, "Formula of Concord Article VI," 147. See Rom 2:15.

[165] Scaer, "Formula of Concord Article VI," 147. See also SD VI, 3; *BS* 963; *Trig* 963.

[166] Scaer, "Formula of Concord Article VI," 148; emphasis in the original.

[167] See SD II, 72; *BS* 901; *Trig* 909.

[168] "The Lutheran Confessions stand against the idea that the Gospel must be construed as the removal of the Law itself. The Gospel is the removal of sin and guilt and the resulting curse, for all this was shouldered by the Lamb of God" (Ken Schurb, " 'The Law Always Accuses' in the Augsburg Confession and the Apology," *CJ* 23 [October 1997]: 349).

[169] Scaer, "Formula of Concord Article VI," 148.

[170] See Forde, "Christian Life," in *Christian Dogmatics;* and Forde, *Law-Gospel Debate*.

[171] Scaer, "Formula of Concord Article VI," 149.

[172] See pp. 103–07.

[173] See SD VI, 4, 14; *BS* 963, 966; *Trig* 963, 967.

[174] Scaer, "Formula of Concord Article VI," 149.

[175] See Scaer, "Formula of Concord Article VI," 149.

[176] Deut 32:39.

[177] See pp. 103–07. The theologians of the Valparaiso school reduced the divine revelation to the Gospel. Barth viewed the scriptural revelation as all equal in its applicability, whether Law or Gospel, both being revelation. Orthodox Lutheranism held that all of Scripture was equally divine, yet the contents of Scripture could be distinguished in their significance to the church on the basis of Law and Gospel. The question to be answered, among others, is, "Is this word of God *pro me?*" not "Is it a word of God at all?"

[178] Scaer, "Formula of Concord Article VI," 149.

[179] See p. 191.

[180] See Scaer, "Formula of Concord Article VI," 150.

[181] Scaer, "Formula of Concord Article VI," 151.

[182] This point is similar to the view of David S. Yeago, see pp. 178–85. Ken Schurb reviewed the teaching of the Augsburg Confession and the Apology of the Augsburg Confession with Yeago's view in mind. He concluded that the Law's accusatory power resides in the sinfulness of humans. "The Law accuses people, but not simply because it is Law. After all, before the first sin Adam had the Law, but he was not accused by it. The Law accuses people as it points to their sin and thus shows them to be sinners" (Schurb, " 'The Law Always Accuses,' " 349).

[183] Scaer expressed this same point elsewhere as well. See David P. Scaer, "Law and Gospel in Lutheran Theology," *Grace Theological Journal* 12 (Fall 1991): 172.

[184] Scaer, "Law and Gospel in Lutheran Theology," 172.

[185] Rom 7:15–25.

[186] Scaer, "Formula of Concord Article VI," 151. Here Scaer is very much like Althaus who characterizes the difference between *Gesetz* and *Gebot* on the basis of the response of the Christian.

[187] Scaer, "Formula of Concord Article VI," 151.

[188] This is why Scaer rightly suggests that Article VI of the Formula of Concord is not properly titled. "Article VI of the Formula of Concord would better be entitled 'The Three Uses of the Law' and not simply 'The Third Use of the Law' " (Scaer, "Sanctification in the Lutheran Confessions," 179).

[189] Scaer, "Sanctification in the Lutheran Confessions," 154.

[190] David P. Scaer, "Sanctification in Lutheran Theology," *CTQ* 49 (April–July 1985): 187.

[191] Scaer, "Sanctification in Lutheran Theology," 187.

[192] Scaer, "Sanctification in Lutheran Theology," 187.

[193] See Scaer, "Sanctification in Lutheran Theology," 181. "*Ich glaube, daß Jesus Christus, wahrhaftiger Gott, vom Vater in Ewigkeit geboren, und auch wahrhaftiger Mensch, von der Jungfrauen Maria geboren, sei mein HERR, der mich verlornen und verdammpten Menschen erlöset hat, erworben, gewonnen und von allen Sunden, vom Tode und von der Gewalt des Teufels, nicht mit Gold oder Silber, sondern mit seinem heiligen, teuren Blut und mit seinem unschüldigen Leiden und Sterben, auf daß ich sein eigen sei und in seinem Reich unter ihm lebe und ihme diene in ewiger Gerechtigkeit, Unschuld und Seligkeit, gleichwie er ist auferstanden vom Tode, lebet und regieret in Ewigkeit; das ist*

gewisslich wahr" (SC II, 2; *BS* 511; *Trig* 543).

[194] Scaer, "Sanctification in Lutheran Theology," 185.

[195] In a thought-provoking article about the use of the norming authority of the Lutheran Confessions, Charles P. Arand and James W. Voelz make the same point. "The Christological principle, in turn, provides the foundation for the confessional distinction between Law and Gospel. Put another way, the distinction between Law and Gospel is another expression of the Christological principle" (Arand and Voelz, "The Lutheran Confessions as Normative Guides for Reading Scripture," *CJ* 21 [October 1995]: 373).

[196] This, too, may be part of the Melanchthonian legacy. See Robert Kolb, "The Ordering of the *Loci Communes Theologici*: The Structuring of the Melanchthonian Dogmatic Tradition," *CJ* 23 (October 1997): 317–37.

HOW HAS
THE THIRD USE FARED?

The information presented here leads to several conclusions about the doctrine of the third use of the Law in American Lutheranism. Those conclusions will be reviewed under nine headings: (1) Luther Renaissance, (2) European Theology, (3) Theological Hermeneutics, (4) Theological Method and Church Authority, (5) Third Use and Gospel Reductionism, (6) Modern Antinomianism and the Third Use, (7) The *Simul*, (8) The *Semper*, and (9) *Quo Vadis?*

LUTHER RENAISSANCE

The Luther renaissance had a great impact on Lutheran theology in America. Beginning in the 1940s, American Lutheran theologians explored the results of burgeoning Luther studies and in doing so were faced with a new picture of Luther—a Luther quite different from the one portrayed in the literature of orthodoxy, including in the Lutheran Confessions. Many American Lutheran theologians enthusiastically embraced the existentialistic Luther of the Luther renaissance. Some, such as Jaroslav Pelikan and Richard R. Caemmerer, brought this new Luther into the heart of Old Lutheran orthodoxy in The Lutheran Church— Missouri Synod. Since Luther studies have always had an enormous influence on Lutheran systematic theology, the new Luther of the Luther renaissance caused reassessments of significant points of Lutheran theology. Law and Gospel was certainly one of those points.

The reassessment of the place and meaning of Law and Gospel in Lutheran theology resulted in the third use of the Law coming under intense scrutiny. The Luther renaissance had determined that the genuine Luther had rejected the Law as an eternal expression of the divine will.

However, this conclusion had more to do with the existentialistic presuppositions of the Luther scholars than Luther's own views. Nonetheless, the light of this new Luther lifted the putatively oppressive orthodoxy of the mid–20th century in favor of "Neo-Lutheranism." Many Lutheran theologians spurned Melanchthon and his Aristotelian rigidity and denigrated his contributions to the Lutheran Reformation as less than Lutheran.

Lutheran theologians began to dissolve the tensions created by Law and Gospel in favor of the Gospel. Under this process the third use of the Law was considered sub-Christian and unLutheran.

In the late 1950s the results of the Luther renaissance began to undergo revision. This work was confined to the Luther scholars and historians until well into the 1970s, when the theological community began to take notice of their work. Increasingly Luther scholars and theologians abandoned the existentialistic presuppositions of the Luther renaissance for a more positive assessment of church organization, discipline, and Law in the work of Luther.

European Theology

Neo-orthodoxy dominated European theology during the 1940s. Neo-orthodoxy was influenced by existentialism, just as Luther studies were. Neo-orthodoxy focused on the importance of the encounter with God and, like the Luther renaissance, downplayed the importance of ontological categories or static "doctrines." The place of the Law and the third use of the Law in Lutheran theology suffered under this thinking.

Karl Barth's views on the relationship of Law and Gospel, shaped as they were by Calvin, generated a great deal of polemical discussion within European theology. Lutheran theologians such as Elert fled from the slightest taint of Calvinism. Since Calvin taught a third use of the Law, the Lutheran doctrine of the third use came under suspicion. Previous discussion in this book has shown that there are substantial differences between Calvin's doctrine and the Lutheran doctrine of the third use of the Law. However, many American Lutherans studied in Germany under Elert and other Lutherans and returned to America ready to reject the third use of the Law as Calvinistic.[1]

Theologians of the ELCA and the Valparaiso school rejected the third use of the Law. The old Missourians, such as F. E. Mayer, were opposed to the developments in Lutheran theology caused by contact with neo-orthodoxy and existentialism, but they were not unaffected by either. Later Missourians repudiated neo-orthodoxy and existentialism.

Ecclesiastical conflict erupted between the Missourians and the Valparaiso theologians in the LCMS over the third use of the Law (among other things) because of the different presuppositions held by the two groups. The circumstances of the ecclesiastical conflict may also have served to increase the differences, as party politics sometimes does. For example, the theologians of the Valparaiso school often made more distinct statements rejecting the third use of the Law than the ELCA theologians did working from similar presuppositions. The *rabies theologorum* was not eradicated in the 16th century. Distinct battle lines were drawn between the camps. Only as Luther scholars reassessed the positive contributions of the later Luther were there any signs of rapprochement, and that primarily by younger ELCA theologians who had not been involved in the bitter disputes of the 1960s and 1970s.

Theological Hermeneutics

Two major hermeneutical issues arose from the conflicts about the third use. First, the theologians of the Valparaiso school argued that Law and Gospel function as a biblical hermeneutic. They saw Law and Gospel as an interpretive filter through which all exegetical conclusions are strained. They claimed that this filter was to serve as a Lutheran modification to the historical critical method of biblical interpretation. In actuality, however, it served merely to deflect criticism of the unLutheran nature of the historical critical methodology. More significant, in Lutheran theology the Law and Gospel hermeneutic is not an exegetical tool, but a theological tool. Scripture gives the data for Law and Gospel, not vice versa. Scripture shapes Law and Gospel; therefore, Law and Gospel can shape Lutheran dogmatic and confessional theology. Thus, these theologians had diverted the Law and Gospel construct from its theological purpose.

Second, Law and Gospel are not the only interpretive guides to be taken into account when shaping the Lutheran theological process. Some theologians took a narrow view of the Law and Gospel theological hermeneutic, so narrow in fact that they ignored or greatly minimized other central theological concerns, such as the incarnation. David S. Yeago of the ELCA and David P. Scaer of the Missouri Synod opposed this tendency.

THEOLOGICAL METHOD AND CHURCH AUTHORITY

Where the third use of the Law was rejected, the whole notion of the church's authority over doctrinal expression fell into disrepair. If the Gospel frees, it was argued, it certainly frees from church authority. The Missourians were concerned about preserving the substance of the faith. Therefore, they emphasized the ways in which the third use of the Law defended the doctrine of the church and guided the church's teachers away from destructive approaches to theology. Younger ELCA theologians also became concerned about the need for teaching authority in the church. David S. Yeago strenuously argued for this.

THIRD USE AND GOSPEL REDUCTIONISM

The theologians of the Valparaiso school reduced the dialectic of Law and Gospel so significantly that their approach was labeled "Gospel reductionism." Now only the Gospel had any normative authority in the church. Unfortunately, this was a truncated Gospel, often nothing more than a vague bromide of "good news for a bad situation." The Law had no place in the life of the Christian.

When the Law is nothing more than that which accuses, it cannot provide direction to the Christian for living in Christ. The lack of the Law in the preaching of the church sends theologians looking for ways to describe the Bible's own moral directives without using the term *Law*. Several different schemes were put forward, the most useful of which was the *Gebot* doctrine of Paul Althaus. However, commonly the Law was reintroduced to Lutheran theology by calling it parenesis or Gospel imperative. Few Lutheran theologians who denied the third use of the Law avoided this dangerous confusion of Law and Gospel.[2]

Gospel reductionism has a negative effect on many points of Lutheran theology. A doctrine that does not pass through the narrow Gospel reductionistic defile is ripe for rejection. Central Lutheran teachings can be jettisoned because they are "not-the-Gospel." This theological method was used also by ELCA theologians, though most often with less radical results than when used by those of the Valparaiso school. Increasingly, during the 1980s and 1990s, the Missourians and also some younger ELCA theologians rejected Gospel reductionism. The corrosive results of Gospel reductionism upon central points of doctrine had warned theologians. The third use of the Law as a sign of doctrinal discipline for teachers of the church has begun to return to favor among American Lutherans.

MODERN ANTINOMIANISM AND THE THIRD USE

Supporters of the third use of the Law warned that by denying it the church would be in jeopardy of falling into moral laxity. This moral laxity was predicted to bring an antinomianism deeper than the 16th-century version. Both Missourians and some alarmed ELCA theologians are now concluding that this prediction was correct. The ELCA's attempts to give direction about sexual ethics outside of a proper understanding of Law and Gospel have again stirred up the issue of the normative character of the Law.

THE *SIMUL*

The *simul justus et peccator* provides the anthropological shape to the application of Law and Gospel. The Valparaiso and ELCA theologians tended to discount the importance of anthropology, whereas the Missourians had a developed sense of human sinfulness and thus the abiding importance of the Law in the Christian life. Forde in particular tried to leapfrog the datum of human depravity with his eschatological view of the human situation. Forde suggested that the converted person was so firmly set in the kingdom to come that the Law no longer applied because it belonged only to the old age. However, the *simul* still obtains because the Christian remains in the old age and the new age, as sinner and righteous, simultaneously. The Christian needs both the Gospel and the Law until he draws his dying breath.

The Law applies to the Christian *quatenus* she or he is still a sinner. The Gospel applies to the Christian *quatenus* he or she is a believer in Christ. The *quatenus* applies in the *simul* to the whole person, what the Missourians called the *concretum*. This is the Missourian response, drawn from the Formula of Concord, to an inadequate anthropology.

THE *SEMPER*

The Valparaiso and ELCA theologians interpreted the dictum of the Apology of the Augsburg Confession *semper accusat lex* so as to rule out a third use of the Law. They argued that if the Law accused it could not also be a guide or rule for life. However, no Lutheran theologian had ever argued that the Law did not accuse even if it functioned as a rule for life. As the Christian lives in the *simul* the Law always accuses, condemning the old Adam while instructing and delighting the new Adam with God's eternal will. The *semper* does not rule out a third use of the Law. God uses the Law for his purposes in his time. The younger ELCA theologians, such as Yeago, have begun teaching a positive use of the Law while not rejecting the *semper*.

Quo Vadis?

The younger ELCA theologians are now moving toward the Missourians on the third use of the Law. How this convergence will progress still remains to be seen. Unfortunately, other significant theological issues still need resolution, such as the authority of Scripture, the meaning of the real presence, and the significance of the teaching office.[3]

Conclusion

The different approaches to the third use of the Law reflected differing approaches to prolegomena and affected other doctrines. During the first period of this study (1940–60), the Missourians, on the one hand, and the theologians of the ELCA and the Valparaiso school, on the other hand, worked with differing definitions of *Law*, differing views on the relationship of Law and Gospel in the Christian life, and differing convictions on the authority of the Bible and the Lutheran Confessions in the theology and life of the church. This period was characterized by a rediscovery of the importance of the Law and Gospel dialectic to Lutheran theology and tentative attempts to understand how the third use of the Law functions in Lutheran theology.

In the second period (1961–76), the ELCA and Valparaiso theologians distinctly rejected the third use of the Law. The position of the groups on the third use of the Law revolved around the doctrinal controversy centered in the LCMS. A hardening of the differences was exhibited in this period. The LCMS theologians defended the third use more strongly than they had in the previous period. Conflicting views about prolegomena also became clearer at this time. The ELCA and Valparaiso theologians accepted the historical critical method of interpreting the Bible, and the LCMS theologians rejected the historical critical method. This had an impact on the way each group used Law and Gospel.

During the third period (1977–98), approaches to the third use of the Law changed from the previous period. The position of younger ELCA theologians grew closer to the position of the Missourians, as the opposing points of view of the previous period were too extreme to defend and also damaging to important theological truths embodied in the issues of prolegomena and the character and integrity of the Gospel. Many American Lutheran theologians found a legitimate place for the third use of the Law in contemporary Lutheran theology.

NOTES

[1] The students of these German-trained Americans still speak of the third use as Calvinistic, though they are now supporting a "positive use" of the Law.

[2] The exception was Gerhard O. Forde, who saw the confusion of Law and Gospel inherent in Paul Althaus's *Gebot* approach.

[3] See Ralph A. Bohlmann, "Missouri Lutheranism, 1945 and 1995," *Lutheran Forum* 30 (February 1996): 17.

BIBLIOGRAPHY

BOOKS

Adams, James E. *Preus of Missouri and the Great Lutheran Civil War.* New York: Harper & Row, 1977.

Aland, Kurt, ed. *Martin Luther's Ninety-Five Theses.* Translated by P. J. Schroeder. St. Louis: Concordia, 1967.

ALC/LCMS Commission on Fellowship. *The American Lutheran Church and The Lutheran Church—Missouri Synod: A Statement on Doctrinal Differences.* St. Louis: The Lutheran Church—Missouri Synod, 1980.

Althaus, Paul. *The Divine Command.* Translated by Franklin Sherman. Philadelphia: Fortress, 1966.

———. *The Ethics of Martin Luther.* Translated by Robert C. Schultz. Philadelphia: Fortress, 1972.

———. *Gebot und Gesetz Zum Gesetz und Evangelium.* Beiträge zur Förderung christlicher Theologie 46. Edited by Paul Althaus and Joachim Jeremias. Gütersloh: C. Bertelsmann, 1952.

Anderson, George H., T. Austin Murphy, and Joseph A. Burgess, eds. *Justification by Faith.* Lutherans and Catholics in Dialogue VII. Minneapolis: Augsburg, 1985.

Aulén, Gustaf. *Church, Law and Society.* With an Introduction by Nels F. S. Ferré. New York: Charles Scribner's Sons, 1948.

———. *The Faith of the Christian Church.* Translated by Eric H. Wahlstrom and G. Everett Arden. Philadelphia: Muhlenberg, 1948.

Baier, John William. *Compendium Theologiae Positivae.* Edited by C. F. W. Walther. 2 vols. St. Louis: Concordia, 1879.

Bainton, Roland H. *Here I Stand: A Life of Martin Luther.* Nashville: Abingdon, 1950.

Barth, Karl. *Epistle to the Romans.* 6th ed. Translated by Edwyn Hoskyns. London: Oxford University Press, 1933.

———. *Evangelium und Gesetz.* Theologische Existenz Heute 32. Edited by Karl Barth and Eduard Thurneysen. Munich: Chr. Kaiser, 1935.

———. "Gospel and Law." In *Community, State, and Church.* Translated by A. M. Hall. Garden City: Doubleday Anchor, 1960.

————. *Nein! Antwort an Emil Brunner*. Theologische Existenz Heute 14. Edited by Karl Barth and Eduard Thurneysen. Munich: Chr. Kaiser, 1934.

Bartling, Walter J. "Hermeneutics and Pauline Parenesis." In *A Project in Biblical Hermeneutics*. Edited by Richard Jungkuntz. St. Louis: The Commission on Theology and Church Relations of The Lutheran Church—Missouri Synod, 1969.

Becker, Siegbert. "The Gospel." In *The Abiding Word*. Vol. 2. Edited by Theodore Laetsch. St. Louis: Concordia, 1946.

Behnken, John W. *This I Recall*. St. Louis: Concordia, 1964.

Die Bekenntnisschriften der evangelischen-lutherischen Kirche. Göttingen: Vandenhoeck & Ruprecht, 1979.

Bente, Friedrich. "Historical Introduction to the Symbolical Books." In *Concordia Triglotta*. St. Louis: Concordia, 1921.

Bente, Friedrich., and W. H. T. Dau, trans. and eds. *Concordia Triglotta*. St. Louis: Concordia, 1921.

Bergendoff, Conrad. *The Church of the Lutheran Reformation*. St. Louis: Concordia, 1967.

Bernthal, August. "Learn from Jesus—God's Own Formula of Concord." In *Confession and Congregation. The Cresset Occasional Paper, III*. Edited by David G. Truemper. Valparaiso: Valparaiso University Press, 1978.

Bertram, Robert W. "A Time for Confessing: When Is the Church a Confessional Movement?" In *Confession and Congregation. The Cresset Occasional Paper, III*. Edited by David G. Truemper. Valparaiso: Valparaiso University Press, 1978.

————, ed. *The Lively Function of the Gospel*. St. Louis: Concordia, 1966.

————, ed. *Theology in the Life of the Church*. Philadelphia: Fortress, 1963.

Bigane, Jack, and Kenneth Hagen. *Annotated Bibliography of Luther Studies, 1967–1976*. Sixteenth Century Bibliography 9. St. Louis: Center for Reformation Research, 1977.

Board of Control of Concordia Seminary, St. Louis, Mo., The. *The. Exodus from Concordia*. St. Louis: Concordia College, 1977.

Bohlmann, Ralph A. *Principles of Biblical Interpretation in the Lutheran Confessions*. Rev. ed. St. Louis: Concordia, 1983.

————. "Principles of Biblical Interpretation in the Lutheran Confessions." In *Crisis in Lutheran Theology*. Vol. 2. Edited by John W. Montgomery. Grand Rapids: Baker, 1967. 2d rev. ed., Minneapolis: Bethany Fellowship, 1973.

Böhmer, Heinrich. *Luther in the Light of Recent Research*. Translated by Carl F. Hutch Jr. New York: The Christian Herald, 1916.

Bonhoeffer, Dietrich. *Ethics*. Edited by Eberhard Bethge. Translated by N. H. Smith. New York: Macmillan, 1962.

Bornkamm, Heinrich. *Luther and the Old Testament*. Edited by Victor I. Gruhn.

Translated by Eric W. and Ruth C. Gritsch. Philadelphia: Fortress, 1969.

———. *Luther in Mid-Career, 1521–1530*. Edited by Karin Bornkamm. Translated by E. Theodore Bachmann. Philadelphia: Fortress, 1983.

Bouman, Walter R. "Piety in a Secularized Society." In *Confession and Congregation. The Cresset. Occasional Paper, III.* Edited by David G. Truemper. Valparaiso: Valparaiso University Press, 1978.

Braaten, Carl E. *The Future of God.* New York: Harper & Row, 1969.

———. *No Other Gospel.* Minneapolis: Fortress: 1992.

Brecht, Martin. *Martin Luther: The Preservation of the Church, 1532–1546.* Translated by James L. Schaaf. Minneapolis: Fortress, 1993.

———. *Martin Luther: Shaping and Defining the Reformation, 1521–1532.* Translated by James L. Schaaf. Minneapolis: Fortress, 1990.

Bretscher, Paul G. *After the Purifying.* River Forest: Lutheran Education Association, 1975.

Brooks, Peter Newman, ed. *Seven-Headed Luther.* New York: Oxford University Press, 1983.

Brunner, Emil. *The Divine Imperative.* Translated by Olive Wyon. Philadelphia: Westminster, 1947.

———. *Man in Revolt.* Translated by Olive Wyon. Philadelphia: Westminster, 1947.

Buber, Martin. *I and Thou.* Translated by Ronald Gregor Smith. New York: Scribner, 1957.

Calov, Abraham. *Systema Locorum Theologicorum.* 12 vols. Wittenberg, 1655–77.

Calvin, John. *Institutes of the Christian Religion.* Translated by Henry Beveridge. 2 vols. Grand Rapids: Eerdmans, 1970.

———. *"Institutio Christianae Religionis."* In *Opera Selecta.* Vol. 3. Edited by Peter Barth and William Niesel. Munich: Christian Kaiser, 1928.

Chemnitz, Martin. *Loci Theologici.* 2 vols. Frankfurt: Christian Henry Schumacher, 1690.

———. *Loci Theologici.* Translated by J. A. O. Preus. 2 vols. St. Louis: Concordia, 1989.

Childress, James F., and John Macquarrie, eds. *The Westminster Dictionary of Christian Ethics.* Philadelphia: Westminster, 1986. Rev. ed. of *A Dictionary of Christian Ethics.* Philadelphia: Westminster, 1967.

Childs, James M., Jr. *Christian Anthropology and Ethics.* Philadelphia: Fortress, 1978.

Cochrane, Arthur C. "The Act of Confession/Confessing." In *Confession and Congregation. The Cresset Occasional Paper, III.* Edited by David G. Truemper. Valparaiso: Valparaiso University Press, 1978.

———. *The Church's Confession under Hitler.* Philadelphia: Westminster, 1962.

Commission on Theology and Church Relations. *Gospel and Scripture.* St. Louis:

The Lutheran Church—Missouri Synod, 1972.

Cragg, Gerald R. *The Church and the Age of Reason 1648–1789.* The Pelican History of the Church 4. New York: Penguin, 1960.

Creighton, James E. *An Introductory Logic.* 4th ed. New York: Macmillan, 1920.

Damm, John S., ed. *The Teaching of Religion.* River Forest: Lutheran Education Association, 1965.

Danker, Frederick W. *No Room in the Brotherhood.* St. Louis: Clayton Publishing House, 1977.

Denifle, Heinrich. *Luther und Luthertum in der Ersten Entwicklung.* Mainz: Kirchheim, 1904.

Dewar, Lindsay. *The Holy Spirit and Modern Thought.* New York: Harper, 1959.

Dodd, C. H. *Gospel and Law.* New York: Columbia University Press, 1951.

Dünnhaupt, Gerhard, ed. *The Martin Luther Quincentennial.* Detroit: Wayne State University Press, 1985.

Ebeling, Gerhard. *Word and Faith.* Translated by James W. Leitch. Philadelphia: Fortress, 1963.

Edwards, Mark U., Jr. *Luther and the False Brethren.* Stanford: Stanford University Press, 1975.

———. *Luther's Last Battles.* Leiden: E. J. Brill, 1983.

Edwards, Paul, ed. *The Encyclopedia of Philosophy.* 8 vols. Repr. ed. New York: Macmillan, 1972.

Elert, Werner. *Law and Gospel.* Translated by Edward H. Schroeder. Philadelphia: Fortress, 1967.

———. *The Christian Ethos.* Translated by Carl J. Schindler. Philadelphia: Muhlenberg, 1957.

———. *The Christian Faith.* 5th ed. Translated by Martin H. Bertram and Walter R. Bouman. Master's Thesis. Luther Seminary Library, St. Paul, 1974.

———. *Der christliche Glaube: Grundlinien der lutherischen Dogmatik.* 5th ed. Edited by Ernst Kinder. Hamburg: Furche-Verlag, 1956.

———. *The Structure of Lutheranism.* Translated by Walter A. Hansen. St. Louis: Concordia, 1962.

Elwell, Walter A., ed. *Handbook of Evangelical Theologians.* Grand Rapids: Baker, 1993.

Fagerberg, Holsten. *A New Look at the Lutheran Confessions.* Translated by Gene J. Lund. St. Louis: Concordia, 1972.

Fendt, Edward C., ed. *What Lutherans Are Thinking.* Columbus: Wartburg, 1947.

Fletcher, Joseph. *Moral Responsibility.* Philadelphia: Westminster, 1967.

Forde, Gerhard O. "Christian Life." In *Christian Dogmatics.* Vol. 2. Edited by Carl E. Braaten and Robert W. Jenson. Philadelphia: Fortress, 1984.

———. *Justification by Faith.* Philadelphia: Fortress, 1982.

———. "Law and Gospel as the Methodological Principle of Theology." In *Theological Perspectives*. Decorah: Luther College Press, 1967.

———. *The Law-Gospel Debate*. Minneapolis: Augsburg, 1969.

———. *Theology Is for Proclamation*. Minneapolis: Fortress, 1990.

———. *Where God Meets Man*. Minneapolis: Augsburg, 1972.

Forell, George W. *Ethics of Decision*. Philadelphia: Muhlenberg, 1955.

———. *Faith Active in Love*. Minneapolis: Augsburg, 1954.

———. "Law and Gospel." In *Marburg Revisited*. Edited by Paul C. Empie and James I. McCord. Minneapolis: Augsburg, 1966.

Franzmann, Martin H. *Bad Boll 1949*. St. Louis: The Lutheran Church— Missouri Synod, 1950.

Frör, Kurt. *Biblische Hermeneutik: zur Schriftauslegung in Predigt und Unterricht*. Munich: Kaiser, 1961.

Geihsler, Walter. "The Law and the Gospel." In *The Abiding Word*. Vol. 1. Edited by Theodore Laetsch. St. Louis: Concordia, 1946.

Gerhard, John. *Loci Theologici*. Edited by Eduard Preuss. 9 vols. Berlin: Schlawitz, 1867.

Gerrish, Brian A. *Grace and Reason*. Oxford: Clarendon Press, 1962.

Gonzalez, Justo L. *A History of Christian Thought*. Vol. 3. Nashville: Abingdon, 1975.

Graebner, Theodore. *The Borderland of Right and Wrong*. Rev. ed. St. Louis: Concordia, 1956.

Green, Lowell C. *How Melanchthon Helped Luther Discover the Gospel*. Fallbrook: Verdict Publications, 1980.

Grenz, Stanley J., and Roger E. Olsen. *Twentieth-Century Theology*. Downers Grove: InterVarsity, 1992.

Gritsch, Eric W., and Robert W. Jenson. *Lutheranism*. Philadelphia: Fortress, 1976.

Grisar, Hartmann. *Luther*. 3 vols. Freiburg im Breisgau: Herder, 1911–12.

Haikola, Lauri. *Gesetz und Evangelium bei Matthias Flacius Illyricus*. Studia Theologica Lundensia 1. Lund: C. W. K. Gleerup, 1952.

———. "*Melanchthons und Luthers Lehre von der Rechtfertigung.*" In *Luther and Melanchthon in the History and Theology of the Reformation*. Edited by Vilmos Vajta. Philadelphia: Muhlenberg, 1961.

———. *Studien zu Luther und sum Luthertum*. Uppsala Universitets Årsskrift 1958:2. Uppsala: B. Lundequistska Bokhandeln, 1958.

Hals, Ronald M. *Grace and Faith in the Old Testament*. Minneapolis: Augsburg, 1980.

Hamann, Henry P. "Article V: Law and Gospel." In *A Contemporary Look at the Formula of Concord*. Edited by Robert D. Preus and Wilbert Rosin. St. Louis: Concordia, 1978.

Harnack, Adolf von. *What Is Christianity?* Translated by Thomas Bailey Sanders. New York: G. P. Putnam's Sons, 1904.

Harnack, Adolf von, and Hans Lietzmann. *Karl Holl: Zwei Gedächtnisreden.* Berlin: Walter de Gruyter, 1926.

Harran, Marilyn J. *Luther on Conversion: The Early Years.* Ithaca: Cornell University Press, 1983.

————, ed. *Luther and Learning.* Selinsgrove: Susquehanna University Press, 1985.

Hebart, Friedemann. *One in the Gospel: The Formula of Concord for Our Day.* Adelaide: Lutheran Publishing House, 1979. Repr., St. Louis: Concordia, 1980.

Heinecken, Martin J. *The Moment before God.* Philadelphia: Muhlenberg, 1956.

————. *We Believe and Teach.* Edited by Harold W. Rast. Philadelphia: Fortress, 1980.

Hermann, R. "The Decalog and the Close of the Commandments." In *The Abiding Word.* Vol. 1. Edited by Theodore Laetsch. St. Louis: Concordia, 1946.

Holl, Karl. *The Cultural Significance of the Reformation.* Translated by Karl and Barbara Hertz and John H. Lichtblau. New York: Meridian Books, 1959.

————. *Die Rechtfertigungslehre im Licht der Geschichte des Protestantismus.* Sammlung gemeinverständlicher Vorträge und Schriften aus dem Gebiet der Theologie und Religionsgeschichte 45. Tübingen: J. C. B. Mohr, 1922.

————. *What Did Luther Understand by Religion?* Edited by James Luther Adams and Walter F. Bense. Translated by Fred W. Meuser and Walter R. Wietzke. Philadelphia: Fortress, 1977.

Hordern, William. *Living by Grace.* Philadelphia: Westminster, 1975.

Hoyer, Theodore. "The Grace of God." In *The Abiding Word.* Vol. 2. Edited by Theodore Laetsch. St. Louis: Concordia, 1946.

Jenson, Robert. "Faith, Dogma and Theology." In *Theological Perspectives.* Decorah: Luther College Press, 1967.

Joest, Wilfried. *Gesetz und Freiheit: Das Problem des tertius usus legis bei Luther und die neutestamentliche Parainese.* Göttingen: Vandenhoeck & Ruprecht, 1951.

Jordahl, Leigh D. "American Lutheranism: Ethos, Style, and Polity." In *The Lutheran Church in North American Life.* Edited by John E. Groh and Robert H. Smith. St. Louis: Clayton Publishing House, 1979.

Jungkuntz, Richard, ed. *A Project in Biblical Hermeneutics.* St. Louis: The Commission on Theology and Church Relations of The Lutheran Church—Missouri Synod, 1969.

Jungkuntz, Theodore R. "Ethics in a Relativizing Society: Between the Relativisms of Moralism and Antinomianism." *In Confession and Congregation. The Cresset Occasional Paper, III.* Edited by David G. Truemper. Valparaiso: Valparaiso University Press, 1978.

———. *Formulators of the Formula of Concord.* St. Louis: Concordia, 1977.

———. "Response to Dr. Lazareth." In *Confession and Congregation. The Cresset Occasional Paper, III.* Edited by David G. Truemper. Valparaiso: Valparaiso University Press, 1978.

———. "Shaping Society-Social Action." In *Evangelical Directions for the Lutheran Church.* Edited by Erich H. Kiehl and Waldo J. Werning. Chicago: Lutheran Congress, 1970.

Kantonen, T. A. *Resurgence of the Gospel.* Philadelphia: Muhlenberg, 1948.

Keller, Walter E. "Response to Dr. Bertram." In *Confession and Congregation. The Cresset Occasional Paper, III.* Edited by David G. Truemper. Valparaiso: Valparaiso University Press, 1978.

———. "When Confession Is Called For: Indifferent Things and the Case of Confession." In *Confession and Congregation. The Cresset Occasional Paper, III.* Edited by David G. Truemper. Valparaiso: Valparaiso University Press, 1978.

Kierkegaard, Søren. *Fear and Trembling.* Translated by Walter Lowrie. Princeton: Princeton University Press, 1941. Repr., Garden City: Doubleday Anchor, 1954.

Kinder, Ernst. *Gottes Gebot und Gottes Gnade im Wort vom Kreuz.* Munich, 1949.

Kittelson, James M. *Luther the Reformer.* Minneapolis: Augsburg, 1986.

Klann, Richard. "Luther on Teaching Christian Ethics." In *A Lively Legacy.* Edited by Kurt E. Marquart, John R. Stephenson, and Bjarne W. Teigen. Fort Wayne: Concordia Theological Seminary Press, 1985.

Klug, Eugene F. "The Third Use of the Law." In *A Contemporary Look at the Formula of Concord.* Edited by Robert D. Preus and Wilbert Rosin. St. Louis: Concordia, 1978.

Klug, Eugene F., and Otto F. Stahlke. *Getting into the Formula of Concord.* St. Louis: Concordia, 1977.

Knight, George A. F. *Law and Grace.* Philadelphia: Westminster, 1962.

Köberle, Adolf. *The Quest for Holiness.* Translated by John C. Mattes. Minneapolis: Augsburg, 1936. Repr., St. Louis: Concordia, 1982.

Koch, G. C. *Law and Gospel.* Adelaide: Lutheran Publishing Co., 1925.

Koelpin, Arnold J., ed. *No Other Gospel.* Milwaukee: Northwestern, 1980.

Kolb, Robert. *The Christian Faith.* St. Louis: Concordia, 1993.

———. "Historical Background of the Formula of Concord." In *A Contemporary Look at the Formula of Concord.* Edited by Robert D. Preus and Wilbert Rosin. St. Louis: Concordia, 1978.

———. "Not without the Satisfaction of God's Righteousness: The Atonement and the Generation Gap between Luther and His Students." In *Die Reformation in Deutschland und Europa.* Archiv für Reformationsgeschichte. Sonderband. Edited by Hans R. Guggisberg and Gottfried G. Krodel. Gütersloh: Gütersloher, 1993.

Korby, Kenneth F. "Naming and Healing the Disorders of Man: Therapy and Absolution." In *Confession and Congregation. The Cresset Occasional Paper, III.* Edited by David G. Truemper. Valparaiso: Valparaiso University Press, 1978.

———. "Response to Dr. Schultz." In *Confession and Congregation. The Cresset Occasional Paper, III.* Edited by David G. Truemper. Valparaiso: Valparaiso University Press, 1978.

Krauth, Charles P. *The Conservative Reformation and Its Theology.* Philadelphia: The United Lutheran Publication House, 1913.

Kretzmann, Adalbert R. A. *Law and Gospel.* St. Louis: Faith Forward Executive Committee, The Lutheran Church—Missouri Synod, n.d.

Krodel, Gerhard A. "The Kingdom of Caesar and the Kingdom of God." In *The Left Hand of God.* Edited by William H. Lazareth. Philadelphia: Fortress, 1976.

Krötke, Wolf. *Das Problem "Gesetz und Evangelium" bei W. Elert und P. Althaus.* Zürich: EVZ-Verlag, 1965.

Laetsch, Theodore, ed. *The Abiding Word.* 2 vols. St. Louis: Concordia, 1946.

Lazareth, William. "Foundation for Christian Ethics: The Question of the 'Third Use' of the Law." In *Confession and Congregation. The Cresset Occasional Paper, III.* Edited by David G. Truemper. Valparaiso: Valparaiso University Press, 1978.

———. *Luther on the Christian Home.* Philadelphia: Muhlenberg, 1960.

———. *A Theology of Politics.* New York: Board of Social Ministry, Lutheran Church in America, 1965.

———, ed. *The Left Hand of God.* Philadelphia: Fortress, 1976.

Lazareth, William, and Péri Rasolondraibe. *Lutheran Identity and Mission.* Minneapolis: Augsburg Fortress, 1994.

Leith, John H. "Creation and Redemption: Law and Gospel in the Theology of John Calvin." In *Marburg Revisited.* Edited by Paul C. Empie and James I. McCord. Minneapolis: Augsburg, 1966.

Loetscher, Lefferts A. *Twentieth Century Encyclopedia of Religious Knowledge.* 2 vols. Grand Rapids: Baker, 1955.

Lohse, Bernhard. *Martin Luther: An Introduction to His Life and Work.* Translated by Robert C. Schultz. Philadelphia: Fortress, 1986.

Lotz, David W. *Ritschl and Luther.* Nashville: Abingdon, 1974.

Lueker, Erwin L., ed. *Lutheran Cyclopedia.* Rev. ed. St. Louis: Concordia, 1975.

Lund, Eric. "The Reformation Roots of Objective Justification." In *A Lively Legacy.* Edited by Kurt E. Marquart, John R. Stephenson, and Bjarne W. Teigen. Fort Wayne: Concordia Theological Seminary Press, 1985.

Luther, Martin. *Commentarium in Epistolam S. Pauli ad Galatas.* Edited by J. C. Irmischer. 3 vols. Erlangen: Charles Heyder, 1844.

ography</

ography</

———. *D. Martin Luthers Werke: Kritische Gesamtausgabe.* 107 vols. Weimar: Hermann Böhlaus Nachfolger, 1883–1999.

———. *Luther's Works.* Edited by Jaroslav Pelikan and Helmut T. Lehmann. 55 vols. Philadelphia: Fortress, 1955–1986.

———. *Sämmtliche Schriften.* Edited by J. G. von Walch. 23 vols. St. Louis: Concordia, 1881–1910.

Lutheran Council in the U. S. A., Division of Theological Studies. *The Function of Doctrine and Theology in Light of the Unity of the Church.* New York: Lutheran Council in the U. S. A., 1978.

Mackinnon, James. *Luther and the Reformation.* 4 vols. New York: Russell & Russell, 1962.

Mackintosh, Hugh Ross. *Types of Modern Theology.* London: Nisbet, 1937.

Marquart, Kurt E. *Anatomy of an Explosion.* Concordia Seminary Monograph Series 3. Fort Wayne: Concordia Theological Seminary Press, 1977.

Marsden, George M. *Understanding Fundamentalism and Evangelicalism.* Grand Rapids: Eerdmans, 1991.

Marty, Martin E. *Being Good and Doing Good.* Philadelphia: Fortress, 1984.

———. *The Hidden Discipline.* St. Louis: Concordia, 1962.

Mayer, F. E. *The Religious Bodies of America.* 4th ed. Revised by Arthur Carl Piepkorn. St. Louis: Concordia, 1961.

———. *The Story of Bad Boll.* St. Louis: Concordia, 1949.

McDonough, Thomas M., O.P. *The Law and the Gospel in Luther.* Oxford Theological Monographs. Oxford: Oxford University Press, 1963.

McGiffert, A. C. *Protestant Thought before Kant.* London: Gerald Duckworth, 1911. Repr., New York: Harper Torch Books, 1961.

McGrath, Alister E. *Iustitia Dei.* 2 vols. New York: Cambridge University Press, 1986.

———. *Luther's Theology of the Cross.* Oxford: Basil Blackwell, 1985.

McQuilkin, Robert C. *God's Law and God's Grace.* Grand Rapids: Eerdmans, 1958.

Melanchthon, Philip. *Commentary on Romans.* Translated by Fred Kramer. St. Louis: Concordia, 1992.

———. *Loci Communes.* Translated by J. A. O. Preus. St. Louis: Concordia, 1992.

———. *Loci Communes Theologici.* Edited by Wilhelm Pauck. Translated by Lowell J. Satre. Library of Christian Classics 19. Philadelphia: Westminster, 1969.

———. *"Philippi Melanthonis [sic] Opera quae supersunt Omnia."* In *Corpus Reformatorum.* Edited by Karl G. Bretschneider and Heinrich E. Bindseil. 28 vols. Halle: Schwetschke, 1834–60.

Meuser, Fred W., and Stanley D. Schneider. *Interpreting Luther's Legacy.* Minneapolis: Augsburg, 1969.

Meyer, Carl S. *Log Cabin to Luther Tower.* St. Louis: Concordia, 1965.

———, ed. *Moving Frontiers.* St. Louis: Concordia, 1964.

Migne, J.-P., ed. *Patrologiae Latinae.* 34 vols. Paris: Garnier Fratres, 1887.

Montgomery, John Warwick. *Crisis in Lutheran Theology.* Vol. 1. Grand Rapids: Baker, 1967. 2d rev. ed., Minneapolis: Bethany Fellowship, 1973.

———, ed. *Crisis in Lutheran Theology.* Vol. 2. Grand Rapids: Baker, 1967. 2d rev. ed., Minneapolis: Bethany Fellowship, 1973.

———. "Law and Justice." In *Applying the Scriptures.* Edited by Kenneth S. Kantzer. Grand Rapids: Academie Books, 1987.

Nelson, E. Clifford. *Lutheranism in North America: 1914–1970.* Minneapolis: Augsburg, 1972.

———. "The New Shape of Lutheranism 1930–." In *The Lutherans in North America.* Edited by E. Clifford Nelson. Philadelphia: Fortress, 1975.

———, ed. *The Lutherans in North America.* Philadelphia: Fortress, 1975.

Nelson, John Oliver. *Work and Vocation.* New York: Harper, 1954.

Nygren, Anders. *Agape and Eros.* Translated by Philip S. Watson. London: S. P. C. K., 1954.

———. *The Gospel of God.* Translated by L. J. Trinterud. Philadelphia: Westminster, 1951.

Oberman, Heiko A. *Forerunners of the Reformation.* Philadelphia: Fortress, 1981.

———. *The Dawn of the Reformation.* Edinburgh: T. & T. Clark, 1986.

———. *The Harvest of Medieval Theology.* Rev. ed. Grand Rapids: Eerdmans, 1967.

———. *The Impact of the Reformation.* Grand Rapids: Eerdmans, 1994.

———. *Luther: Man between God and the Devil.* Translated by Eileen Walliser-Schwartzbart. New Haven: Yale University Press, 1989.

———. *The Roots of Anti-semitism in the Age of Renaissance and Reformation.* Philadelphia: Fortress, 1984.

Olivier, Daniel. *Luther's Faith: The Cause of the Gospel in the Church.* Translated by John Tonkin. St. Louis: Concordia, 1982.

Pannenberg, Wolfhart. "Protestant Piety and Guilt Consciousness." In *Christian Spirituality.* Philadelphia: Westminster, 1983.

Pauck, Wilhelm. *The Heritage of the Reformation.* Rev. ed. New York: Oxford University Press, 1968.

———. Introduction to *"Loci Communes Theologici,"* by Philip Melanchthon. In *Melanchthon and Bucer.* The Library of Christian Classics 19. Philadelphia: Westminster, 1969.

Pelikan, Jaroslav. *Fools for Christ.* Philadelphia: Muhlenberg, 1955.

———. *From Luther to Kierkegaard.* St. Louis: Concordia, 1950.

———. *Obedient Rebels.* New York: Harper & Row, 1964.

———. *Spirit Versus Structure.* New York: Harper & Row, 1968.

Pieper, Francis. *Christian Dogmatics.* Translated by Walter W. F. Albrecht. 3 vols. St. Louis: Concordia, 1950–53.

Pieper, Franz. *Christliche Dogmatik.* 3 vols. St. Louis: Concordia, 1917–24.

———. *What Is Christianity?* Translated by John Theodore Mueller. St. Louis: Concordia, 1933.

Pittelko, Roger D. "Confession and Congregation: Resources for Parish Life and Work." In *Confession and Congregation. The Cresset Occasional Paper, III.* Edited by David G. Truemper. Valparaiso: Valparaiso University Press, 1978.

Pinomaa, Lennart. *Faith Victorious.* Translated by Walter J. Kukkonen. Philadelphia: Fortress, 1963.

Prenter, Regin. *Spiritus Creator.* Translated by John M. Jensen. Philadelphia: Muhlenberg, 1953.

Preus, J. A. O. "A Statement of Scriptural and Confessional Principles." Quoted in Frederick W. Danker. *No Room in the Brotherhood.* St. Louis: Clayton Publishing House, 1977.

———. "Translator's Preface" to *Loci Communes*, by Philip Melanchthon. Translated by J. A. O. Preus. St. Louis: Concordia, 1992.

Preus, Robert D. "Confessional Subscription." In *Evangelical Directions for the Lutheran Church.* Edited by Erich H. Kiehl and Waldo J. Werning. Chicago: Lutheran Congress, 1970.

———. *Getting into the Theology of Concord.* St. Louis: Concordia, 1977.

———. "The Hermeneutics of the Formula of Concord." In *No Other Gospel.* Edited by Arnold J. Koelpin. Milwaukee: Northwestern, 1980.

———. *The Theology of Post-Reformation Lutheranism.* 2 vols. St. Louis: Concordia, 1970–72.

Preus, Robert D., and Wilbert Rosin, eds. *A Contemporary Look at the Formula of Concord.* St. Louis: Concordia, 1978.

Quenstedt, John Andrew. *Theologia Didactico-Polemica, Sive Systema Theologicum.* 2 vols. Wittenberg: Matthew Henckel, 1685.

Ritschl, Albrecht. *The Christian Doctrine of Justification and Reconciliation.* Translated by Hugh Ross Mackintosh and A. B. Macaulay. Clifton: Reference Book Publishers, 1966.

Rogge, Joachim. *Johann Agricolas Lutherverständnis: Unter besonderer Berücksichtigung des Antinomismus.* Berlin: Evangelische Verlaganstalt, 1960.

Rogness, Michael. "Dusting Off the Book of Concord." *In Confession and Congregation. The Cresset Occasional Paper, III.* Edited by David G. Truemper. Valparaiso: Valparaiso University Press, 1978.

Rudnick, Milton L. *Authority and Obedience in the Church.* River Forest: Lutheran Education Association, 1977.

Rupp, Gordon. *The Righteousness of God.* 3d ed. London: Hodder & Stoughton, 1968.

Saarnivaara, Uuras. *Luther Discovers the Gospel.* St. Louis: Concordia, 1951.

Sasse, Hermann. *Here We Stand.* Translated by Theodore G. Tappert. Minneapolis: Augsburg, 1946.

———. *This Is My Body.* Minneapolis: Augsburg, 1959. Rev. ed., Adelaide: Lutheran Publishing House, 1977.

———. *Was Heisst Lutherisch?* Munich: Chr. Kaiser, 1934.

Scharlemann, Martin H. *The Church's Social Responsibilities.* St. Louis: Concordia, 1971.

———. *The Ethics of Revolution.* St. Louis: Concordia, 1971.

Schlink, Edmund. *Gesetz und Evangelium.* Theologische Existenz Heute 53. Edited by Karl Barth and Eduard Thurneysen. Munich: Chr. Kaiser, 1937.

———. *Theology of the Lutheran Confessions.* Translated by Paul F. Koehneke and Herbert J. A. Bouman. Philadelphia: Fortress, 1961.

———. *"Die Verborgenheit Gottes des Schöpfers nach lutherischer Lehre."* In *Theologische Aufsätze, Karl Barth zum 50. Geburtstag.* Munich: Chr. Kaiser, 1936.

Schmauk, Theodore E., and C. Theodore Benze. *The Confessional Principle and the Confessions of the Lutheran Church.* Philadelphia: General Council Publication Board, 1911.

Schmid, Heinrich. *The Doctrinal Theology of the Evangelical Lutheran Church.* 3d rev. ed. Translated by Charles A. Hay and Henry E. Jacobs. Philadelphia: United Lutheran Publication House, 1875. Repr., Minneapolis: Augsburg, 1961.

Schmucker, Samuel S. *The American Lutheran Church.* Springfield: D. Harbaugh, 1851. Repr., New York: Arno Press, 1969.

Schroeder, Edward H. "Family Ethos in the Light of the Reformation" In *Family Relationships and the Church.* Edited by Oscar E. Feucht. St. Louis: Concordia, 1970.

———. "Is There a Lutheran Hermeneutics?" in *The Lively Function of the Gospel.* Edited by Robert W. Bertram. St. Louis: Concordia, 1966.

———. "The Relationship between Dogmatics and Ethics: An Investigation into the Theologies of Elert, Barth *und* [*sic*] Troeltsch." Th.D. diss., The University of Hamburg, 1963.

Schroeder, Edward H., and Stephen Hitchcock. *"A Statement" a Misstatement.* St. Louis: Evangelical Lutherans in Mission, n.d.

Schuetze, Armin W. "On the Third Use of the Law: Luther's Position in the Antinomian Debate." In *No Other Gospel.* Edited by Arnold J. Koelpin. Milwaukee: Northwestern, 1980.

Schultz, Robert C. *Gesetz und Evangelium in der lutherischen Theologie des 19.*

Jahrhunderts. Arbeiten zur Geschichte und Theologie des Luthertums 4. Edited by Wilhelm Maurer, Karl H. Rengstorf, and Ernst Sommerlath. Berlin: Lutherisches Verlaghaus, 1958.

———. "Pastoral Theology." In *The Lively Function of the Gospel.* Edited by Robert W. Bertram. St. Louis: Concordia, 1966.

———. "Therapy and Absolution: Issues of Healing and Redemption." In *Confession and Congregation. The Cresset Occasional Paper, III.* Edited by David G. Truemper. Valparaiso: Valparaiso University Press, 1978.

Schwarz, Hans. *Responsible Faith.* Minneapolis: Augsburg, 1986.

———. "The Dynamics of the Word." In *Christian Dogmatics.* Vol. 2. Edited by Carl E. Braaten and Robert W. Jenson. Philadelphia: Fortress, 1984.

Schweitzer, Albert. *The Mysticism of Paul the Apostle.* Translated by William Montgomery. New York: Macmillan, 1931.

Seeberg, Reinhold. *Lehrbuch der Dogmengeschichte.* Vol. 4/1. Basel: Benno Schwabe, 1960.

Silcock, Jeffrey G. "Law and Gospel in Luther's Antinomian Disputations, with Special Reference to Faith's Use of the Law." Th.D. diss., Concordia Seminary, 1996.

———. "Luther and the Third Use of the Law, with Special Reference to His Great *Galatians Commentary.*" S.T.M. diss., Concordia Seminary, 1993.

Sittler, Joseph. *The Structure of Christian Ethics.* Baton Rouge: Louisiana State University Press, 1958.

Spitz, Lewis W., and Wenzel Lohff, eds. *Discord, Dialogue, and Concord.* Philadelphia: Fortress, 1977.

Sponheim, Paul R. "The Knowledge of God." In *Christian Dogmatics.* Edited by Carl E. Braaten and Robert W. Jenson. Philadelphia: Fortress, 1984.

Strickland, Wayne G. et al. *The Law, the Gospel, and the Modern Christian: Five Views.* Grand Rapids: Zondervan, 1993.

Stöckhardt, George. *Law and Gospel According to Their Several Effects.* Translated by Walter H. Bouman. Valparaiso Pamphlet Series 9. Valparaiso: Valparaiso University Association, 1946.

Stuempfle, Herman G. *Preaching Law and Gospel.* Philadelphia: Fortress, 1978.

Suelflow, August R., ed. *Editorials from "Lehre und Wehre."* Translated by Herbert J. A. Bouman. Selected Writings of C. F. W. Walther. St. Louis: Concordia, 1981.

Tappert, Theodore G. "The Significance of Confessional Subscription." In *Essays on the Lutheran Confessions Basic to Lutheran Cooperation.* New York: The Lutheran Church—Missouri Synod and National Lutheran Council, 1961.

———. "The Symbols of the Church." In *What Lutherans Are Thinking.* Edited by Edward C. Fendt. Columbus: Wartburg, 1947.

———, ed. *Lutheran Confessional Theology in America, 1840–1880.* New York:

Oxford University Press, 1972.

Tappert, Theodore G. et al. *The Mature Luther.* Martin Luther Lectures 3. Edited by Gerhard L. Belgum. Decorah: Luther College Press, 1959.

Tavard, George H. *Justification: An Ecumenical Study.* New York: Paulist Press, 1983.

Teigen, Bjarne W. *I Believe: A Study of the Formula of Concord.* Mankato: Bethany Lutheran College, 1977.

Thielicke, Helmut. *Theological Ethics.* Edited by William H. Lazareth. 2 vols. Philadelphia: Fortress, 1966.

Tietjen, John H. *Which Way to Lutheran Unity?* St. Louis: Concordia, 1966.

Tillich, Paul. *Systematic Theology.* Vol. 1. Chicago: University of Chicago Press, 1951.

Tjernagel, Neelak S., ed. *The Lutheran Confessions: A Harmony and Resource Book.* Mankato: The Evangelical Lutheran Synod, 1979.

Troeltsch, Ernst. *The Social Teaching of the Christian Churches.* Translated by Olive Wyon. 2 vols. New York: Macmillan, 1931. Repr., New York: Harper Torchbooks, 1960.

Truemper, David G. "Confession and Congregation: An Approach to the Study of the Formula of Concord." In *Confession and Congregation. The Cresset Occasional Paper, III.* Edited by David G. Truemper. Valparaiso: Valparaiso University Press, 1978.

———. "Piety in a Secularized Society: A Faith-Full Lifestyle; or, The Piety of the Presence of Christ." In *Confession and Congregation. The Cresset Occasional Paper, III.* Edited by David G. Truemper. Valparaiso: Valparaiso University Press, 1978.

———. "Response to Dr. Bouman." In *Confession and Congregation. The Cresset Occasional Paper, III.* Edited by David G. Truemper. Valparaiso: Valparaiso University Press, 1978.

Vajta, Vilmos, ed. *Luther and Melanchthon in the History and Theology of the Reformation.* Philadelphia: Muhlenberg, 1961.

Walch, John George. *Introductio in Libros Ecclesiae Lutheranae Symbolicos.* Jena: Meyer, 1732.

Walther, C. F. W. *The Proper Distinction between Law and Gospel.* Translated by W. H. T. Dau. St. Louis: Concordia, 1986.

———. *Die Rechte Unterscheidung von Gesetz und Evangelium.* St. Louis: Concordia, 1897.

Watson, Philip S. *Let God Be God.* Philadelphia: Muhlenberg, 1949.

Weber, Otto. *Foundations of Dogmatics.* Translated by Darrell L. Guder. 2 vols. Grand Rapids: Eerdmans, 1981.

Wengert, Timothy J. *Law and Gospel.* Grand Rapids: Baker, 1997.

Wentz, Abdel Ross. *A Basic History of Lutheranism in America.* Philadelphia:

Muhlenberg, 1955. Repr., Philadelphia: Fortress, 1964.

Wingren, Gustaf. *The Christian's Calling: Luther on Vocation.* Translated by Carl C. Rasmussen. Edinburgh: Oliver & Boyd, 1958.

————. *Creation and Law.* Translated by Ross Mackenzie. Edinburgh: Oliver & Boyd, 1961.

————. *Gospel and Church.* Translated by Ross Mackenzie. Philadelphia: Fortress, 1964.

————. *The Living Word.* Translated by Victor C. Pogue. Philadelphia: Muhlenberg, 1960.

————. *Theology in Conflict: Nygren, Barth, Bultmann.* Translated by Eric H. Wahlstrom. Edinburgh: Oliver & Boyd, 1958.

Wolf, E. *Historical Introduction to the Formula of Concord.* Translated by Arthur Carl Piepkorn. St. Louis: Concordia Seminary, 1958.

JOURNAL ARTICLES

Arand, Charles P. "Luther on the God behind the First Commandment." *Lutheran Quarterly* 8 (1994): 397–423.

Arand, Charles P., and James W. Voelz. "The Lutheran Confessions as Normative Guides for Reading Scripture." *Concordia Journal* 21 (October 1995): 366–84.

Arndt, William F. "In Memoriam." *Concordia Theological Monthly* 25 (September 1954): 641–46.

————. "The Wrath of God and the Grace of God in Lutheran Theology." Translated by F. E. Mayer. *Concordia Theological Monthly* 23 (August 1952): 569–82.

Barth, Karl L. "Cardinal Principles of Lutheranism and 'Evangelical Theology.' " *Concordia Journal* 7 (March 1981): 50–57.

Berkemeyer, F. "Law and Grace." *Lutheran Church Review* 14 (January 1895): 54–63.

Bloesch, Donald G. "Law and Gospel in Reformed Perspective." *Grace Theological Journal* 12 (Fall 1991): 179–88.

Bohlmann, Ralph A. "Missouri Lutheranism, 1945 and 1995." *Lutheran Forum* 30 (February 1996): 12–17.

Bouman, Henry J. "Conference Paper on Romans 4:5." *Concordia Theological Monthly* 18 (May 1947): 338–47.

Bouman, Herbert J. A. "The Doctrine of Justification in the Lutheran Confessions." *Concordia Theological Monthly* 26 (November 1955): 801–19.

Bouman, Walter R. "The Concept of the 'Law' in the Lutheran Tradition." *Word and World* 3 (Fall 1983): 413–22.

————. "The Law of God: Response to Professor David Yeago." *Lutheran Forum* 29 (November 1995): 12–15.

————. "Walter Bouman on HSII." *Lutheran Forum* 29 (May 1995): 12–14.

Braaten, Carl E. "Whatever Happened to Law and Gospel?" *Currents in Theology and Mission* 14 (April 1987): 111–18.

Breen, Quirinus. "The Terms 'Loci Communes' and 'Loci' in Melanchthon." *Church History* 16 (December 1947): 197–209.

Bretscher, Paul G. "The Log in Your Own Eye." *Concordia Theological Monthly* 43 (November 1972): 645–86.

Bretscher, Paul M. "Professor D. Dr. Werner Elert, 1885–1954." *Concordia Theological Monthly* 26 (March 1955): 211–14.

————. "Review of *'Bad Boll'* Conferences." In *Concordia Theological Monthly* 25 (November 1954): 834–38.

Brondos, Joel A. "Sanctification and Moral Development." *Concordia Journal* 17 (October 1991): 419–39.

Caemmerer, Richard R. "The Educational Use of Scripture in the Light of the Doctrine of the Holy Spirit." *Concordia Theological Monthly* 28 (March 1957): 211–19.

————. "Kerygma and Didache in Christian Education." *Concordia Theological Monthly* 32 (April 1961): 197–208.

————. "The Melanchthonian Blight." *Concordia Theological Monthly* 18 (May 1947): 321–38.

————. "Training the Parish for Christian Citizenship." *Concordia Theological Monthly* 24 (October 1953): 740–48.

————. Review of John Oliver Nelson, ed., *Work and Vocation*. *Concordia Theological Monthly* 27 (March 1956): 335–36.

————. Review of Ewald M. Plass, *This Is Luther*. *Concordia Theological Monthly* 20 (March 1949): 234.

Childs, James M., Jr. "The Third Use of the Law and Constructive Ethics." *Currents in Theology and Mission* 2 (February 1975): 35–40.

Coates, Thomas. "The Barthian Inversion: Gospel and Law." *Concordia Theological Monthly* 26 (July 1955): 481–91.

Coiner, Harry G. "Law and Gospel in Christian Education." *Concordia Theological Monthly* 35 (November 1964): 622–31.

Danker, Frederick W. "Faith with Works." *Concordia Theological Monthly* 27 (July 1956): 513–35.

————. "Faith with Works." *Concordia Theological Monthly* 27 (August 1956): 593–612.

Das, A. Andrew. "Oneness in Christ: The *Nexus Indivulsus* between Justification and Sanctification in Paul's Letter to the Galatians." *Concordia Journal* 21 (April 1995): 173–86.

Dayton, Donald W. "Law and Gospel in the Wesleyan Tradition." *Grace Theological Journal* 12 (Fall 1991): 233–43.

Diebert, Joseph A. "Law-Gospel or Gospel-Law." *Scottish Journal of Theology* 15 (September 1962): 225–34.

Diem, Hermann. "Is Doctrinal Discipline Possible?" *Lutheran Forum* (February 1971): 11–15.

Drevlow, Arthur. "Is the Formula of Concord Still Relevant?" *Concordia Journal* 6 (January 1980): 9–12.

Drickamer, John M. "Did Melanchthon Become a Synergist?" *Springfielder* 40 (September 1976): 95–101.

Dyck, C. J. "The Luther Quincentennial." *Journal of Ecclesiastical History* 35 (October 1984): 597–613.

Ebeling, Gerhard. *"Zur Lehre vom triplex usus legis in der reformation Theologie."* *Theologische Literaturzeitung* 75 (1950): 235–46.

Eggold, Henry J., Jr. "The Third Use of the Law." *Springfielder* 27 (Spring 1963): 15–23.

Engelder, Theodore. "Contrition." Translated by Herbert J. A. Bouman and Erwin Lueker. *Concordia Theological Monthly* 28 (May and July 1957): 321–48, 504–22.

Engelder, Theodore. "Objective Justification." *Concordia Theological Monthly* 4 (July, August and September 1933): 507–17, 564–77, 664–75.

Estep, W. R. "Law and Gospel in the Anabaptist/Baptist Tradition." *Grace Theological Journal* 12 (Fall 1991): 189–214.

Fendt, E. C. "The Theology of the 'Common Confession.' " *Lutheran Quarterly* 2 (August 1950): 308–23.

Forde, Gerhard O. "The Exodus from Virtue to Grace: Justification by Faith Today." *Interpretation* 34 (January 1980): 32–44.

———. "The Formula of Concord Article V: End or New Beginning?" *Dialog* 15 (Summer 1975): 184–91.

———. "Justification by Faith Alone." *Dialog* 27 (Fall 1988): 260–67.

———. "Outside the Gate: Atonement as Actual Event." *Dialog* 18 (Autumn 1979): 247–54.

Forell, George W. "Confessional Lessons for Today's Church." *Lutheran Forum* (Reformation 1977): 12–16.

———. "Why Recall Luther Today?" *Word and World* 3 (Fall 1983): 337–43.

Franzmann, Martin H. "Reconciliation and Justification." *Concordia Theological Monthly* 21 (February 1950): 81–93.

Fry, C. George. "Luther and Melanchthon in America." *Concordia Theological Quarterly* 44 (July 1989): 148–54.

Gerrish, Brian A. "The Chief Article—Then and Now." *The Journal of Religion* 63 (October 1983): 355–75.

Gibbs, Jeffery. "The Grace of God as the Foundation for Ethics." *Concordia Theological Quarterly* 48 (April–July 1984): 185–202.

Gogarten, Friedrich. *"Theologie und Wissenschaft: Grundsätzliche Bemerkungen zu Karl Holls 'Luther.'"* *Die Christliche Welt* 38 (1924): 34–42, 71–80.

Green, Lowell C. "The Relationship of Werner Elert and America." *Concordia Historical Institute Quarterly* 70 (Summer 1997): 75–93.

———. "Toward a New Lutheran Dogmatics." *Concordia Theological Quarterly* 50 (April 1986): 109–18.

———. " 'What Does This Mean?' Luther's Exposition of the Decalogue in Relation to Law and Gospel, with Special Reference to Johann Michael Reu." *Logia* 7 (Eastertide 1998): 3–10.

———. Review of Gerhard Ebeling, *Dogmatik des Christlichen Glaubens. Concordia Theological Monthly* 52 (January 1988): 53–59.

Greenough, Geoffrey H. "The Reformers Attitude to the Law of God." *Westminster Theological Journal* 39 (Fall 1976): 81–99.

Griffin, Dale E. "The Christian Answer to the Ethical Problem." *Concordia Theological Monthly* 30 (October 1959): 733–60.

Hagen, Kenneth. "Changes in the Understanding of Luther: The Development of the Young Luther." *Theological Studies* 28 (September 1968): 477.

Hägglund, Bengt. "Melanchthon Versus Luther: The Contemporary Struggle." *Concordia Theological Quarterly* 44 (July 1980): 123–33.

Haikola, Lauri. "A Comparison of Melanchthon's and Luther's Doctrine of Justification." *Dialog* 2 (Winter 1963): 32–39.

Hamann, Henry P. "Aspects of Law and Gospel, FC V." *Lutheran Theological Journal* 11 (August 1977): 40–48.

———. "Justification by Faith in Modern Theology." *Concordia Theological Monthly* 29 (January-April 1958): 25–37, 98–113, 187–99, 261–76.

Harran, Marilyn J. "The Contemporary Applicability of Luther's Pedagogy: Education and Vocation." *Concordia Journal* 16 (October 1990): 319–32.

Hein, Steven A. " 'A Scrutiny' Scrutinized." *The Cresset* 36 (January 1973): 21–23.

Hermelink, Heinrich. *"Ein Wendepunkt in der Lutherforschung."* *Die Christliche Welt* 38 (1924): 99–108.

Hinlicky, Paul R. "Christ Was Made to Be Sin—Atonement Today." *Currents in Theology and Mission* 14 (June 1987): 177–84.

Hinrichs, Everard. "Are We Preaching a Gospel Free from Law?" *Concordia Theological Monthly* 24 (June 1958): 401–420.

Hoerber, Robert G. "Implications of the Imperative in the Sermon on the Mount." *Concordia Journal* 7 (May 1981): 100–03.

Hoyer, Paul M. "Law and Gospel: With Particular Attention to the Third Use of the Law." *Concordia Journal* 6 (September 1980): 189–201.

Hoyer, Robert J. "On Law and Gospel." *The Cresset* 29 (February 1966): 8–9.

———. "On Second Thought." *The Cresset* 32 (March 1968): 17.

———. "On Second Thought." *The Cresset* 32 (November 1968): 17.

———. "On Second Thought." *The Cresset* 32 (June 1969): 20.

———. "On Second Thought." *The Cresset* 35 (April 1972): 5.

Hummel, Horace. "Are Law and Gospel a Valid Hermeneutical Principle?" *Concordia Theological Quarterly* 46 (April-July 1982): 181–208.

———. "The Debate Continues on the Nature of Gospel and Confession." *Lutheran Forum* (March 1970): 8–10.

———. "Law and Gospel in the Old Testament." Mimeographed Conference Essay, 4. Quoted in Scaer, "The Law Gospel Debate in the Missouri Synod," *Springfielder* 36 (December 1972): 159.

———. "No Other Gospel!" *Lutheran Forum*. (October 1969): 4–9.

Huxhold, Harry N. "A Little Response to Klein." *Lutheran Forum* 29 (August 1995): 13–15.

Ickert, Scott. "*Iustitia Dei*. A History of the Christian Doctrine of Justification." *Dialog* 27 (Fall 1988): 308–16.

———. "The Uses of the Law." *Lutheran Forum* 25 (February 1991): 20–23.

Jersild, Paul. "Situationism and Law in Christian Ethics." *Concordia Theological Monthly* 40 (November 1969): 692–701.

Ji, Won Yong. "To Be Lutheran: Lutheran Identity and Task in Light of the Doctrine of Justification and the Responsibility for the World." *Concordia Journal* 18 (October 1992): 315–38.

Junghans, Helmar "Interpreting the Old Luther (1526–1546)." *Currents in Theology and Mission* 9 (1982): 271–81.

Jungkuntz, Theodore R. "Gamesmanship or Dialogue?" *Lutheran Forum* (Lent 1978): 22.

———. "The 'Third Use of the Law': Looking for Light on the Heat." *Lutheran Forum* (May 1978): 10–12.

Kaiser, Walter C., Jr. "Evangelical Hermeneutics." *Concordia Theological Quarterly* 46 (April-July 1982): 167–80.

———. "God's Promise Plan and His Gracious Law." *Journal of the Evangelical Theological Society* 33 (September 1990): 289–302.

Keller, Walter E. "A Scrutiny of 'A Statement on Scripture.' " *The Cresset* 35 (June 1972): 6–9.

Keller, Walter E. et al. Review of J. A. O. Preus, "A Statement of Scriptural and Confessional Principles." *The Cresset* 36 (May 1973): 6–19.

Kittelson, James M. "Luther, the Church Bureaucrat." *Concordia Journal* 13 (October 1987): 294–306.

Klann, Richard. "Contemporary Lutheran Views of Justification." *Concordia Theological Quarterly* 45 (October 1981): 281–96.

———. "Helmut Thielicke Appraised." *Concordia Journal* 6 (July 1980): 155–63.

————. "Reflections on Disputes Regarding the Proper Distinction between Law and Gospel." *Concordia Journal* 1 (January 1975): 34–45.

————. "Righteousness and Holiness: A Study of Articles III–VI of the Formula of Concord." *Concordia Journal* 5 (March 1979): 44–54.

Klein, Leonard. "Back Home Again in Indiana." *Forum Letter* 21 (4 March 1992): 2–5.

————. "Disaster Averted, Disaster Invited." *Lutheran Forum* 29 (February 1995): 4.

Klug, Eugene F. "Confessional Emphasis on Law and Gospel for Our Day." *Concordia Theological Quarterly* 42 (July 1978): 241–57.

————. "Luther on Law, Gospel and the Third Use of the Law." *Springfielder* 38 (September 1974): 155–67.

Köberle, Adolf. "Reconciliation and Justification." Translated by F. E. Mayer. *Concordia Theological Monthly* 21 (September 1950): 641–58.

Koehler, John Philip. "Legalism in an Evangelical Church." *Concordia Theological Monthly* 40 (March 1969): 131–48.

Koenig, Richard E. "Post-mortem on the Showdown in the LCMS: The Issue was Conscience." *Lutheran Forum* (September 1976): 6–11.

————. "What's after the Showdown in the LCMS? Epilogue to New Orleans." *Lutheran Forum* (November 1973): 10–12.

————. "What's behind the Showdown in the LCMS? Church and Tradition in Collision." *Lutheran Forum* (November 1972): 17–20.

————. "What's behind the Showdown in the LCMS? Conservative Reaction: 1965–69." *Lutheran Forum* (May 1973): 18–21.

————. "What's behind the Showdown in the LCMS? Missouri Turns Moderate: 1938–65." *Lutheran Forum* (February 1973): 19–20, 29.

Kolb, Robert. "Christian Civic Responsibility in an Age of Judgement." *Concordia Journal* 19 (January 1993): 10–34.

————. "Luther's Smalcald Articles: Agenda for Testimony and Confession." *Concordia Journal* 14 (April 1988): 115–37.

————. "The Ordering of the *Loci Communes Theologici*: The Structuring of the Melanchthonian Dogmatic Tradition." *Concordia Journal* 23 (October 1997): 317–37.

————. "Philip Melanchthon: Reformer and Theologian." *Concordia Journal* 23 (October 1997): 309–16.

Kolden, Marc. "Luther on Vocation." *Word and World* 16 (Fall 1983): 382–97.

————. "Posing a Question." *Forum Letter* 23 (7 October 1994): 6–8.

————. "The Scope of Forgiveness." *Word and World* 16 (Summer 1996): 309–19.

Krodel, Gottfried G. "Erasmus-Luther: One Theology, One Method, Two Results." *Concordia Theological Monthly* 41 (November 1970): 648–67.

Künneth, Walter. "Responsibility for Doctrine Today." *Lutheran Forum* (February 1971): 8–10.

Lange, Jonathan G. "Using the Third Use: Formula of Concord and the Preacher's Task." *Logia* 3 (January 1994): 19–25.

Lazareth, William. "The 'Two Kingdom' Ethic Reconsidered." *Dialog* 1 (Autumn 1962): 30–35.

———. Review of Paul L. Lehmann, *The Decalogue and a Human Future: The Meaning of the Commandments for Making and Keeping Human Life Human. Lutheran Forum* 29 (November 1995): 61–63.

Lohff, Wenzel. "Justification and Anthropology." Translated by B. A. Asen and Edward H. Schroeder. *Concordia Theological Monthly* 44 (January 1973): 31–47.

Lueker, Erwin. "Justification in the Theology of Walther." *Concordia Theological Monthly* 32 (October 1962): 598–606.

———. "Luther and Melanchthon." *Concordia Theological Monthly* 31 (August 1960): 476–78.

Lull, Timothy F. "The Doctrine of Justification Today." *Dialog* 27 (Fall 1988): 250–59.

Lund, Eric. "The Impact of Lutheranism on Popular Religion in Sixteenth-Century Germany." *Concordia Journal* 13 (October 1987): 331–41.

Luther, Martin. "The Distinction between Law and Gospel: A Sermon by Martin Luther." Translated by William L. Burce. *Concordia Journal* 18 (April 1992): 153–63.

Maier, Paul L. "Bohlmann and the 44: A Response." *Lutheran Forum* 30 (February 1996): 20–21.

Marshall, Ronald F. "Four Lutheran Rules on False Teaching." *Lutheran Forum* 29 (May 1995): 18.

Mayer, Frederick E. "The Function of the Law in Christian Preaching." *Concordia Theological Monthly* 21 (February 1950): 123–29.

———. "Human Will in Bondage and Freedom: A Study of Luther's Distinction between Law and Gospel." *Concordia Theological Monthly* 22 (October and November 1951): 719–48, 785–819.

———. "*De Ministerio Ecclesiastico.*" *Concordia Theological Monthly* 21 (December 1950): 881–95.

———. "The Proper Distinction between Law and Gospel and the Terminology 'Visible and Invisible Church.' " *Concordia Theological Monthly* 25 (March 1954): 177–98.

———. Review of T. A. Kantonen, *Resurgence of the Gospel. Concordia Theological Monthly* 20 (April 1949): 313–16.

McGrath, Alister E. "The Article by which the Church Stands or Falls." *The Evangelical Quarterly* 58 (July 1986): 207–28.

————. "Divine Justice and Divine Equity in the Controversy between Augustine and Julian of Eclanum." *The Downside Review* 101 (October 1983): 312–19.

————. "Justice and Justification: Semantic and Juristic Aspects of the Christian Doctrine of Justification." *Scottish Journal of Theology* 35.5 (1982): 403–18.

————. "Justification: Barth, Trent, and Küng." *Scottish Journal of Theology* 34.6 (1981): 517–29.

McNeill, John T. "Natural Law in the Thought of Luther." *Church History* 10 (1941): 211–27.

Meilander, Gilbert. "The Place of Ethics in the Theological Task." *Currents in Theology and Mission* 6 (August 1979): 196–203.

Meyer, Carl S. "Christian Humanism and the Reformation: Erasmus and Melanchthon." *Concordia Theological Monthly* 41 (November 1970): 637–47.

Moellering, H. Armin. "A Rejoinder with Repristinating Notes." *Currents in Theology and Mission* 2 (February 1975): 10–18.

————. "Spirituality Defined, Dissected, Recommended, Schematized." *Concordia Journal* 17 (April 1991): 176–83.

Montgomery, John Warwick. "The Law's Third Use: Sanctification." *Christianity Today* 7 (26 April 1963): 6–8.

Mueller, John Theodore. "The Law in the Light of the Gospel." *Concordia Theological Monthly* 28 (June 1957): 452.

————. "Moral Theology and the Criminal Law." *Concordia Theological Monthly* 27 (November 1956): 894–95.

Mueller, Rick. "LCMS & ELCA: Patience, Please." *The Lutheran* (August 1996): 40–41.

Murray, Scott. "Law and Gospel: The Lutheran Ethic." *Logia* 4 (July 1995): 15–24.

————. "Luther in Newman's 'Lectures on Justification.' " *Concordia Theological Quarterly* 54 (April-July 1990): 155–78.

Nessan, Craig L. "Justification in its Reformation Context: Beyond Confessional Fundamentalism." *Word and World* 12 (Summer 1992): 278–91.

Nestingen, James Arne. "The Catechism's *Simul.*" *Word and World* 3 (Fall 1983): 364–72.

————. "Distinguishing Law and Gospel: A Functional View." *Concordia Journal* 22 (January 1996): 27–34.

————. "Luther in Front of the Text: The Genesis Commentary." *Word and World* 14 (Spring 1994): 186–94.

Neuhaus, Richard John. "To Serve the Lord of All: Law, Gospel, and Social Responsibility." *Dialog* 30 (Spring 1991): 140–49.

Niebanck, Richard J. "Law and Gospel: Essential Proprium or Embarrassing Peculiarity?" *Lutheran Forum* 29 (November 1995): 44–46.

Nygren, Anders. "Christianity and Law." *Dialog* 1 (Autumn 1962): 36–45.

Oetting, Walter W. Review of Brian A. Gerrish, *Grace and Reason*. *Concordia Theological Monthly* 34 (May 1963): 307.

Pelikan, Jaroslav. "Doctrine of Man in the Lutheran Confessions." *The Lutheran Quarterly* 2 (February 1950): 34–44.

————. "The Origins of the Object-Subject Antithesis in Lutheran Dogmatics." *Concordia Theological Monthly* 21 (February 1950): 94–104.

————. "Some Word Studies in the Apology." *Concordia Theological Monthly* 24 (August 1953): 580–96.

Peters, Curtis H. "How Important Are Historical Events for Religion?" *Currents in Theology and Mission* 4 (August 1977): 229–34.

Pieper, August. "The Difference between the Reformed and the Lutheran Interpretation of the So-Called Third Use of the Law." *Wisconsin Lutheran Quarterly* 81 (Spring 1990): 108–22.

Piepkorn, Arthur Carl. "Walther and the Lutheran Symbols." *Concordia Theological Monthly* 32 (October 1961): 606–20.

————. Review of Lauri Haikola, *Gesetz und Evangelium bei Matthias Flacius Illyricus*. *Concordia Theological Monthly* 27 (March 1956): 225–26.

Preus, J. A. O. "Chemnitz on Law and Gospel." *Concordia Journal* 15 (October 1989): 406–22.

Preus, Herman A. Review of Werner Elert, *The Structure of Lutheranism*. *Una Sancta* 22 (1965): 49–53.

Preus, Robert D. "The Doctrine of Justification and Reconciliation in the Theology of Karl Barth." *Concordia Theological Monthly* 31 (April 1960): 236–44.

————. "Justification of a Sinner before God as Taught in Later Lutheran Orthodoxy." *Scottish Journal of Theology* 13 (September 1960): 262–77.

————. "Melanchthon the Theologian." *Concordia Theological Monthly* 31 (August 1960): 469–75.

————. "The Significance of Luther's Term *Pure Passive* as Quoted in Article II of the Formula of Concord." *Concordia Theological Monthly* 29 (August 1958): 561–70.

Raabe, Paul R., and James W. Voelz. "Why Exhort a Good Tree?: Anthropology and Paraenesis in Romans." *Concordia Journal* 22 (April 1996): 154–63.

Reimann, Henry W. "Matthias Flacius Illyricus." *Concordia Theological Monthly* 35 (February 1964): 69–93.

Reumann, John. "Sex *et alia* and Law/Gospel Preaching." *Dialog* 34 (Summer 1995): 180–86.

Reynolds, Terrence. "Ritschl's Appropriation of Luther: A Reappraisal." *Concordia Theological Quarterly* 55 (April-July 1991): 105–30.

Roeber, A. G. "Almost Persuaded." *Lutheran Forum* 30 (February 1996): 22–27.

Rosin, Robert. "Melanchthon and 'The Preacher': A Theology for Life."
    Concordia Journal 23 (October 1997): 295–308.

Rosin, Wilbert H. "In Response to Bengt Hägglund: The Importance of
    Epistemology for Luther's and Melanchthon's Theology." *Concordia
    Theological Quarterly* 44 (July 1980): 134–40.

Saltzman, Russell E. "A Discredited Debacle." *Forum Letter* 22 (28 December
    1993): 1–3.

Sasse, Hermann. Review of E. Clifford Nelson, ed., *The Lutherans in North
    America*. *Lutheran Theological Journal* 10 (August 1976): 60.

Sayler, Gwen. "Werner Elert and the Law/Gospel Dialectic." *Currents in
    Theology and Mission* 2 (February 1975): 41–43.

Scaer, David P. "Christ or the Bible?" *Christianity Today* 12 (10 November 1967):
    113–14.

———. "Formula of Concord Article VI: The Third Use of the Law." *Concordia
    Theological Quarterly* 42 (April 1978): 145–55.

———. "Law and Gospel in Lutheran Theology." *Grace Theological Journal* 12
    (Fall 1991): 163–78.

———. "The Law and the Gospel in Lutheran Theology." *Logia* 3 (January
    1994): 27–34.

———. "The Law Gospel Debate in the Missouri Synod." *Springfielder* 36
    (December 1972): 156–71.

———. "The Law Gospel Debate in the Missouri Synod Continued."
    Springfielder 40 (September 1976): 107–18.

———. "Sanctification in the Lutheran Confessions." *Concordia Theological
    Quarterly* 53 (July 1989): 165–82.

———. "Sanctification in Lutheran Theology." *Concordia Theological Quarterly* 49
    (April-July 1985): 181–98.

———. "Three Cheers for Hummel." *Lutheran Forum* (December 1969): 16–17.

———. "The Two Sides of Justification." *Christianity Today* 25 (26 June 1981):
    44.

Scharlemann, Martin H. "Human Relations According to 'Ephesians.' "
    Concordia Theological Monthly 24 (October 1953): 703–48.

Schmidt, Stephen A. "Law-Gospel: Toward a Model of Moral Education."
    Religious Education 65 (November-December 1970): 474–82.

Schöne, Jobst. "Law and Gospel in Hermann Sasse." *Logia* 4 (October 1995):
    25–29.

Schroeder, Edward H. "Critique of President Preus' [sic] Statement." TMs
    [Mimeograph]. Archive Stacks. Ludwig Fuerbringer Library. Concordia
    Seminary, St. Louis, n.d.

———. "Current Implications of the 'We Condemn' Statements in the Lutheran
    Confessions." *Currents in Theology and Mission* 2 (February 1975): 5–9.

———. "A Dogmatics that Makes Sense." Review of Regin Prenter, *Creation and Redemption*. *The Cresset* 30 (September 1967): 24–25.

———. "Law-Gospel Reductionism in the History of The Lutheran Church—Missouri Synod." *Concordia Theological Monthly* 43 (April 1972): 232–47.

———. "The Relationship between Dogmatics and Ethics." *Concordia Theological Monthly* 36 (December 1965): 744–71.

Schulze-Kadelbach, Gerhard. "The Grace of God Gives Us Christ for Justification." Translated by Lewis W. Spitz. *Concordia Theological Monthly* 24 (February 1953): 112–29.

Schuessler, Paul E. "A Pastor's Reflection on Law and Gospel." *Lutheran Forum* 25 (February 1991): 24–26.

———. "Using the Law." *Lutheran Forum* (May 1978): 23–24.

Schultz, Robert C. "An Alternative to the Formula of Concord?" Review of Holsten Fagerberg, *A New Look at the Lutheran Confessions*. *The Cresset* 36 (March 1973): 10–15.

———. "The Distinction between Law and Gospel." *Concordia Theological Monthly* 32 (October 1961): 591–97.

———. "Missouri Synod History and Doctrine: Variant Readings." *The Cresset* 35 (October 1972): 29–33.

———. "Reflections on the Current Controversy in The Lutheran Church—Missouri Synod: An Attempt to Express Pastoral Concern." *The Cresset* 35 (October 1972): 7–12.

Schurb, Ken. "Twentieth-Century Melanchthon Scholarship: With Particular Reference to 'The Melanchthonian Blight.' " *Concordia Theological Quarterly* 62 (October 1998): 287–307.

———. " 'The Law Always Accuses' in the Augsburg Confession and the Apology." *Concordia Journal* 23 (October 1997): 338–49.

Sedgwick, Peter. " 'Justification by Faith': One Doctrine, Many Debates?" *Theology* (January-February 1990): 11.

Shearier, Jeffrey. "The Ethics of Obedience: A Lutheran Development." *Concordia Journal* 12 (March 1986): 55–63.

Shoemaker, Dennis E. "They Toughed It Out in Style: Watching Missouri Wage War." *Lutheran Forum* (September 1975): 20–21.

Spitz, Lewis W., Jr. "Current Accents in Luther Studies: 1960–1967." *Theological Studies* 28 (1967): 549–73.

———. "Images of Luther." *Concordia Journal* 11 (March 1985): 43–51.

Stevens, Gerald L. "Paul and the Law in Galatians." *The Theological Educator* 50 (Fall 1994): 95–104.

Truemper, David G. "Shaping Theology Evangelically: Thirty Theses on the Gospel." *The Cresset* 42 (February 1979): 16–17.

———. Review of Robert D. Preus and Wilbert Rosin, eds., *A Contemporary*

Look at the Formula of Concord. The Cresset 43 (February 1980): 22–30.

Wagner, Walter H. "Luther and the Positive Use of Law." *Journal of Religious History* 11 (January 1980): 45–63.

Warneck, Richard H. "Law and Gospel Preaching." *Concordia Journal* 16 (April 1990): 99–120.

Wehmeier, Waldemar W. "Missouri and Public Doctrine." *Currents in Theology and Mission* 2 (February 1975): 23–34.

Wengert, Timothy. " 'Fear and Love' in the Ten Commandments." *Concordia Journal* 21 (January 1995): 14–27.

Werning, Walter H. "In Defense of F. Pieper." *Lutheran Forum* (September 1973): 28.

Westhelle, Vítor. "Proclamation and Obligation: On the Demonstration of the Spirit and of Power." *Word and World* 16 (Summer 1996): 328–39.

Wingren, Gustaf F. "Justification by Faith in Protestant Thought." *Scottish Journal of Theology* 9 (December 1956): 374–83.

Wriedt, Markus. "Between Angst and Confidence: Melanchthon as a Man of the Sixteenth Century." *Concordia Journal* 23 (October 1997): 277–94.

Yeago, David S. "Bouman on the Law: *Amica Responsio*." *Lutheran Forum* 29 (August 1995): 10–12.

———. "Bouman on Yeago on Bouman on the Law: A Brief Rejoinder." *Lutheran Forum* 29 (November 1995): 16.

———. "Gnosticism, Antinomianism, and Reformation Theology." *Pro Ecclesia* 2 (Winter 1993): 37–49.

Zorn, Hans. "The Confessors Meet Aristotle." *Currents in Theology and Mission* 9 (October 1982): 291–95.

INDEX OF NAMES

INDEX OF SUBJECTS